MOTHER OF ROYALTY

אִמָּהּ שֶׁל מַלְכוּת

Mother of Royalty

An exposition of the Book of Ruth
in the light of the sources

by

Yehoshua Bachrach

Translated from the third Hebrew edition by
LEONARD OSCHRY

FELDHEIM PUBLISHERS
Jerusalem / New York

Published in cooperation with the

JERUSALEM COLLEGE FOR WOMEN

מכללה ירושלים

First published 1973
Newly corrected edition, 1980
ISBN 0-87306-018-0

Distributed by

Feldheim Publishers Ltd
POB 6525 / Jerusalem, Israel

Philipp Feldheim Inc
96 East Broadway
New York, NY 10002

Printed in Israel

In Blessed Memory
of
my dearly beloved mother
who sent me to study Torah
far away from home
though of tender age and precious to her —
this too, then, is hers.

TABLE OF CONTENTS

THE SCROLL OF OBED

FOREWORD

With the advent of Yehoshua Bachrach's *Ima Shel Malchut* on the scene of Biblical Exegesis some two decades ago, students of Tanach found a new era of understanding opened before them. Yehoshua Bachrach presents to the intelligent student of the Tanach not a new commentary, nor new ideas, but a radically new approach to our most ancient study.

Educated in the Lithuanian yeshivot — the first of which was Sha'arei Torah, of the renowned Rabbi Shim'on Shkop, of blessed memory, in Grodno — Bachrach combines the qualities of the erudite Lithuanian *talmid chacham* with the nobility and the piety of the religious poet. It is a new approach to the study of Tanach that Bachrach has opened and expounded so eloquently in his books and publications, an approach that, in its particularly pleasant and yet deep fashion, has shattered the idols of biblical study so reverently held by so many for so long. In an era devoted and almost enslaved to the dictates of *Pshat* — so incorrectly identified with the simple grammatical and syntactical meaning of the verse — and so willing to ignore the beauty and depths of the inner meaning of the text, it is Bachrach who turned once again to the wealth and richness of the Midrashic literature, to delve deep down into the unfathomed waters of the Talmud and Midrash, to give new light and new meaning to the eternal study of Tanach that seemed destined to loose its vitality in the strait jacket of grammatical, historical and archaeological interpretation.

It is not merely the beauty of Midrashic interpretation that Bachrach has brought to Bible students, however, but something greater and of even more lasting value. It is a new approach to the study of Tanach vis-à-vis the study of Midrash. He never imposes his views on his reader, but simply poses questions, so simple yet so strong, so that under the pressure of the gradual onslaught of didactically worded questions and intellectually stimulating problems, the great walls dividing the realms of *Pshat* and *Drash* tremble and disintegrate. Those worlds of Biblical studies (*Pshat* and *Drash*) that had been forced by so many to become mutual enemies, soon found themselves enveloped in harmonious unity, as the tones of *Drash* are superimposed on the basic forms of *Pshat*. The world of *Drash* came once again into its own, not to be suffered as artificial and extraneous commentaries of the Rabbis to the resisting tenons and fibres of the text, and not even to be welcomed as precious breaths of cool air on the warm desert heat of the day as they revive the soul parched for spiritual uplifting. *Drash*, as Bachrach shows, is an integral part of Torah, a direct result of a deeper understanding of *Pshat* — a necessary conclusion to be reached, as the problems of *Pshat* fade away and disappear in the solution offered by the *Drash*. Bachrach does not attack his reader, nor push nor force nor cajole him into any new situation. He merely reads the verse again and again, asking question after question, until the intelligent reader is forced to raise his hands in despair if he thinks to find satisfaction in grammar, history and archaeological excavations. Bachrach leads the reader to the conclusion that in order to understand *Pshat* in its depth, one must of necessity have recourse to *Drash*. *Drash*, as he presents it, seems the simple, logical answer to the problems left unsolved by reading with *Pshat* alone. *Pshat* leads to *Drash*, and *Drash* brings one back again to the deeper level of *Pshat*.

Hebrew speaking students of the Tanach have enjoyed Bachrach's works for years now, since his first publication, which is herewith translated. Bachrach has since gone from strength to strength. As senior lecturer in Nevi'im Rishonim at the Jerusalem

College for Women (Michlalah) he has published — as a direct result of his teaching experience — his monumental study of David and Saul, the first two kings of Israel's monarchy. He has also published a book on Jona the prophet and Elijah — *Yona ben Amitai veEliyahu* — and at present he is publishing his interpretation of Megilat Esther. He has also written numerous articles, primarily in the field of Nevi'im Rishonim and Megilot. The translation of Bachrach's works into other languages has long been missing and its want has been felt, particularly in the English speaking world.

This present publication comes, then, as a major contribution to the English speaking student of the Tanach, and it is hoped that the impact on him will be no less than the impact on the Hebrew speaking student during the past two decades. Feldheim Publishers did wisely in retaining portions of the original Hebrew text as a gentle reminder to the English reader that when all is said and done there is no full substitute for the beauty and the eloquence and the particular music of the language of the Bible and *Chazal*. Rabbi Leonard Oschry did a fine job of translating and the assistance of Rabbi Moshe Litoff must also be noted. Thanks are due to Yaakov Feldheim and Toby Klein, a student of the author, for their painstaking review of the manuscript and their astute observations.

We hope and trust that as a result of this translation there will be given the encouragement and stimulus to translate Bachrach's other works into the English language.

Yehudah Copperman,
Dean
Jerusalem College for Women

Yerushalayim
Rosh Chodesh Cheshvan, 5733

Stars refer to corresponding supplementary notes at the end of the book.

THE RULING EMANATING FROM THE PROPHET SAMUEL'S BETH DIN

Samuel wrote his own book, the Book of Judges and Ruth. (Bava Bathra 14b)

Says Abraham [Ibn Ezra]: Since David was the progenitor of the Israelite Monarchy, the Holy Scriptures recounted his ancestry.

It was most fitting for Samuel to have written the Book of Ruth. It was in honor of David * that he did so.

For Samuel had been so seldom together with David. And even that short period had been marred by Samuel's love for Saul, the first royal tree he had planted,* to the extent that David seemed at first to have been cast aside by the very prophet by whom he had been anointed.

> "And *Hashem* said to Samuel:
>
> How long will you mourn for Saul, seeing that I have rejected him from being king over Israel?
>
> Fill your horn with oil, and go, I will send you to Jesse the Bethlehemite; for I have provided Me a king among his sons"
> (1 Sam. 16.1).

Against his will, the prophet fulfilled this mission. For in spite of all that had taken place, Samuel still loved Saul.

Indeed, at first, when the populace had clamored for a king, Samuel had regarded their request as evil. Yet once ***Hashem*** had consented and had prepared him to wait expectantly for the arrival of the appointed one, and a young man came seeking his father's donkeys in the land of Zuf, the prophet became fondly attached to Saul. And through this love, Samuel endowed Saul with all that was precious and desirable in Israel.*

> "Then Samuel took the vial of oil and poured it upon his head, and kissed him,
> and said: "Is it not that *Hashem* has anointed you to be prince over His inheritance!'" (*Ibid.* 10.1)

> וישקהו [אהרן למשה] כמנשק דבר קדוש, כעניין ויאמר הלא כי משחך ה'.
> (ספורנו שמות, ד כז)

> "And he (Aaron) kissed him (Moses)" — as if kissing a holy object, and in a similar context: "And he said: 'Is it not that *Hashem* has anointed you!'" (Seforno, Exod. 4.27)

Samuel stood alone with Saul on the roof, to sanctify him there as king over Israel.

> Rashi: Admonishing him and teaching him to fear the Holy One, blessed be He.

On this day, however, Samuel was ordered to execute the sentence against Saul — to uproot with his very own hands what he himself had planted. Was not Samuel moved by a redoubled love and compassion for Saul that day?

> "And God has given it to a neighbor of yours that is better than you." (I Sam. 15.28)

Who would this better person than Saul be?

> איך אלך ?
>
> "How can I go?" * (I Sam. 16.2).

Do we not discern here that Samuel was offering an excuse for not going, begging that he not be sent this time?

"And it was, when they were come, that he beheld Eliav and said: 'Surely God's anointed is before Him.'" (*Ibid.* 16.6).

R. David Kimhi: Some explain the remark as a petition on behalf of Saul, that his kingdom not be confiscated. Noticing that Eliav was no more handsome than Saul, Samuel begged God not to replace Saul. God accordingly replied: "Look not upon his countenance or the height of his stature, because I have rejected him"—the rejected one being Saul who was handsome in appearance and tall of stature.
"For it is not as man sees;
For man looks on the outward appearance, but God looks on the heart." (*Ibid.* 16.7).

Here was a stinging rebuke to Samuel, who had not, at first, approved of David as king.

The Sifri related in the name of R. Joshua of Sikhnin, who reported the remarks of R. Joshua b. Levi: "Even though you have called yourself 'seer'—you told Saul: 'I am the seer'—I have shown you here that you do not see."

וישלח ויביאהו והוא אדמוני עם־יפה עינים וטוב ראי
ויאמר יי קום משחהו כי־זה הוא. (ש"א. טז, יב)

רד"ק: קום — ענין זרוז. ורבותינו ז"ל דרשו: אמר לו הקב"ה:
קום מלפניו! משיחי עומד — ואתה יושב? קום משחהו. (שו"ט לא, יז)

"And he sent and brought him in. Now he was ruddy, and withal of beautiful eyes, and goodly to look upon.
And *Hashem* said: 'Arise, anont him; for this is he.'" (I Sam. 16. 12) R. David Kimhi: "Arise"—urging him. Our Rabbis have further explained: "Stand up before him! My anointed is standing—and you remain seated?! Stand up and anoint him!" (Mid. *Shoḥer Tov*)
"And Samuel took the horn of oil, and anointed him in the

> presence of his brethren... So Samuel rose up and went to Ramah." (*Ibid.* 16.13)

He did not, however, bless the new king. Neither was the prophet's kiss bestowed on David, nor was he vouchsafed the blessing that had been conferred on Saul when the latter was anointed king.

> "So Samuel rose up and went to Ramah."

There the prophet remained in seclusion, alone, communing with himself in his grief and disappointment.

Perhaps it was there that he roused himself and wrote down this glorious testament, the tacit blessing which he accorded to David, for this is the Book which delineates David's origins and affirms its faith in the glorious destiny reserved for him in Israel.

How strange does it strike us that Samuel should have so utterly isolated himself, from that day onwards to his very death! Why did he make no attempt to calm the storms of hatred beating down upon the heads of the two he had anointed? The prophet seemed to have been responsible for what was happening, yet was powerless to intervene. He realized that God had made him the prime cause of Saul's unfortunate harassment of David. For, that very day, when Samuel had taken David, had spirited him away from his sheep and had poured two drops of oil * on his head, marked the beginning of the round of agony that turned on him and Saul as well.

This, perhaps, was the very reason for the prophet's isolation, for locking himself up in Ramah.

> "And the spirit of God came mightly upon David from that day onward... Now the spirit of God had departed from Saul, and an evil spirit from God terrified him." (1 Sam. 16.13-14)

Yet Samuel must have felt obliged to protect David, the persecuted, in all that was transpiring.

Samuel certainly realized that his assignment, as the first prophet to establish the permanent Israelite monarchy, had now been fulfilled.* And David was also hounded by the fact that the law applying to his status had not yet become common knowledge in that generation.

ר׳ אבא בר כהנא פתח : רגזו ואל תחטאו (תהלים ד, ח). אמר דוד לפני הקב״ה : עד אימתי הם מתרגזים עלי ואומרים, לא פסול משפחה הוא, לא מרות המואביה הוא ? (רות רבה ח, ז)

R. Abba b. Kahana opened [his exposition] with the verse: "Tremble and sin not" (Ps. 4.5). David said to the Holy One, blessed be He: "How long will they rage against me and say: Is he not of tainted descent? Is he not a descendant of Ruth the Moabitess?" (Ruth Rabba, 8.7)

בן מי־זה העלם ?

אמר לו דואג : עד שאתה משאיל עליו אם הגון הוא למלכות אם לאו, **שאל** עליו אם הגון הוא לבוא בקהל אם לאו — מאי טעמא ? דקאתי מרות המואביה.
בעי לאכרוזי עליו [ביקשו להכריז עליו שהוא פסול].
מיד חגר עמשא חרבו כישמעאלי ואמר : כל מי שאינו שומע **הלכה זו** — ידקר בחרב ! **כך** מקובלני מבית דינו של שמואל הרמתי : **עמוני — ולא עמונית, מואבי — ולא מואבית.** (יבמות עו:עז.)

"Who is this lad?" (1 Sam. 17.56)

Doeg then said to him: "Instead of inquiring whether he is fit to be king or not, inquire rather whether he is permitted to enter the community (of Israel) or not!" What is the reason? Because he is descended from Ruth, the Moabitess. He wanted publicly to proclaim him [unfit].

Immediately Amasa girded on his sword like an Ishmaelite and exclaimed: "Whoever will not obey the following ruling will be stabbed with the sword: This rule emanated from the Prophet Samuel's Beth Din. An Ammonite (is unfit), but not an Ammonitess; a Moabite but not a Moabitess." (Yevamoth 76b, 77a)

Now Samuel himself succeeded in disseminating the knowledge of this law, and in glorifying it in Israel for all generations. He, however, accomplished his purpose peacefully and forthrightly, writing this charming and idyllic Book of Ruth the Moabitess, by portraying her as she really was, in essaying her first steps as she entered the community of Israel and showing her merit and receiving her reward in full measure from *Hashem,* God of Israel, under Whose wings she had come to take refuge.

And, indeed, this book is pervaded by hidden love for her grandson David, and from this book a crown is placed on the royal house of the Messiah.*

ותקראנה שמו עובד. הוא אבי־ישי אבי דוד.

אמר רבי יוחנן:
למה נקרא שמה רות?
שיצא ממנה דוד, שריווה להקב"ה בשירות ותשבחות. (ב"ב יד:)

"AND SHE CALLED HIS NAME OBED; HE IS THE FATHER OF JESSE, THE FATHER OF DAVID." (Ruth 4.17)

Said R. Johanan:
"Why was her name called Ruth?"
Because there issued from her David, who satiated the Holy One, blessed be He, with hymns and praises." (Bava Bathra 14b)

Our Rabbis, of blessed memory, must have sensed what transpired during the short meeting between Samuel and David, at the time when David was fleeing from Saul, and this also deserves mention. It was there that Samuel placed the royal crown upon David by entrusting him with the fulfillment of the commandment that would consummate the holiness of the nation on the mountain of their inheritance — the mitzvah of building the Holy Temple.*

ודוד ברח וימלט ויבא אל שמואל הרמתה וכו׳
וילך הוא ושמואל וישבו בניות.
וכתיב: הנה דוד בניות ברמה. (שם יט. יח)

אמר רבא: וכי מה ענין ניות אצל רמה? אלא שהיו יושבים ברמה,
(בעירו של שמואל) ועוסקים בנויו של עולם.
רש״י: למצוא מקום לבית הבחירה מן התורה. (זבחים נד:)

"Now David fled and escaped and came to Samuel in Ramah... And he and Samuel dwelt in Naioth." (1 Sam. 19.18)
"'Behold David is in Naioth in Ramah.'" (*Ibid.*)
Rava said: What connection then had Naioth with Ramah? It means that they sat in Ramah and were occupied with the beautiful place (*naioth*) of the world. (Zevaḥim 54b)
Rashi: To find a reference in the Torah to the place of the Temple.

How loftly and sublime is this observation! For Scripture has also related Ruth to the holy Temple.

אריאל מואב. (ש״ב כג, כו)

אריאל. — זה בית המקדש,
שנאמר: הוי אריאל אריאל קרית חנה דוד. (ישעיה כט)
מואב. — על שם שבנאו דוד, דאתי מרות המואביה. (ברכות יח.)

"Ariel Moab" (2 Sam. 23.20).

Ariel — refers to the Temple.

As it is said: "Ah, Ariel, Ariel, city where David encamped." (Isa. 29)

Moab refers to David, architect of the Temple, the descendant of Ruth, the Moabitess. (Berakhoth 18a)

THE SIN OF SELFISHNESS

אא. וַיְהִי בִּימֵי שְׁפֹט הַשֹּׁפְטִים וַיְהִי רָעָב בָּאָרֶץ
וַיֵּלֶךְ אִישׁ מִבֵּית לֶחֶם יְהוּדָה לָגוּר בִּשְׂדֵי מוֹאָב
הוּא וְאִשְׁתּוֹ וּשְׁנֵי בָנָיו׃

ב. וְשֵׁם הָאִישׁ אֱלִימֶלֶךְ וְשֵׁם אִשְׁתּוֹ נָעֳמִי וְשֵׁם שְׁנֵי־בָנָיו
מַחְלוֹן וְכִלְיוֹן אֶפְרָתִים מִבֵּית לֶחֶם יְהוּדָה
וַיָּבֹאוּ שְׂדֵי־מוֹאָב וַיִּהְיוּ־שָׁם׃

ג. וַיָּמָת אֱלִימֶלֶךְ אִישׁ נָעֳמִי וַתִּשָּׁאֵר הִיא וּשְׁנֵי בָנֶיהָ׃

ד. וַיִּשְׂאוּ לָהֶם נָשִׁים מֹאֲבִיּוֹת שֵׁם הָאַחַת עָרְפָּה
וְשֵׁם הַשֵּׁנִית רוּת וַיֵּשְׁבוּ שָׁם כְּעֶשֶׂר שָׁנִים׃

ה. וַיָּמֻתוּ גַם־שְׁנֵיהֶם מַחְלוֹן וְכִלְיוֹן
וַתִּשָּׁאֵר הָאִשָּׁה מִשְּׁנֵי יְלָדֶיהָ וּמֵאִישָׁהּ׃

1.1 AND IT WAS IN THE DAYS WHEN THE JUDGES JUDGED, THAT THERE WAS A FAMINE IN THE LAND. AND A CERTAIN MAN OF BETH-LEHEM IN JUDAH WENT TO SOJOURN IN THE FIELD OF MOAB, HE, AND HIS WIFE, AND HIS TWO SONS.

2 AND THE NAME OF THE MAN WAS ELIMELECH, AND THE NAME OF HIS WIFE, NAOMI, AND THE NAMES OF HIS TWO SONS, MAHLON AND CHILION, EPHRATHITES OF BETH-LEHEM IN JUDAH. AND THEY CAME TO THE FIELD OF MOAB, AND CONTINUED THERE.

3 AND ELIMELECH NAOMI'S HUSBAND DIED; AND SHE WAS LEFT AND HER TWO SONS.

4 AND THEY TOOK THEM WIVES OF THE WOMEN OF MOAB: THE NAME OF THE ONE WAS ORPAH, AND THE NAME OF THE OTHER, RUTH; AND THEY DWELT THERE ABOUT TEN YEARS.

5 AND MAHLON AND CHILION DIED, BOTH OF THEM; AND THE WOMAN WAS LEFT OF HER TWO CHILDREN AND HER HUSBAND.

The prophet has condensed a lengthy account into a few sentences. Only the severe retribution meted out to this family is emphasized: death, widowhood, orphancy, bereavement, excision.

"AND MAHLON AND CHILION DIED, BOTH OF THEM."

ולמה נקרא שמם מחלון וכליון?

מחלון — שעשו עצמם חולין, וכליון — שנתחייבו כליה.
ד"א: מחלון וכליון — שנמחו וכלו מן העולם. (ב"ב צא, רו"ר, ילק"ש ת"ר)

And why were they named Mahlon and Chilion?

Mahlon — (*halal* — *profane*) because they profaned their bodies.
Chilion — (*kalah* — destroyed) because they were judged worthy of destruction.

Another interpretation: Mahlon and Chilion — because they were completely wiped out and disappeared from the earth. (Bava Bathra 91a; Ruth Rabba, Yalkut Shim'oni 600)

"AND THE WOMAN WAS LEFT OF HER TWO CHILDREN AND HER HUSBAND."

Bereaved of her two children, and widowed of her husband (Targum).

By leading us so far, Scripture desired to provoke this question: What grave transgression had they committed, that their retribution was so severe?
Was it for having deserted Eretz Israel and going elsewhere? Scripture attests to there having been a famine in the land.
Abraham, our forefather, facing similar circumstances, had also left the land.

> "And there was a famine in the land; and Abram went down to Egypt to sojourn there, for the famine was sore in the land." (Gen. 12.10)

[Note: The comparison of passages bearing similarities is an important pedagogical technique generally, but of even greater importance in Bible study. Scripture is a single entity, one passage supplementing and illuminating another.
Here, for instance, the two passages use similar language; there are only two differences, a slight omission and a slight addition. With proper and intelligent guidance, students can be stimulated to discover the differences between the two incidents, the persons involved and the surrounding circumstances. In this way they can gain new insights into the respective natures of the two episodes.]
Perhaps in this instance the famine was not so severe. The Book of Judges does not mention any crippling famine. Moreover, why did the family choose Moab? It was not watered by the Nile, like Egypt. And why were they the only ones departing from Eretz Israel?

הלכה :

ת"ר : אין יוצאין מארץ לחוץ־לארץ אלא אם כן עמדו סאתיים בסלע ; אמר ר' שמעון אימתי, בזמן שאינו מוצא ליקח, אבל בזמן שמוצא ליקח, אפילו עמדה סאה בסלע לא יצא.

וכן היה ר' שמעון בן יוחאי אומר : אלימלך, מחלון וכליון גדולי הדור היו, ופרנסי הדור היו, ומפני מה נענשו ? מפני שיצאו מארץ לחוץ־לארץ. (ב"ב צא. ב"ר כח ג)

> The law:
>
> Our Rabbis taught: It is not permitted to go forth from Eretz Israel to a foreign country unless two seahs are sold for one selah:
>
> R. Shimon said: This is permitted only when one cannot find [anything] to buy, but when one is able to find something to buy, even if one seah costs a selah, one must not depart.
>
> And so said R. Shimon bar Yoḥai: Elimelech, Mahlon and Chilion were among the notables of their generation, and they were also leaders of the generation. Why, then, were they punished? Because they left Eretz Israel for a foreign country. (Bava Bathra 91a; Gen. Rabba 28.3)

In the eyes of the law, then, their principal transgression was their leaving Eretz Israel. So Maimonides ruled (Law of Kings 5.9). They ought not to have been guided by the letter of the law, but should have elected to act more righteously, even where they were permitted to leave, since they were the outstanding leaders of their generation. They left to escape a disaster — and, in God's judgment, were deemed deserving of destruction.

> Said Rav Ḥanan bar Rava in the name of Rav:
>
> Elimelech and Salmon and the *Peloni Almoni* (the anonymous person in the Book of Ruth) and the father of Naomi were all descended from Nachshon the son of Aminadab. What does he come to teach us by this statement? — That even the merit of one's ancestors is of no avail when one leaves Eretz Israel for a foreign land. (*Ibid.* 92b; Yalkut Shim'oni 599)

By comparing their conduct with what is related in detail elsewhere, viz. concerning the returning Babylonian exiles, our Rabbis discovered further evidence of this guilt in the fact that they left Eretz Israel alone and incognito.

> And a certain man... went — like a mere stump (empty-handed). See how the Holy One, blessed be He, favors the entry into Eretz Israel over the departure therefrom. In the former case it is written, "Their horses... their mules... their camels" (Ezra 2.66), but, in this case, it is written, "a certain man went" — like a mere stump. (Ruth Rabba 1.5)

Others have attributed their guilt to their having settled permanently in Moab.

> "and they came into the field of Moab and continued there."
>
> Although they originally left with the intention of merely sojourning temporarily in the field of Moab, once they came there, they remained — the import being that they consented to reside there permanently. (Malbim; R. Mosheh Alshekh, at length.)
>
> R. Joshua b. Korḥa said: Why, then, was punishment inflicted on them ? — Because they should have begged mercy for their generation, and they did not do so; for it is said: 'When thou criest, let them that you have gathered deliver you." (Bava Bathra, *Ibid.*)
>
> Maharsha: When you cry out to Heaven on account of the suffering of the "gathering" — the group (for the group is always referred as a "gathering"), Heaven will deliver you. So the Rabbis have asserted, "Whoever prays for mercy on behalf of his neighbor will himself be answered first."

R. Joshua b. Korḥa did not choose this verse at random and interpret it out of context. In it, he discerned the cry of the individual integrated in his group and joined with his people. And he contrasted this with the behavior of Elimelech, departing and abandoning his community, walking away while the rest of Israel was suffering in adversity.

Does not Heaven ordain every famine, afflicting the land, with the intention of thereby impelling the inhabitants to petition for Divine mercy? How was it possible to flee from the Divine decree? *

Whoever flees excludes himself from the community, since he believes that he will thereby escape the communal hardship.

> ואמרו רבותינו ז״ל : בזמן שישראל שרויין בצער ופירש אחד מהם, באים שני מלאכי השרת ומניחין לו את ידיהם על ראשו ואומרים : פלוני זה שפירש עצמו מן הצבור, אל יראה בנחמת ציבור. אלא בזמן שהציבור שרוי בצער, אל יאמר אלך לביתי ואוכל ואשתה ושלום עליך נפשי, ואם עושה כן, עליו הכתוב אומר : (ישעיה כב) ״והנה ששון ושמחה הרוג בקר ושחוט צאן אכול בשר ושתות יין וגו׳ ״ מה כתיב בתריה ? ״ונגלה באזני ה׳ צבאות אם יכופר העון הזה לכם עד תמותון אמר ה׳ צבאות״. (תענית יא, תנדבא״ז פ״א)

> Our Rabbis of blessed memory have taught: When Israel is in trouble and one of them separates himself from them, then the two ministering angels who accompany every man come and place their hands upon his head and say: So and so, who separated himself from the community, shall not behold the consolation of the community. When the community is in trouble, let not a man say: I will go to my house, and I will eat and drink and all will be well with me! For of him does Scripture say (Isa. 22.13): "And behold joy and gladness, and slaying oxen and killing sheep, eating flesh and drinking wine . . ." What follows after this verse? — "And the Lord of Hosts revealed Himself in my ears: Surely this iniquity shall not be expiated by you till you die, says the Lord of Hosts." (Ta'anith 11a; Tanna debay Eliyahu Zuta, 1)

A heinous crime is committed by anyone who leaves the land of Israel, and great is the iniquity of anyone excluding himself from the community. Yet the punishment befalling Elimelech's family: death, widowhood, childlessness and excision, still seems inordinately severe to us. Nowhere have we found such retribution inflicted except for sins between man and man, in the case of the affliction of the widow and the orphan, and then only as measure for measure.

> "You shall not afflict the widow or fatherless child.
> If you afflict them in any wise — for it they cry at all unto Me, I will surely hear their cry. —
> My wrath shall wax hot, and I shall kill you with the sword;
> And your wives shall be widows and your children fatherless."
> (Exod. 22.21-23)

Therefore, our Rabbis declared that Elimelech and his family had also committed a very grave social crime:

והא תניא: בשעת דבר כנס רגליך, בשעת רעב פזר רגליך, ולמה נענש [אלימלך]? **לפי שהפיל לבן של ישראל.**
משל לבליוטוס [שר העצה] של מלך, שהיה שרוי במדינה והיו בני המדינה בטוחים עליו, שאם תבוא שנת בצורת, שיוכל לפרנס המדינה עשר שנים. וכיון שבאה שנת בצורת היתה שפחתו עומדת בסירקי וקופתה בידיה. (ילקוט שמעוני רות)

אלימלך מגדולי המדינה ומפרנסי הדור היה, וכיון שבאו שני רעבון, אמר: עכשיו יהיו כל ישראל מסבבים על פתחי, זה בא בקופתו וזה בא בכפיפו [בסלו], מה עשה? עמד וברח מפניהם. (שם)

But the Baraitha teaches: At the time of pestilence draw back your feet and at the time of famine set them in motion. Why then was he (Elimelech) punished? — Because he caused the people of Israel to lose heart.
His act may be compared to that of a king's counsellor, stationed in a certain country. All the inhabitants of the country placed their reliance on his being able to sustain the country for ten years in the event of famine. Yet when a famine did break out, his own maidservant had to stand in the circus holding her almsbox in her hands. (Yalkut Shim'oni, Ruth)

Elimelech was among the outstanding personalities of the country, as well as one of its leading providers. When the years of famine set in, he claimed: Now all Israel will gather at my gates. One will come with his box, the other with his basket. What did he do? He arose and ran away from them. (*Ibid.*)

"Because he caused the people of Israel to lose heart."

We can gain an added insight into his misdeed by bearing in mind that, in those days, the people of Israel had settled in the land according to their tribal divisions, their families and fathers' houses. Certainly all the inhabitants of Beth-lehem were related to each other in some way or other, for brothers, uncles and cousins had all taken up residence in the same area.

Now, in the days of trouble, Elimelech's family had deserted its relatives and run away. Elimelech's family was very wealthy. Their fields, they left behind, but their gold and silver, they took along with them to Moab. There, they would be able to live in peace and quiet. No hungry relatives would see or disturb them.

Wealthy and distinguished, they were appropriately received in the neighboring land.

Had they been poor, they would not have dared to leave. They would have lived on standards similar to the rest of the population even in times of famine. What could the impoverished expect to obtain in a foreign country?

And in those days, Moab was subservient to Israel. So it had been from the days of Ehud ben Gera, from the time of Jephthah of Gilead until Ibzan of Beth-lehem (Ibzan, according to the Rabbis, was Boaz).

> "Ephrathites" — distinguished persons. Similarly (1 Sam. 1.1): "The son of Tohu, the son of Zuf, an Ephrathite" — *eugenus.* See how important he was. Eglon, King of Moab, married off his daughter to Mahlon, as the master has said: Ruth was the daughter of Eglon.*
>
> The Targum, too, adds: nobles, masters (for Ephrathim); "And they continued there" — as princes.

It follows, then, that their fate was finally sealed only on account of their selfishness, their lack of consideration for their distressed brothers and relatives.

Their punishment began while they were transgressing, and one transgression led to another.

> And they took for themselves Moabite wives.
> — And the Holy One, blessed be He, was angry at him (Elimelech) for he was the prince of his generation.

> The Holy One, blessed be He, said: These persons have deserted my children and left My land to its desolation. — What is written there? — "And Elimelech, Naomi's husband died." — Should not the sons have learned a lesson from the father (his death) and returned to the land of Israel? What did they do? They also [sinned]. They married Moabite women and did not even induce their wives to undergo ritual purification and conversion. (Tanḥuma, *Bahar.*)

They did not return. Was it so simple for them to return and marry women of their own people and tribe? Would they not be regarded as deserters there? They would have been ashamed to return. Therefore they further increased the distance between themselves and their people — involuntarily — by taking to wife daughters of that nation which was forbidden to enter the Israelite community.

> It was taught in the name of R. Meir: They did not induce their wives to convert and to undergo ritual purification. Nor were they aware of the law soon to be resuscitated that only an Ammonite male, and not a female, only a Moabite male, and not a female, was prohibited. (Yalkut Shim'oni 600)

Our Rabbis held that they had acted out of despair.

> It is written (1 Chron. 4.22): "And Yoash and Saraph who had dominion in Moab. Rav and Samuel offered interpretations. One held that their names were really Mahlon and Chilion; so why were they called Yoash and Saraph? Yoash— —to signify that they had despaired (*nithya-ashu*) of redemption; Saraph — to signify that they had deserved the Divine retribution of burning (*serefah*). (Bava Bathra 91b)

And our Rabbis have afforded us another profound insight here:

> What caused them to marry Moabite wives?
>
> Like Ammon and Moab, they had acted out of selfish motives, "because they [Ammon and Moab] met you not with bread, and with water in the way when you came forth from Egypt." (Deut. 23.5; Yalkut Shim'oni *Ibid.*)

See how severe is the retribution for selfishness! To the end of all generations did these nations have to answer for their selfishness; they can never enter the community of Hashem —

> "You shall seek neither their peace nor their prosperity for all your days, for ever." (*Ibid.*)

Nahmanides attributes the fate of these nations to their ingratitude:

> "And it appears to me that Scripture had condemned these two brothers (Ammon and Moab), since they had been the beneficiaries of Abraham's charitableness. He had rescued their father and mother from the sword and from captivity. On account of his merit, they escaped the overthrow (of Sodom) — they were, therefore, duty bound to be kind to Israel..." (*Ibid.*)

Ingratitude is the diametric opposite of kindness. To be kind means to go beyond the requirements of the law and to lean towards compassion. Ingratitude signifies the failure to fulfill even what the bare law expressly ordains — and entails cruelty. Kindness and compassion go beyond the requirements of the law. For this very reason, perhaps, the Torah demands that we act with kindness, more insistently, more extremely, and punishes unkind behavior severely.

> No man leaves orphans unless he is selfish with his money. For so Scripture avers (Ps. 109.10,16): "His children shall be vagabonds and beg" — and why? — "because he remembered not to do kindness." (*Ibid.*)

Let us examine this chapter of the Psalms, from where the Rabbis have extracted the verse they have used in the above passage. There we shall find a description of the transgression of Elimelech and his household, as well as of their punishment.

"Let his days be few; let another take his charge.
Let his children be fatherless and his wife a widow.

Let his children be vagabonds and beg;
And let them seek their bread out of their desolate places."

Rashi: Concerning them, all will ask: what happened to so and so, because the report of his misfortune had been circulating (*shielu* being understood here is "inquiring"). And *shielu* may also be understood as an intensive form denoting "begging."

"Let the creditor distrain all that he has.
And let strangers make spoil of his labor.
Let there be none to extend kindness unto him;
Neither let there be any to be gracious unto his fatherless children.

Let his posterity be cut off;
In the generation following let their names be blotted out.
Let the iniquity of his fathers be brought to remembrance unto the Lord;
And let not the sin of his mother be blotted out.

Let them be before the Lord continually,
That he may cut off the memory of them from the earth.
Because that he remembered not to do kindness." (Ps. 109.8-18)

THE WOMAN WAS LEFT ALONE

"AND ELIMELECH, NAOMI'S HUSBAND, DIED;
AND SHE WAS LEFT AND HER TWO SONS
"AND... BOTH OF THEM DIED;
AND THE WOMAN WAS LEFT OF HER TWO CHILDREN
AND HER HUSBAND."

A student once asked me: Seeing that the Holy One, blessed be He, is long suffering and abundant in goodness, why did he levy punishment in full, blow by blow, and without giving any warning? (The brevity of the narrative led him to overlook the fact that punishment was not inflicted all at once nor the blows in immediate succession.)

We have already noted that reading this far for the first time, we pay attention only to the deaths and bereavements. Reading more slowly a second time, we discover that here too *Hashem* was long suffering and patient. We become aware that ten years were to pass before the sons died.

> "And they dwelt there about ten years" — this teaches that a decree is held in abeyance for ten years. (Ruth Zuta 5)

The Rabbis went even further and observed:

> R. Hunya and R. Joshua bar Avin and R. Zavda, R. Levi's son-in-law:
> The Merciful One never exacts retribution of a man's life to begin with. Where is this taught? — From Job, as it is said (Job 1.1): "There came a messenger unto Job and said: The oxen were plowing..."

> And so it was with Mahlon and Chilion also. First, all of their horses, their donkeys and their camels died, then Elimelech and lastly the two sons. (Midrash Rabba Ruth 2; Pesikta Rabbathi 16; Tanḥuma *Bahar*)

If we examine these two proximate verses once more, the concluding clause of each would seem redundant. The two add nothing to what we already know.

Now these statements were not written down for stylistic embellishment only, but in order to divert our attention from the dead to the survivors. "And she was left... And she was left..."

> "And Elimelech, Naomi's husband, died." — The death of a man is felt by none but his wife. (Sanhedrin 22b)
>
> And the woman was left — a widow; and her two sons — orphans. (The additions by the Targum)

The emphasis is especially evident in the last verse which, as it were, sums up the entire account so far:

> "And the woman was left of her two children and her husband." R. Hanina said: She was like the remnants of the remnants.

The story spans ten years of the life of a family in a foreign country. How many episodes did they experience? How many tribulations did they endure? All this has been distilled by Scripture into the tears of the surviving woman. She wept at one and the same time for all her loved ones, since on this day, her consciousness of her widowhood had been reawakened, and her pain was redoubled.

"Of her two children"... They had grown up, but to the compassionate feelings of their bereaved mother, they were still young and had, as it were, reverted to their childhood once again.*

"AND THE WOMAN WAS LEFT."

The cry of the bereaved and cut off can be discerned in this verse, just as the cry of the woman of Tekoa in her plea to David:

> "And they will destroy the heir also. Thus they will quench my coal which is left, and will leave my husband neither name nor remainder upon the face of the earth." (2 Sam. 14.7)

More than once Naomi asked herself why she had survived.

Had she not sinned along with them, and as much as they?

Perhaps her sin was greater, and so her punishment was greater. That was why she had been left desolate to bear the burden of sorrow of the entire family.

From now on, then, all her life would be devoted to serve this one purpose, to bear the burden of their guilt. She took upon herself the task, to make known how bitterly they had been punished. With this guilt in her heart, she would return to the people of Beth-lehem. They would stare at her, realizing what had overtaken her, and they would write it down for the generations to come —

> "For the hand of *Hashem* is gone forth against me." (v. 13)
> The Divine decree — has so gone forth that its effect is now clearly evident. (Ibn Ezra)

Naomi could not yet have known, she could hardly have dared to believe at the time, that she had been preserved alive through the kindness and compassion of *Hashem*. The Righteous Judge had allowed the spark of life of Elimelech's family to remain glowing in her and had not extinguished its light — How did she deserve this?

It is a story of a single family stretching back for ten years, and even before, a story that is not recorded in the Bible.

It is the story of the happenings in the home of Elimelech and Naomi, of their deliberations, of the suffering they endured, till they finally made up their minds to leave and go to live in the fields of Moab. Generally, students are disposed to side with Naomi, to believe that she was sorely distressed, that she was opposed to leaving, that she could not, nevertheless, raise her voice in protest. Against her will, then, she followed her husband and children all of whom she loved so well.*

> "And a certain man went" — he and his wife.
> He was the prime mover; his wife secondary to him. (Ruth Rabba 1)

Is all this good ascribed to her on account of the traits she revealed later? Or does this judgement emanate from the disposition to assume that a woman is more inclined to compassion than a man — more involved in charity than he? (See Rashi, 2 Kings 22.14; Megillah 14b)

Perhaps, too, because the woman is more closely tied up with her immediate surroundings — her relatives and neighbors — and it is more difficult for her to travel abroad to become an alien.

Our Rabbis have also found an indication of her virtue in her name.

> Naomi (*no'am* pleasant) — for her deeds were pleasing and sweet. (Ruth Rabba *Ibid.*)

This being so, we can understand that Naomi's heart was torn between her love for her family, on the one hand, and for her people, on the other, during all those years.

How much must she have castigated herself for that transgression—she whose whole being was permeated with kindness and compassion! For all we know, these very agonies may have rendered her worthy to survive. So she became the remnant.*

"AND THE WOMAN WAS LEFT OF HER TWO CHILDREN AND HER HUSBAND."

"In that day, says the Lord, will I assemble her that halts, and I will gather her that I have afflicted;

And I will make her that halted a remnant." (Micah 4.6-7)

THE RETURN JOURNEY BEGINS

או. וַתָּקָם הִיא וְכַלֹּתֶיהָ וַתָּשָׁב מִשְּׂדֵי מוֹאָב
כִּי שָׁמְעָה בִּשְׂדֵה מוֹאָב כִּי־פָקַד יְיָ אֶת־עַמּוֹ
לָתֵת לָהֶם לָחֶם׃

1.6 "THEN SHE AROSE WITH HER DAUGHTERS-IN-LAW, THAT SHE MIGHT RETURN FROM THE FIELDS OF MOAB; FOR SHE HAD HEARD IN THE FIELD OF MOAB HOW THAT GOD HAD REMEMBERED HIS PEOPLE IN GIVING THEM BREAD."

"THEN SHE AROSE!"

What was driving her to depart from there? Or else, what was drawing her back to Eretz Israel? Is the only reason the one recorded in Scripture: "for she had heard . . ."?

It is incorrect to read this sense only into the text. R. Moses Alshekh has remarked, astonished:

> Scripture ascribes an unworthy reason to her in stating "for she had heard" — since it seems to convey that she returned for the sake of food alone.
> And that it was not enough for her to return out of love for the holy land of Israel, even with a lack of food.

The truth is that "the fields of Moab" — "the field of Moab", repeated "superfluously" here, were the real factor impelling her to return.

> "From the fields (pl.) of Moab" — to indicate that she had torn herself away completely from all the towns of Moab. (*Ibid.*)

Only now did she realize how utterly alien the locality was to her. True; the graves of her husband and sons were precious to her, but was she to linger there, waiting for her own grave to be dug?

No! — she would return to her former home, to Beth-lehem, there to live out the rest of her days in the midst of her own people. There would she be buried — among the graves of Israel.
[These thoughts may be ascertained by examining Ruth's remarks to Naomi (see verses 16-17).]

But — how was she to go back?

She still remembered the day, or was it night, of their departure, when she, her husband and sons had run away. In her mind's eye she could once more detect the angry, contemptuous looks and the cursing which the men of Beth-lehem had sent on after them.

How was she able to go back? How could she have the effrontery to face them, while their anger was still smouldering in their hearts?

Yet perhaps now she would be forgiven, since she had been stricken with anguish and widowhood, and had been bereaved of her children. Perhaps they would forgive and forget her iniquity. They too had been forgiven:

> THAT *HASHEM* HAD REMEMBERED HIS PEOPLE IN GIVING THEM BREAD."

> And she arose...and returned — in her thoughts. (Ibn Ezra)

[The entire verse merely reports her thoughts — the actual journey is recounted in the following verse.]

In her thoughts, she had already uprooted herself from the fields of Moab, and was contemplating herself standing in Beth-lehem, to where she had wanted to return.

Yet Beth-lehem itself is not mentioned either in this, or the succeeding, verse. Instead, Scripture merely records that they went to return to the land of Judah.

Perhaps she was, after all, still afraid of Beth-lehem? — —

In some situations, we only reveal a fraction of our thoughts and hide the rest away. Yet the latter are by far the more important. Beth-lehem is not expressly mentioned, but is definitely alluded to by the final word *leḥem* — bread.

We know all too well that it was not for bread alone that Naomi longed — but for her home!

She was returning from the field of Moab to the house of (Beth-)*leḥem,* from the field to her home.
Interestingly, the entire account of the famine and the flight moves between Beth-lehem and the *field* of Moab. Throughout this entire Book, Moab is always designated as a field, which, contrasted with home, indicates mobility, a lack of stability.

A novel interpretation was suggested by overseas students in a teachers' seminary class. Their observation was particularly suited to them.

They noticed that here it is not simply related that Naomi had heard that the famine had ceased from the land. Instead the information is presented with special joy and exaltation:

> "FOR SHE HAD HEARD IN THE FIELD OF MOAB, HOW THAT *HASHEM* HAD REMEMBERED HIS PEOPLE IN GIVING THEM BREAD."

Today, too, whenever a Diaspora Jew hears good tidings concerning Eretz Israel, he rejoices and is especially encouraged, for national pride becomes exceptionally strong in foreign lands. Diaspora Jewry identifies itself with the people in Israel as a whole.

Perhaps their view coincides with the opinion of the Rabbis.

כי פקד ה׳ את עמו.
כי לא יטוש ה׳ עמו ונחלתו לא יעזוב. (תהלים נ״ד)
כי לא יטוש ה׳ עמו בעבור שמו הגדול. (שמואל א׳ יב)

"How that *Hashem* had remembered His people."

"For *Hashem* will not cast off His people, neither will He forsake His inheritance." (Ps. 94.14)

"For *Hashem* will not cast off His people for His Name's sake." (1 Sam. 12-22)

אמר ר׳ שמואל בר נחמיה: פעמים שהוא עושה בעבור עמו ונחלתו, ופעמים שהוא עושה בעבור שמו הגדול.

אמר ר׳ איבי: כשישראל זכאין — בעבור עמו ונחלתו, וכשאין ישראל זכאין — בעבור שמו הגדול.

ורבנן אמרי: בארץ ישראל — בשביל עמו ונחלתו! בחוץ לארץ בעבור שמו הגדול. שנאמר: (ישעיה מח) ״למעני למעני אעשה״. (רו״ר ב, יא)

R. Samuel b. Nehemiah said: Sometimes He does it for the sake of His people and His inheritance and sometimes He does it for the sake of His great Name.

R. Ibbi said: When Israel merits it, He does it for the sake of His people and His inheritance, but when Israel does not deserve it, He does it for the sake of His great Name.

Rabanan said: In the land of Israel, He does it for the sake of His people and His inheritance; in the Diaspora, for the sake of His great Name, as it is said (Isa. 48.11): "For My own sake, for My own sake will I do it." (Ruth Rabba 2.11)

In the field of Moab, Naomi, too, had heard the good tidings, that God had remembered His people, God had done so, and she wanted to share in that good fortune. If they had been remembered, she would be remembered too.* Come, see! Here was a person in whom all hope had been extinguished — her entire family had perished; her sons were gone. Yet now the echo of public rejoicing reawakened her to life. She roused herself from her anguish to seek the refuge of her former spacious home, her people and God.

> "I dwell among my own people" (2 Kings 4.13-14), the great woman of Shunem replied, as if forgetting that she was childless. It follows from here that one should take his place in the midst of the people and not be counted alone. (Zohar Ḥadash Ruth; Zohar, *Vayetze* 169)

Her desire to return to her people had now become an obsession. She had, apparently, broached the subject to her daughters-in-law, and they had accordingly answered: "But we will return with you unto your people" (v. 10), "Your people is my people — your God, my God" (v. 16). Her return journey was her path of repentance.

It is fitting here to recall the verse quoted by R. Joshua ben Korḥa (see p. 12)

> "When you cry, let them that you have gathered deliver you." (Isa. 57.13)

"THEN SHE AROSE WITH HER TWO DAUGHTERS-IN-LAW."

What were her daughters-in-law doing, remaining with her after the deaths of their husbands?

> The halakhah presumes that there is antagonism between the daughter — and mother-in-law — hence they cannot testify against each other. (Maimonides, Laws of Divorce, 12.16)

Nevertheless, they rose to follow her to an unknown land, to a people they had never known before. Why? Was it so easy to leave everything behind in Moab, to forfeit any chance to rebuild their lives among their own people? Did they not have any doubts? Did they not discuss and debate this move at home — with each other, and each with her own self?

Were they prepared to do so merely out of pity for the desolate, old woman, the mother of their late husbands? (see v. 8). Why did they make no attempt to restrain her, to persuade her to remain in Moab, and to assure her of their love and respect for the rest of her life?

The feeling engendered by the text is that they were not tormented by any misgivings, that they were attached to Naomi and clung lovingly to her. If she went, so would they go.
From this verse onwards, a new, wondrous ray of grace and humility seems to shed its light upon Naomi, as the two Moabite women accompanied her repaying her for all she had given to them.

> A ray of *ḥesed* illuminates the path of these two daughters of Moab and is reflected, indirectly, upon Mahlon and Chilion who had, by now, receded behind the horizon. The Book of Ruth does not disclose the nature of the inner life of this family. Yet the passionate devotion of the daughters-in-law to the mother of their departed husbands allows us to appraise the purity and warmth permeating the family life of these two Ephrathites of Judah. Otherwise the strong ties binding the women to this family would be utterly incomprehensible. If, then, the influence of Mahlon and Chilion was also manifest posthumously, the very disparagement of their other traits serves to point up their virtues.
> The strongest influence, however emanates from Naomi. She was "refined in word and deed." Orpah and Ruth were drawn towards her like planets gravitating towards the sun. (Rabbi I. Z. Lipowitz,* Naḥal Yosef).

The Zohar Ḥadash discusses whether Orpah and Ruth had been converted prior to their being married or not. The tendency is to view them as having become Jewish, the proof lying in Naomi's remark (v. 15):

> "BEHOLD YOUR SISTER-IN-LAW IS GONE BACK TO HER PEOPLE AND TO HER GOD."

That became the occasion for Ruth to reaffirm, with even greater conviction and sincerity, her submission to the authority of the Torah.

We found the contrary view in the Zohar, (*Balak*) — the view of R. Meir (see p. 16); however another passage there sheds light on this matter:

> פתח ואמר : (דברים ב׳ ט) ויאמר ד׳ אלי אל תצר את מואב ואל תתגר בם מלחמה. כל דא אתפקד למשה — דלא נפקו עדיין אינון מרגלאן טבאן, דהא ביומיהון דשופטים נפקא רות, וכו׳.
>
> תרגום ע״פ ה״סולם״
> כל זה נצטוה למשה — שלא יצאו עדיין אלו מרגליות הטובות, כי בימי השופטים יצאה רות , ובת עגלון מלך מואב היתה. מת עגלון, שהרגו אהוד ונתמנה מלך אחר, נשארה בת עגלון זו, והיתה בבית אומנת ובשדה מואב, כיון שבא שמה אלימלך לקחה לבנו.
>
> ואי תימא דגיירא אלימלך תמן — לא, אלא כל אורחי **ביתא ומיכלא ומשתיא אוליפת —**
> ואם תאמר שאלימלך גייר אותה שם — לא, אלא כל דרכי הבית, ואכילה ושתייה למדה. ומתי נתגיירה ? אחר כך, כשהלכה עם נעמי אז אמרה עמך עמי ואלהיך אלהי. (זהר פ׳ בלק)
>
> It begins by saying (Deut. 2.9): "And God said unto me: Be not at enmity with Moab, neither contend with them in battle." Moses was given this order — because the two precious jewels had not yet crystallised, for Ruth only emerged in the period of the Judges — she was the daughter of Eglon, King of Moab. Eglon died at the hand of Ehud. Another king was appointed. This daughter of Eglon remained a ward in the house and in the field of Moab. When Elimelech came there, he took her for his son.

> And if you think that Elimelech converted her there — the answer is, no. She did, however, learn all the ways of that household, even its eating and drinking habits. When did she convert? — When she went with Naomi. Then she affirmed: "Your people is my people and your God is my God." (Zohar *Balak*)

These daughters of Moab saw how the Jewish household was conducted and became educated in its practices. The ties connecting them to that household became transformed into bonds of love, of the longing to join that people and its God.

Here too was a miniature messianic episode, one that will recur when the fame of the children of Israel will become widespread in the world.

> "And they shall take hold of the skirt of him that is a Jew, saying: We will go with you." (Zech. 8.23)

The seeds for such eventualities were planted by Abraham, our forefather, the progenitor of a multitude of nations, when he first went down with his family to Egypt.

> When Paraoh saw what was done on Sarah's behalf in his own house, he took his daughter and gave her to Sarah, saying: Better let my daughter be a handmaid in this house than a mistress in another... as it is written (Ps. 45.10): "Kings' daughters are among your favorites." (Gen. Rabba 45.2)

Such then was Naomi. She imparted to her daughters-in-law all the beautiful practices of the Hebrew home — even in eating and drinking.

Together with the pleasantness of her manner, they must have noticed her inner grief at the absence of *ḥesed* (kindness and benevolence), brought about by their departure from Beth-lehem. Who knows — perhaps it was these invisible lines of *ḥesed* which had raised the two precious jewels from the depths of Moab to place them in the royal crown of Israel.

"AND SHE AROSE AND HER TWO DAUGHTERS-IN-LAW."

נפולה היתה, וקמה לה בחזירה לארץ־ישראל. (מדרש לקח־טוב)

Fallen, she had now lifted herself up by returning to Eretz Israel. (Midrash Lekaḥ Tov.)

THE ROAD BACK

אז. וַתֵּצֵא מִן־הַמָּקוֹם אֲשֶׁר הָיְתָה־שָׁמָּה
וּשְׁתֵּי כַלֹּתֶיהָ עִמָּהּ
וַתֵּלַכְנָה בַדֶּרֶךְ לָשׁוּב אֶל־אֶרֶץ יְהוּדָה׃

1.7 "AND SHE WENT FORTH OUT OF THE PLACE WHERE SHE WAS, AND HER TWO DAUGHTERS-IN-LAW WITH HER;
AND THEY WENT ON THE WAY TO RETURN UNTO THE LAND OF JUDAH."

When even the most clear-cut decision has to be carried out, doubts begin to arise. There are second thoughts and misgivings, especially where the implementation entails the tribulation of a lengthy journey and the endurance of considerable anguish. This verse, then, is not to be read as imparting any new information, but as portraying the difficulties in Naomi's departing from the locality where she resided.

And so our reading of their journey on the road back to the land of Judah is slowed down.
For there, on the way, doubts began, or returned, to gnaw at Naomi's heart.
And perhaps her daughters-in-law were no longer of one mind; for "her daughters-in-law" of the previous verse now become "her *two* daughters-in-law."

Wending her way back, on the road to Beth-lehem, Naomi began reflecting, pondering on her reentry, in the company of her two daughters-in-law, into the city of her birth.

To what end were they accompanying her? To see her disgrace? — To add to it?

They were, after all, Moabites.

מפני מה היתה מחזרת אותן ? כדי שלא תתבייש בהן, שכן מצינו ; כמה שווקים היו בירושלים ולא היו מערבין אלו עם אלו ; שוק של מלכים, שוק של נביאים, שוק של כהנים, שוק של לויים, שוק של ישראל.

ניכרים בלבושיהם בשווקים, מה שאלו לובשים לא היו אלו לובשים. (רות זוטא ח)

Why, then, was she sending them back? So as not to suffer shame on their account, for so we have found: There were many markets in Jerusalem, but they (the customers) of the one would not mix with the customers of the other. There was a market for kings, for prophets, for priests, for Levites, for Israelites.

People were recognizable, in the market places, by the clothes they wore. No one single group wore the same clothes as any other. (Ruth Zuta 8)

Here she halted, looked at them, and as if merely continuing her train of thought, her inner thoughts spoken aloud in their presence.

ח. וַתֹּאמֶר נָעֳמִי לִשְׁתֵּי כַלֹּתֶיהָ
לֵכְנָה שֹּׁבְנָה אִשָּׁה לְבֵית אִמָּהּ
יַעַשׂ יְיָ עִמָּכֶם חֶסֶד כַּאֲשֶׁר עֲשִׂיתֶם עִם־הַמֵּתִים
וְעִמָּדִי:

8 "AND NAOMI SAID UNTO HER TWO DAUGHTERS-IN-LAW: 'GO, RETURN EACH OF YOU TO HER MOTHER'S HOUSE; THE LORD DEAL KINDLY WITH YOU, AS YOU HAVE DEALT WITH THE DEAD AND WITH ME.'"

She continued further:

ט. יִתֵּן יְיָ לָכֶם וּמְצֶאןָ מְנוּחָה אִשָּׁה בֵּית אִישָׁהּ

9 "THE LORD GRANT THAT YOU FIND REST, EACH OF YOU IN THE HOUSE OF HER HUSBAND."

The implication: you are able, and even obliged, to rebuild your lives in the midst of your own people.

וַתִּשַּׁק לָהֶן וַתִּשֶּׂאנָה קוֹלָן וַתִּבְכֶּינָה׃

"AND SHE KISSED THEM AND THEY LIFTED UP THEIR VOICE AND WEPT."

Three women standing by the wayside weeping.
Till now they had suffered their sorrow in common. Now Naomi boldly made their separate reckonings for them.
She presented her argument with all womanly and motherly skill.
Slowly, slowly, but with clarity and precision, she marked out the proper course for them to follow.

And they answered her, tearfully:

י. וַתֹּאמַרְנָה לָּהּ, כִּי־אִתָּךְ נָשׁוּב לְעַמֵּךְ׃

10 "NAY BUT WE WILL RETURN WITH YOU TO YOUR PEOPLE."

They did not, perhaps, know how fervently Naomi desired them to stay with her. Did they not, the widows of Mahlon and Chilion, bring her memories of her sons? Had they, at least, been of her own people, she could still have found solace in them, and even hope. For then, a redeemer would surely be found, one who would establish a name in Israel. For so the Torah ordains:

> "If bretheren dwell together, and one of them die, and have no child,
> the wife of the dead shall not be married abroad unto one not of his kin;
> her husband's brother shall go in unto her, and take her to him to wife and perform the duty of a husband's brother to her.
> And it shall be, the first-born that she bears shall succeed in the name of his brother that is dead;
> that his name not be blotted out of Israel." (Deut. 25.5-6)

Probably, too, they were equally unaware of how ardently Naomi did not want them to accompany her. Were they not a constant reminder of the guilt of her sons and her family? Why should she drag them back to the land of Judah, and so increase her disgrace? There could not be any redeemer for them in Israel.

> "An Ammonite or a Moabite shall not enter into the assembly of God;
> even to the tenth generation shall none of his house enter into the assembly of the Lord for ever.
> You shall not seek their peace or their prosperity all your days for ever." (Deut. 23.4-7)

How could she explain this prohibition to them? She felt bitter because of them — and for them.

אל בנותי — אללי בנותי כי מר לי מאד מכם — **בשבילכן,**
כי יצאה בי ובבני ובבעלי יד ד׳.
(עץ יוסף: דרשו **מכם,** מ״ם הסיבה ולא מ״ם היתרון,
בשבילכן — בשביל מהירות שמיהרו בני לישא אתכן.) (רו״ר ב, יח)

> "Nay (*al*) my daughters — Woe unto me (*alelai*) my daughters, for it grieves me much on account of you — for your sake — for the hand of the Lord is gone forth against me."
> (*Etz Yosef*: The letter *mem* here is not the comparative "more than" but the *mem* of cause, on your account — because of my sons' impulsiveness in marrying you.) (Ruth Rabba 2.18)

Here all the bitterness of her reflections on her lot bursts out with ever mounting force.

יא. וַתֹּאמֶר נָעֳמִי
שֹׁבְנָה בְנֹתַי לָמָּה תֵלַכְנָה עִמִּי
הַעוֹד־לִי בָנִים בְּמֵעַי וְהָיוּ לָכֶם לַאֲנָשִׁים׃

יב. שֹׁבְנָה בְנֹתַי לֵכְןָ
כִּי זָקַנְתִּי מִהְיוֹת לְאִישׁ כִּי אָמַרְתִּי יֶשׁ־לִי תִקְוָה
גַּם הָיִיתִי הַלַּיְלָה לְאִישׁ וְגַם יָלַדְתִּי בָנִים׃

יג. הֲלָהֵן תְּשַׂבֵּרְנָה עַד אֲשֶׁר יִגְדָּלוּ
הֲלָהֵן תֵּעָגֵנָה לְבִלְתִּי הֱיוֹת לְאִישׁ
אַל בְּנֹתַי כִּי־מַר־לִי מְאֹד מִכֶּם כִּי־יָצְאָה בִי יַד־יְיָ׃

11 AND NAOMI SAID:
TURN BACK, MY DAUGHTERS, WHY WILL YOU GO WITH ME?
HAVE I YET SONS IN MY WOMB, THAT THEY MAY BE YOUR HUSBANDS?

12 TURN BACK, MY DAUGHTERS, GO YOUR WAY;
FOR I AM TOO OLD TO HAVE A HUSBAND. IF I SHOULD SAY I HAVE HOPE, SHOULD I EVEN HAVE A HUSBAND TONIGHT, AND ALSO BEAR SONS,

13 WOULD YOU TARRY FOR THEM TILL THEY WERE GROWN?
WOULD YOU SHUT YOURSELVES OFF FOR THEM AND HAVE NO HUSBANDS?
NAY, MY DAUGHTERS; FOR IT GRIEVES ME MUCH FOR YOUR SAKES, FOR THE HAND OF THE LORD IS GONE FORTH AGANST ME.' "

Thus spoke the bereaved mother, devoid of all hope, fated to be cut off, to be childless.
So man cuts up his flesh with his cruel mocking, intensifying his pain to feel it all the more.

14 AND THEY RAISED THEIR VOICES AND WEPT EXCEEDINGLY.

ותשנה קולן ותבכינה עוד :

ויבך על צואריו עוד (בראשית מו, כט) — שם פירש רש"י :
עוד — לשון הרבות בכיה. הרבה (יוסף) והוסיף בבכי יותר על הרגיל.

ותשנה — חסר אלף. תש כוחן מהלכות ובוכות. (ילק"ש תר"א)

"And he wept on his neck more" (Gen. 46. 29) — where Rashi takes "more" to signify weeping copiously — Joseph wept copiously and continuously — more than is usual.

And they raised — the *aleph* in **ותשנה** has been omitted. Their continuous weeping sapped (**תש**) their strength. (Yalkut Shim'oni 601)

A PARTING KISS AND A REFUSAL TO LEAVE

א יד. וַתִּשֶּׂנָה קוֹלָן וַתִּבְכֶּינָה עוֹד
וַתִּשַּׁק עָרְפָּה לַחֲמוֹתָהּ
וְרוּת דָּבְקָה־בָּהּ:

1.14 "AND THEY LIFTED UP THEIR VOICE AND WEPT AGAIN;
AND ORPAH KISSED HER MOTHER-IN-LAW.
BUT RUTH CLUNG TO HER."

This was the parting!
No words. Only a kiss. But not without pain.
Scripture remains silent, not divulging any more.

Did not Orpah kiss Ruth as well? Did she not stand and wait for Ruth? Or did she rush away, as if fleeing involuntarily?

"The name of the one was Orpah" — who turned her back (*oref*) on her mother-in-law. (Ruth Rabba 2)

Orpah left, Naomi looking sorrowfully after her.
[Scripture does not say whether Naomi returned the kiss. See v. 9.]
Naomi watched Orpah drawing away towards the border of Moab, realizing that with Orpah the remnant of her son Chilion's life was also being removed from and lost to her.

כליון — מלשון כליה. (ילק"ש ת"ר)

Chilion — is derived from *kelayah,* extinction. (Yalkut Shim'oni 600)

"BUT RUTH CLUNG TO HER."

How strongly does this expression bring out the feelings of the two for each other! *

"But you that did cling to *Hashem*, your God, are alive every one of you this day." (Deut. 4.4)

"And to cling to Him." (*Ibid.* 11.22)

Ruth too did not speak.
With her eyes, she pleaded, expressing her attachment to Naomi.
But Naomi did not understand. After all, Orpah was right in leaving.

Now she saw the two of them, as contrasted with each other. As against Orpah who had acted reasonably, the spiritual stature of Ruth rises on high, for she had decided to act beyond the call of reason — in obedience to the dictates of kindness of the best sort.

טו. וַתֹּאמֶר הִנֵּה שָׁבָה יְבִמְתֵּךְ אֶל־עַמָּהּ וְאֶל־אֱלֹהֶיהָ
שׁוּבִי אַחֲרֵי יְבִמְתֵּךְ׃

15 "AND SHE SAID: 'BEHOLD YOUR SISTER-IN-LAW (*yevimtekh*) IS GONE BACK TO HER PEOPLE AND UNTO HER GOD; GO BACK AFTER YOUR SISTER-IN-LAW.'"

Perhaps here, too, Naomi's pain at parting is all to evident. She could not hide her feelings.
Perhaps, too, the term *yevimtekh* contains an allusion to the institution of levirate marriage, one which she could not bring herself to mention directly any more. It was a slip of the tongue, forced out by the thoughts suppressed in her inner consciousness.

And Ruth was hurt.

Was her love, then, suspect? Would the people and the God to whom she longed to attach herself refuse to accept her? Why was Naomi so anxious to be rid of her?

She gave her reply, her words issuing forth like some powerful, passionate melody, as she poured out her love and utter devotion.

טז. וַתֹּאמֶר רוּת אַל־תִּפְגְּעִי־בִי לְעָזְבֵךְ לָשׁוּב מֵאַחֲרָיִךְ
כִּי אֶל־אֲשֶׁר תֵּלְכִי אֵלֵךְ וּבַאֲשֶׁר תָּלִינִי אָלִין
עַמֵּךְ עַמִּי וֵאלֹהַיִךְ אֱלֹהָי׃

יז. בַּאֲשֶׁר תָּמוּתִי אָמוּת וְשָׁם אֶקָּבֵר
כֹּה יַעֲשֶׂה יְיָ לִי וְכֹה יֹסִיף
כִּי הַמָּוֶת יַפְרִיד בֵּינִי וּבֵינֵךְ׃

16 "AND RUTH SAID, ENTREAT ME NOT TO LEAVE YOU, AND TO RETURN FROM FOLLOWING AFTER YOU; FOR WHITHER YOU GO, I WILL GO; WHERE YOU LODGE I WILL LODGE; YOUR PEOPLE SHALL BE MY PEOPLE AND YOUR GOD, MY GOD.

17 WHERE YOU DIE, I WILL DIE, AND THERE WILL I BE BURIED; THE LORD DO SO UNTO ME AND MORE ALSO IF AUGHT BUT DEATH PART YOU AND ME."

"ENTREAT ME NOT."

Rashi: Do not urge me. Ibn Ezra: Do not placate me, as in "placate Ephron for me." Or else, perhaps the term signifies "to attack — to fall upon," as in "and he fell upon him and he died." (1 Kings 2.25)

To sense how greatly Ruth was distressed:

> She said to her: You will not sin on account of me. You will not be punished on account of me. — I am fully resolved to become converted, but it is better that it should be at your hands than at those of another.
> When Naomi heard this she began to unfold to her the laws of conversion. (Ruth Rabba 2.23)

With all the grace, compassion and heroism radiating from these verses and illuminating Ruth's personality, we still ask in astonishment: Why did she see fit to act in this way? What did Ruth discover in Naomi, that she took upon herself to utter this oath? Did she want to lavish upon Naomi the love still harbored for her dead husband?

Or did some hidden voice beckon to her, speaking on behalf of the royal family destined to issue from her?

Indeed, Ruth followed her mother-in-law to the land of Judah, carrying, hidden within her, the powerful urge to cling to this family and to expiate their crime, and the hope of the perpetuation of the family in the midst of Israel — that the name of the deceased husband not become expunged, but that a house for him be built in Judah and his name established in Israel.

And to this purpose she dedicated her life.

> שתי נשים מסרו עצמן על שבט יהודה, תמר ורות. תמר היתה צועקת:
> אל אצא מן הבית הזה ריקנית!
> רות, כל שעה שחמותה אמרה לה לכי בתי, היתה בוכה... (ילק"ש תרא)

> Two women dedicated their lives to the perpetuation of the tribe of Judah — Tamar and Ruth. As for Tamar, she kept entreating: Let me not depart from this house empty! And Ruth, the longer her mother-in-law kept ordering her "go, my daughter," the longer she wept... (Yalkut Shim'oni 601)

Naomi, her heart preoccupied with the distress brought on by the return to Beth-lehem, could hardly notice the torrent of emotion raging within the heart of Ruth, the Moabite daughter-in-law, and gushing forth in a hymn of love for the people of Israel and their God. Nor could Naomi, in her heart, foresee or even sense the significance of that occasion, that this particular day was marked in the recesses of Divine prescience, as a new beginning in the unfolding of a messianic future.

Nor could Naomi know that on that selfsame day the iniquity of her house would be expiated, and that Ruth, her daughter-in-law, would be the very one to effect the renascence of her family. Ruth's unbounded kindness and compassion, her clearly and distinctly pronounced vow, by which she entered the community of Israel, effected this change.

"By kindness and truth is iniquity expiated." (Prov. 16.6)

יח. וַתֵּרֶא כִּי־מִתְאַמֶּצֶת הִיא לָלֶכֶת אִתָּהּ
וַתֶּחְדַּל לְדַבֵּר אֵלֶיהָ׃

1.18 "AND WHEN SHE SAW THAT SHE WAS STEADFASTLY MINDED TO GO WITH HER,
SHE LEFT OFF SPEAKING TO HER."

But the God of Israel heard and harkened to the heart of this proselyte, and accepted her.

א״ר חייא: בשעה שהגר מקבל עליו עולו של הקב״ה באהבה וביראה ומתגייר לשם שמים׳ אין הקב״ה מחזירו שנאמר ״ואוהב גר לתת לו לחם ושמלה״. (דברים י, יח; ילק״ש תרא)

אמר ר׳ אבהו; בוא וראה כמה חביבין גרים לפני הקב״ה, כיון שנתנה דעתה להתגייר השוה הכתוב אותה לנעמי שנאמר: ותלכנה שתיהן עד בואנה בית־לחם. (שם)

R. Hiyya said: When a proselyte accepts upon himself the yoke of the Holy One, blessed be He, and converts for the sake of Heaven, the Holy One, blessed be He, does not reject him, as it is said (Deut. 10.18) "...and loves the stranger giving him food and raiment." (Yalkut Shim'oni 611)

R. Abbahu said: Come and see how precious are proselytes to the Holy One, blessed be He. Once she (Ruth) had set her heart on converting, Scripture placed her in the same rank as Naomi, as it is said: "And the two of them went till they came to Beth-lehem." (*Ibid.*)

And He "Who shows mercy unto the thousandth generation" stored up great reward for her generations, commensurate with His consideration for all who love Him.

ותשק ערפה לחמותה ורות דבקה בה — אמר רבי יצחק:
אמר הקב"ה: יבואו בני הנשוקה [גלית] ויפלו בידי בני הדבוקה [דוד].

רש"י: שנגזר עליה שיפלו בניה בחרב בני רות שדבקה בשכינה. (סוטה מב:)

"Orpah kissed her mother-in-law but Ruth clung to her." — Said God: Let the sons (Goliath) of the one who kissed come and fall by the hands of the sons (David) of the one who clung.

Rashi: It was decreed upon her (Orpah) that her sons would fall by the hands of the sons of Ruth who clung to the Divine presence. (Sotah 42b)

FOUR SUPPLEMENTARY CHAPTERS

[A]
LOT THE FATHER OF MOAB

> "And Lot also, who went with Abram, had flocks and herds and tents." (Gen. 13.5)
>
> R. Tobiah b. R. Isaac said:
>
> He had two tents: Ruth, the Moabitess, and Na'amah the Ammonitess." (Gen. Rabba 41.5)

Our Sages, of blessed memory, and the subsequent Torah exegetes who faithfully interpreted the Holy Writ, were true "men of valor," capable of penetrating to the inner meaning of the Biblical text. Rising to their full stature, the brightness of their vision illuminating all around them, they were able to encompass the full scope of Torah, viewing it as a single, complete entity, in which begining and end are interconnected, all fitting together.

They saw, in a single glance, both the fathers and the progeny... Our Rabbis, in their holiness, discovered hidden meanings and secrets of the Torah even in the crowns topping the letters. Where, in the Torah, is Ruth alluded to? — She is specifically referred to in the Book of Genesis!

> "So Abram went, as the Lord had spoken to him; and Lot went with him." (Gen. 12.4)

As Abraham, the progenitor of the nation, took his first steps towards the land God had indicated to him, the messianic design began to unfold.

True, when we first began to study Torah, we did not search for hidden meanings. The bare narrative of Lot's accompanying Abraham is absorbing enough — and the meaning is also significant. By his interpretation, however, R. Tobiah has opened our eyes to the significance of those "tents." From there, two mothers of Israel gaze towards us, so far away and yet so near to us.

These are the mothers of the Jewish monarchy.

For so the One, "Who calls the generations from the beginning," teaches us through His Torah.*

והנה האלהי רשבי אמר: ווי לההוא בר־נש דאמר דהאי אוריתא אתיא לאחואה סיפורים בעלמא. (בעל "עקדת יצחק" בהקדמתו למגילת רות — זהר פ' בהעלותך קנ"ב ע"א)

And so, indeed, the divine R. Shimon bar Yoḥai asserted: Woe to the son of man who declares that this Torah merely tells stories. (R. Isaak Arama in his Introduction to Ruth, quoting the Zohar, *Beha'alothekha* 152a)

[B]

RUTH AND DAVID EMERGED FROM SODOM

דרש רבא : מאי דכתיב (תהלים מ, ח) **אז אמרתי הנה־באתי במגלת ספר כתוב עלי.** —
אמר דוד : אני אמרתי עתה באתי. ולא ידעתי, שבמגילת ספר כתוב עלי . . .

התם כתיב : (בראשית יט, טו) **שתי בנתיך הנמצאת.**
הכא כתיב : (תהלים פט, כא) **מצאתי דוד עבדי בשמן קדשי משחתיו !** — — —
רש"י : אני אמרתי — בשעה שנמשחתי, **עתה באתי לגדולה** ומקרוב פסקו לי גדולה זו, ולא ידעתי שמימי אברהם נכתבה עלי **במגילת ספר.** (יבמות עז)

Rava expounded: What is meaning of the verse (Ps. 40.8): "Then I said: 'Lo, I am come with the scroll of a book which is prescribed for me." — David said: I had thought that I had just come, yet did not know that I was alluded t[illegible] Scroll of a Book...

There (Gen. 19.15) it is written: "and your two daughters that are found here."
Here (Ps. 89.21) it is written: "I have found David My servant; with My holy oil have I anointed him."

Rashi: "I had said" — at the time I was anointed, that I had only now acceded to greatness, that just recently was greatness allotted to me. I did not know that I had been alluded to, from Abraham's time, in the scroll of a book. (Yevamoth 77a)

It becomes clear that even the rescue of Lot and his daughters from the overthrow of Sodom was part of an overall design.

Certainly, even taken in its plain sense, Abraham's prayer possessed both beauty and significance. In the mystic spheres, however, this prayer is of overriding importance. The Holy One, blessed be He, awaited it. He therefore revealed his intentions to His prophet.

ויי אמר המכסה אני מאברהם אשר אני עשה.
ואברהם היו יהיה לגוי גדול ועצום
ונברכו־בו כל גויי הארץ.

כי ידעתיו למען אשר יצוה את־בניו ואת־ביתו אחריו
ושמרו דרך יי׳ לעשות צדקה ומשפט,
למען הביא יי׳ על אברהם את אשר־דבר עליו. (בראשית יח, יז—יט)

[ונברכו — גם מלשון מבריך את הגפן]. (ראה יבמות ס״ג ע״א)

"And *Hashem* said: 'Shall I hide from Abraham that which I am doing;
seeing that Abraham shall surely become a great and mighty nation, and all the nations of the earth shall be blessed in him?

For I have known him to the end that he may command his children and his household after him,
that they may keep the way of *Hashem* to do righteousness and justice;
to the end that God may bring upon Abraham that which He had spoken of to him.' " (Gen. 18.17-19)

Venivrekhu — translated "shall be blessed" also conveys the connotation "will be engrafted" (like grafting a vine). (See Yevamoth 63a)

[C]

LOT AND HIS BELONGINGS

"And they took Lot, Abram's brother's son... and his belongings and they departed,

And Abram heard that his brother was taken captive." (*Ibid.* 14.12-14)

The account of the kings warring against Chedorlamer and of Abraham's energetic pursuit to Dan is impressive enough of itself. It portrays the kindness and faithfulness of Abraham our forefather.

This significance is not, however, lost even if we also discover the account, told here by God, "Who calls the generations from the beginning," of Abram's pursuit as being designed to rescue Lot and, with him, the ancestry of the Messiah.

"And he also brought back his brother, Lot, and his belongings." (*Ibid.* v. 16)

ויקחו את לוט ואת רכושו בן אחי אברם וילכו.
דאף־על־גב דאינהו לא חזו מזליהו חזי,
כי רצונם היה לבטל ישראל ולבטל משיחם ח"ו, ועל זה רדף אברהם אבינו מהר להצילו.
וזה סוד קלסתר פני לוט כפני אברהם, וכמו שאברהם אדם גדול בענקים כך לוט בגימטריא אד"ם — א׳דם, ד׳וד, מ׳שיח.

ולוט רצה להקדים בירושת הארץ כי חשב שהוא יורש את אברהם כמו שפירש"י — הסוד ארור כנען, ואין לו חלק בארץ.
כי לוט בעת ההיא מקולל — כי לוט לשון לטותא.
ואף־־על־פי שקלסתר פניו דומה לאברהם — הוא כקוף בפני אדם ולא אדם ממש.
וזה יהיה עד ביאת דוד ומשיח, ואז יאיר הקלסתר. (של"ה פ׳ נח)

Lot's belonging were the "two tents."

"And they took Lot, Abram's brother's son ... and his belongings and they departed."
Even though they had no idea what they were doing, their inner selves sensed the significance of their act.
Their unconscious desire was to blot out Israel and its Messiah, God forbid; that is why Abraham, our forefather, rushed to the rescue.
Here is the underlying significance of the fact that Lot's facial features resembled Abraham's. Just as Abraham towered above the giants, so did Lot (since the *gimatria* of Lot is ADaM — א'דם, ד'וד, מ'שיח)

Lot wanted to take immediate possession of his inheritance, believing himself to be Abraham's heir, as Rashi commented: the secret meaning is, Canaan is cursed in that he has no portion in the land.
At that time Lot was under a curse — the root of the word "Lot" (לוט) carries this connotation.
Even though, in his features, Lot resembled Abraham, this was only insofar as an ape bears a likeness to a human being.

And so it will continue until the advent of the Messiah, and then his facial features will become illuminated (*Shelah,* Noah).

[D]

THE DAUGHTER EARNS MERIT FOR HER FATHER

> "Ruth the Moabitess — who returned from the field of Moab" (See 1.22).
>
> She was the first to return "from the field of Moab."
> For then the ruling was rediscovered... (Korban Ha'edah, Yerushalmi Yevamoth 8.3)

Ruth, after all, is our kinswoman. She comes down to us from distant generations, for whom she atoned. She cleansed herself of the defilements of idolatry which had contaminated and corrupted her forefathers through all the generations, her forefathers who had sinned against Israel.*

From the cursed valley of Sodom rises the image of Ruth and revives and refurbishes the affection between the ancients, extending back to the time when her original ancestor accompanied Abraham, the forefather of a multitude of nations.
God's blessing was conferred, fittingly, upon Abraham from the first:

> "And all the families of the earth shall be blessed (*nivrekhu*) in you."
>
> The Holy One, blessed be He, said to Abraham: I have two goodly shoots to engraft on you: Ruth the Moabitess and Na'amah the Ammonitess.
> (*nivrekhu* — usually translated shall be blessed, here taken as deriving from *lehavrikh* — to engraft.)
>
> Rashi: Shoots — as bending the shoot of the vine. (Yevamoth 63a; Kilaim 7.1)

> "He that separates himself seeks his own desire,
> And snarls against all sound wisdom.
> A brother offended is harder to be won than a strong city;
> And their contentions like the bar of a castle" (Prov. 18.1,19)

> He that seeks his own desire — is Lot.
> The brother offended that is harder to be won than a strong city — is Lot. (Nazir 23a)

Ruth's original ancestor, Lot, had sinned. He was not steadfast when his faithfulness was tested. He did earn, but also failed to earn, merit. For was not his father Haran's heart still steeped in Terah's idols, surrounded by darkness and doubt?

> Haran thought: Either way — If Abraham is victorious, I will say that I am with Abraham; while if Nimrod is victorious, I will say that I am on Nimrod's side. When Abraham descended into the fiery furnace and was saved, Nimrod asked him: On whose side are you? On Abraham's, he replied. Thereupon Nimrod seized him and cast him into the fire; his innards were scorched and he died in the presence of his father, Terah. (Gen. Rabba 38.19)

[Abraham had allowed himself to be cast into the furnace with the idea of sacrificing his life to sanctify the Name of God — he was accordingly saved by Divine miracle. Haran submitted to the fire, but he expected to be saved. Therefore he was burnt!]
The son had the merit of basking in the light of Abraham, the Hebrew. Lot attached himself to Abraham, who departed from Ur of the Chaldees to go toward the promised land, there to proclaim the Name of God.

Abraham's home was the school in which Lot was educated — the stronghold of love, human kindness and Divine bounty stemming from the God of the universe.

Lot, as it were, "ascended the mountain of God," but was not strong enough to "maintain himself in His holy place." * And so he fell, descending to his erstwhile state.

> "And I am incapable of escaping to the mountain." (Gen. 19.19 Rashi *Ibid.*)

Abraham discerned the first symptoms of evil in his pupil and companion. He saw that there was no antidote for the root that was accursed.

> "And Abram said to Lot: 'Let there be no strife, I pray you between me and you;
> Is not the whole land before you? Separate yourself, I pray you, from me.'" (*Ibid.* 13.8-9)
>
> R. Helbo said: *Hibbadel* is not written here, only *hippared;* just as a *peredah* (mule) cannot fertilize seed, so is it impossible for this man to mix with the seed of Abraham. (Gen. Rabba 41.8)

Grief, bitterness, disappointment. Abraham, father to all proselytes, was compelled to dismiss his first convert, his nephew, his confidant — the soul he had made.*

> "And God said to Abram after that Lot was separated from him." (*Ibid.* 13.14)
>
> R. Judah said:
> There was anger in heaven against our father, Abraham, when his nephew, Lot, parted from him.
> The Holy One, blessed be He, said: He makes every one cling to Me, except his brother's son. (Gen. Rabba 41.10)

"Separate yourself from me!" — a permanent separation, of one root from another, one nation from another.

As for Lot, his root was evil:

> "He moved his tents as far as Sodom —:
> Now the men of Sodom were wicked and sinners against God, exceedingly." (*Ibid.* 13.12,13)

*

הפרד נא מעלי!

"Separate yourself from me!"

Many generations were to pass by, before that daughter of Moab — Lot's descendant — was to effect a reconciliation between the quarrelling brothers:

כה יעשה יי לי וכה יוסיף
כי המות יפריד ביני ובינך.

"The Lord do so to me, and more beside,
If aught but death part you and me." (According to *Shlah, Ibid.*)

*

ויסע לוט מקדם ויפרדו איש מעל אחיו. (בראשית יג, יא)

הסיע עצמו מקדמונו של עולם. אמר:
אי אפשי באברהם אי אפשי באלהיו. (ב"ר מא, י)

"And Lot journeyed east; and they separated themselves the one from the other." (Gen. 13.11)

He betook himself from the Ancient of the world, saying, I want neither Abraham nor his God. (Gen. Rabba 41.10)

(***Kedem,*** normally translated "east," interpreted as *kadmon,* the "Ancient.")
Contrary to him, Ruth returned singing her song of glory to Israel and its God.
All the subsequent generations of Lot responded to her call, Echoing her song in repentance, for all that her heart was pure in attaching herself to the Divine presencc:

עמך עמי ואלהיך אלהי!

"Your people shall be my people; your God, my God."

And the Divine wrath against Abraham was also stayed:

אמר הקדוש־ברוך הוא:
לכל הוא מדבק, ולבן אחיו אינו מדבק. (ב"ר מא, י)

The Holy One, blessed be He, said:
"He makes every one cling to Me except his brother's son." (Gen. Rabba 41.10)

ורות דבקה בה.

But Ruth clung to her.

THE RETURN TO BETHLEHEM

יט. וַתֵּלַכְנָה שְׁתֵּיהֶם עַד־בּוֹאָנָה בֵּית לָחֶם

1.19 "SO THEY TWO WENT TOGETHER UNTIL THEY CAME TO BETH-LEHEM."

So they two went . . . the two together — side by side — slowly wending their long way — traversing paths between fields, crossing rivers, ascending mountains. It is a long way from Moab to Beth-lehem. They crossed the Jordan, too, and passed by the valley of Sodom.

As usual, Scripture has greatly abridged the account of their journey. It tells nothing of what they spoke as they walked along together.

Perhaps no words at all passed between them. Perhaps they spoke only the few that were absolutely necessary.

They walked in silence. Each communed with herself. Each made her own reckoning with her own thoughts and feelings.

Naomi's attention was preoccupied with the journey to Beth-lehem, her recollections of the familiar paths, her seeing the city from afar off. She and her husband had traversed these paths ten years before when they departed in flight —

וַיְהִי כְּבֹאָנָה בֵּית לֶחֶם וַתֵּהֹם כָּל־הָעִיר עֲלֵיהֶן
וַתֹּאמַרְנָה הֲזֹאת נָעֳמִי?

"AND IT WAS WHEN THEY WERE COME TO BETH-LEHEM, THAT ALL THE CITY WAS ASTIR CONCERNING THEM, AND THE WOMEN SAID: 'IS THIS NAOMI?'"

The whole city was astir, excited. Naomi had come back — alone.

Like wildfire, the astounding news spread. The women converged on the city square to see. They did not know what reception to accord Naomi.

This was her punishment! Here, Naomi stood before them, a widow, a bereaved mother, broken. Without uttering a sound, she told them all her grief, her iniquity.

And the women of Beth-lehem, her relatives, her former friends, stood before her in her suffering, and nodded. They could not decide whether to take pity on her, or to gloat over her revengefully.

Was this not the curse that had been sent after her on the day that her flight had become known — the flight that caused Israel to lose heart?

Yet how could one gaze in revenge upon her in her hour of misfortune?

Compassion was certainly uppermost in their minds at the sight of her desolation; all the terrors of the punishment she had suffered were engraved on her face. They could not help recalling how she had looked in her youth and glory. Involuntarily, the cry burst from their lips:

"IS THIS NAOMI?"

זו היא נעמי, שהיתה מגנה את הפז ביפיה?
לשעבר היתה מהלכת באספקטיאות שלה [בעגלת צב מכוסה] — ועכשיו היא מהלכת יחפה...

לשעבר מתכסה בבגדי מלתין — ועכשיו מתכסה בבגדי סמרטוטין ופניה ירוקים מרעבון. (ילק״ש תרא)

Is this Naomi, who had put shining gold to shame by her beauty?
In the past, she had travelled in her canopied carriage — and now she walked barefoot...
In the past she would cloak herself in the finest wool — now she was in rags and tatters, her face pale with hunger. (Yalkut Shim'oni 601)

Some even recalled her former charity and kindness:

הזאת נעמי ? — שהיו בנות בית־לחם משתמשות בתכשיטיה !
הזאת נעמי ? — שהיו מעשיה נאים ונעימים. (שם)

Is this Naomi — who let the daughters of Beth-lehem use her jewelry?
Is this Naomi — whose deeds were pleasing and gracious? (*Ibid.*)

(Naomi is connected here with *naeh* and *na'im.*)

And Naomi was deeply sensitive to the glances cast at her, piercing her heart, hurting her.

כ. וַתֹּאמֶר אֲלֵיהֶן אַל־תִּקְרֶאנָה לִי נָעֳמִי
קְרֶאןָ לִי מָרָא (מרה) כִּי הֵמַר שַׁדַּי לִי מְאֹד:
כא. אֲנִי מְלֵאָה הָלַכְתִּי וְרֵיקָם הֱשִׁיבַנִי יְיָ
לָמָּה תִקְרֶאנָה לִי נָעֳמִי
וַיְיָ עָנָה בִי וְשַׁדַּי הֵרַע לִי:

20 "AND SHE SAID UNTO THEM: 'CALL ME NOT NAOMI, CALL ME MARAH; FOR THE ALMIGHTY HAS DEALT VERY BITTERLY WITH ME.
21 I WENT OUT FULL, AND THE LORD HAS BROUGHT ME BACK EMPTY.
WHY DO YOU CALL ME NAOMI,
SEEING THAT THE LORD HAS TESTIFIED (*anah*) AGAINST ME, AND THE ALMIGHTY HAS AFFLICTED ME?

> *anah* — the attribute of justice, punished, as in (Exod. 22.22) "If you afflict him in any wise," or else,
> *anah* — has testified against me, as in (Deut. 19.19): "...has testified falsely against his brother," or else,
> *anah* — his whole concern (*inyan*) has only been against me. (Ruth Rabba, end of Chap. 3)

This is the utterance of a bitter woman in submitting to her lot, justifying it to those against whom she had sinned. And she was, as it were, pleading for their forgiveness.

Note should be taken of the many times, and the many different forms, in which the verb — *shuv* ("return") appears, a clear allusion to the laws of repentance (*teshuvah*):

> It is highly praiseworthy in a penitent to make public confession, openly avow his transgressions and discover to others his sins against his fellow men; he should say to them: "Truly I have sinned against that person, and did this and that to him." (Maimonides, Laws of Repentance 2.5)

Her remarks were well chosen and poetically framed. Did she prepare her statement on the way? Does it adequately describe all her pain?
See, "the Lord has brought me back" to you, for you to see me, bearing, in my affliction, the iniquity of my destroyed family! God has testified against me — I am the living testimony of His retribution.

> "FOR GOD HAS TESTIFIED AGAINST ME AND THE ALMIGHTY HAS AFFLICTED ME."

This reads like a verse uttered by Job, the prototype of all sufferers.

> "For the arrows of the Almighty are within me, the poison of which my spirit drinks up." (Job 6.4)

Did the women have nothing to say in reply?

Did they accept her, comfort her — or did they shy away, reject her?

For at Naomi's side stood her gentile daughter-in-law — the daughter of Moab, who had sinfully married Naomi's son.

Perhaps Scripture tells us nothing here, because each woman in turn slunk away silently to her own home.
Shunned, Naomi remained alone in the city square, and with her, her daughter-in-law, Ruth, the Moabitess.

כב. וַתָּשָׁב נָעֳמִי וְרוּת הַמּוֹאֲבִיָּה כַלָּתָהּ עִמָּהּ
הַשָּׁבָה מִשְּׂדֵי מוֹאָב
וְהֵמָּה בָּאוּ בֵּית לֶחֶם בִּתְחִלַּת קְצִיר שְׂעֹרִים׃

1.22 "SO NAOMI RETURNED, AND RUTH THE MOABITESS, HER DAUGHTER-IN-LAW WITH HER, WHO RETURNED OUT OF THE FIELDS OF MOAB — AND THEY CAME TO BETH-LEHEM IN THE BEGINNING OF THE BARLEY HARVEST."

What is this statement intended to convey? Was it written merely to round off the chapter which began with a famine and ended with an abundant harvest?

Or is it, perhaps, to relate that the people of Beth-lehem were preoccupied with their bountiful harvest, the first after so many bad years, and that this harvest distracted their attention from their guest and her Moabite daughter-in-law?
Or perhaps, the verse is intended to make us aware of and sense the grief of Naomi as she returned to her home.

Here she was sitting at her window watching, listening to the joy of the harvesting rising from the fields.

And all the while, Elimelech's fields had not been blessed with plenty.

They had been left, untended, desolate with no one to till them, to redeem them.

> "Their children shall be vagabonds, and beg, and seek their bread out of their desolate places." (Ps. 109.10)

THE BREAD OF THE POOR

ב א. וּלְנָעֳמִי מְיֻדָּע (מודע קרי) לְאִישָׁהּ
אִישׁ גִּבּוֹר חַיִל מִמִּשְׁפַּחַת אֱלִימֶלֶךְ וּשְׁמוֹ בֹּעַז:

2.1 "AND NAOMI HAD A KINSMAN OF HER HUSBAND, A MIGHTY MAN OF VALOR, OF THE FAMILY OF ELIMELECH, AND HIS NAME WAS BOAZ."

Rashi: He was Elimelech's brother's son.

A kinsman (*moda'*) —
denoting an especially close relationship, one of true love and affection between one man and another. So Rashi teaches us in his commentary on Genesis.

> "For I have known him (*yeda'tiv*), to the end that he may command his children..." (Gen. 18.19)
> *Yeda'tiv* — I have known, have loved, an expression of affection, as in (Ruth 2.1) "*moda'* — kinsman"; (*Ibid.* 3.2) "Is not Boaz our kinsman (*moda'tenu*)?", and (Exod. 33.17) "I will distinguish you (*va-eida'akha*) by name." The primary meaning of the term, derived from the root *yada'*, is "knowing," for whoever holds a person in close affection, becomes attached to him, and so comes to *know* him well, is thoroughly familiar with him. (Rashi, *Ibid.*) *

Moda' is the reading (*keri*); the spelling (*kethiv*) is *mi-da*, perhaps to convey: Who knows what his relationship will be to her now?

The construction of the sentence should also be noted: "Naomi had a kinsman of her husband."

"A MIGHTY MAN OF VALOR."

Men of valor — rich men, who have no need to flatter or favor. (Rashi, Exodus 18.21)
I have already explained (Exod. 18) that this term encompasses all virtues, among them generosity and the hatred of unjust gain. (Malbim)

"AND HIS NAME WAS BOAZ."

The righteous are introduced in this order: "his name was..." "And his name was Kish" (1 Sam. 9); "and his name was Saul" (*Ibid.*); "and his name was Jesse" (*Ibid.* 17); "and his name was Mordecai" (Esther); "and his name was Elkanah" (1 Sam. 1); "and his name was Boaz" —
Since they resemble their Creator of Whom it is written (Exod. 3) "And my Name, *Hashem*." (Ruth Rabba 4).

What does this verse, standing by itself, at the head of the chapter, convey?

Is its only intention to introduce Boaz to us, that we should make the acquaintance of the principal character in what follows?

Or is it that we should add this item of information to Naomi's innermost thoughts as she sat alone, brooding, till Ruth asked for permission to gather some ears of corn for them...

The two of them, Naomi and Ruth, were sitting at home, isolated from human company, denied human help. And we should again recall that the inhabitants of Beth-lehem were all sons of the tribe of Judah, all interrelated in their inheritance.

Naomi does not turn to them seeking bread and they act as if they do not notice her.

It is difficult to explain the lack of compassion on the part of the people of Beth-lehem.

Perhaps, by general consent, the curse against this family for having made their fellow Jews lose heart was still observed. Perhaps, too, their antagonism was reinforced by their resentment against the Moabitess brought back by Naomi, since the halakhah concerning her status had not yet been clarified.

> "You shall not seek their peace nor their prosperity all your days forever." (Deut. 23.7)

Also Boaz, the relative, the kinsman, Elimelech's former friend, failed to extend consolation to the widow, nor did he provide for her support.

Was he so busily engaged in the harvesting of his fields? Or was he powerless to resist public pressure, even though he was "a mighty man of valor"?

General consent to do harm does not imply that all individuals approve.
On the contrary, it is quite possible that no one really wanted to do harm. Yet, since no one knew what the next person really felt, no one dared to go against public opinion.*

In this way, Boaz's conduct during all those days preceding Ruth's coming to his field to gather corn, becomes comprehensible. Scripture does, after all, assert that he was a "mighty man of valor" — embodying all human virtues, among them generosity. (See *Malbim* previous page).

> "Friend and companion have you put far from me, and my acquaintance into darkness." (Ps. 88.19)

Naomi did not go begging for help. She recalled the former wealth and glory she had enjoyed there, and she justified her lot.

Ruth, as well, saw and understood all. Perhaps she envisioned her fate thus and resigned herself to it: "Where you will lodge, there will I lodge."

Slowly it began to dawn on her that she too may have been to blame.

Yet perhaps she could still not explain why everyone shunned her. With all her heart, she had attached herself to this people — her oath to Naomi was as valid and holy to her as ever: "Your people shall be my people."

And now the two of them hungered, while the harvest was under way.

This was yet another trial for Ruth in her journey to the people she did not know. —

ב ב. וַתֹּאמֶר רוּת הַמּוֹאֲבִיָּה אֶל־נָעֳמִי
אֵלְכָה־נָּא הַשָּׂדֶה וַאֲלַקֳטָה בַשִּׁבֳּלִים
אַחַר אֲשֶׁר אֶמְצָא־חֵן בְּעֵינָיו׃

2.2 "AND RUTH THE MOABITESS SAID UNTO NAOMI: LET ME NOW GO INTO THE FIELD, AND GLEAN AMONG THE EARS OF CORN AFTER HIM IN WHOSE SIGHT I SHALL FIND FAVOR."

As one of the poor, she would glean in the fields, if she would be allowed.

"AFTER HIM IN WHOSE EYES I SHALL FIND FAVOR."

Gleanings are not the property of the owner of the field, but belong to the poor. This is the gift of God to the poor, God Who had now remembered his people to give them bread.

From Naomi, Ruth had most surely learned about the Jewish harvest laws, of their beauty: Gleanings, forgotten sheaves, the corners of the field all belong to the poor and the stranger (the proselyte).*

Was she not a proselyte? Was she not poor?

Naomi reluctantly consented, against her will.
She was distressed. She recalled the joyous harvests in her home. And now her daughter-in-law had to go gather with the poor.

Several days might have had to pass, before she overcame her reluctance and consented — for she was sorely distressed.

וַתֹּאמֶר לָהּ לְכִי בִתִּי׃

"AND SHE SAID UNTO HER: 'GO MY DAUGHTER.'"

A COINCIDENCE

ב ג. וַתֵּלֶךְ וַתָּבוֹא וַתְּלַקֵּט בַּשָּׂדֶה אַחֲרֵי הַקֹּצְרִים
וַיִּקֶר מִקְרֶהָ חֶלְקַת הַשָּׂדֶה לְבֹעַז
אֲשֶׁר מִמִּשְׁפַּחַת אֱלִימֶלֶךְ׃

2.3 "AND SHE WENT, AND CAME AND GLEANED IN THE FIELD AFTER THE REAPERS;
AND IT HAPPENED TO HER TO LIGHT ON THE PORTION OF THE FIELD BELONGING TO BOAZ, WHO WAS OF THE FAMILY OF ELIMELECH."

"And she went, and she came"—said R. Eliezer: She repeatedly went and came until she found decent men with whom to go. (Shabbat 113b)
R. Judah b. R. Simon said: She began to mark out her ways. (Ruth Rabba 4.6)
Rashi: She marked out her route prior to entering a field and would accordingly go and come and return to the city, marking the marks so as not to lose her way in the bypaths, and to know how to return.

The two words ("went," "came") afforded the Rabbis an understanding of Ruth's thoughts as she went out by herself for the first time.

She made her way trembling, fearful, praying. Would she be driven away and put to shame?

Would she, a gentile, be allowed to gather corn along with other poor Jews?

"AND IT HAPPENED TO HER TO LIGHT ON THE PORTION OF THE FIELD BELONGING TO BOAZ."

It was a coincidence that she came first to the field of Boaz of the family of Elimelech. Does not the verse so testify? Naomi did not give Ruth any instructions where to go, did not mark out any route for her. Painfully, she had given her consent: "Go, my daughter."

Had Ruth been aware that the field belonged to Naomi's kinsman, she would certainly have avoided going there. This owner was their rich relative who had ignored them.

It was a coincidence.

Does man realize that the Creator, the Prime Cause of all, designs all the apparently random events and plans their course in advance, to the last detail?*

"A man's goings are of the Lord: What does man understand of his way?" (Prov. 20.24)

TWO SUPPLEMETARY CHAPTERS

[A]
THE GIFTS TO THE STRANGER, THE ORPHAN, THE WIDOW

What a remarkable mitzvah is the commandment to leave the gleanings for the poor!

How this commandment was fulfilled in all its details during the joyous harvest season in the land of Judah is described in the Book of Ruth in distinct and lively color.

Here is a portrayal of our forefathers as they farmed their land long ago, and of their fulfillment of the *mitzvoth* pertaining to the land.

It would be well worthwhile to examine some of the reasons advanced as underlying this precept. In this way, we shall be better able to trace Ruth's path as she went forth to glean in the fields.

"And when you reap the harvest of your land, you shall not wholly reap the corners of your field, neither shall you gather the gleaning of your harvest,
And you shall not glean your vineyard, neither shall you gather the fallen fruit of your vineyard." (Lev. 19.9-10)

ראב"ע: וטעם ובקצרכם אחר זבח שלמים, כאשר נתת לשם האימורים, כן תתנו מקציר ארצכם לכבוד השם, לעני ולגר.
אלשיך: שלא תכלה פאת השדה ותקח בידך הלקט והפרט לתת בידיך לעני, כי יתבייש. רק שתניח הפאה והלקט והפרט והם ילכו כלוקטים משלהם דרך כבוד. וז"א: כי אני ה' אלוקיכם, כמוך העני והגר, לכן תתן לו משלי דרך כבוד. או קרוב לזה כי רצה הוא יתברך ללמד מה רב טוב מתן בסתר אשר לא יבוש המקבלו, וזה מאמרו יתברך: ראה נתתי לכם תבואתכם, בלתי נרגש. — כן גם אתה הזהר מלהתראות כאילו אתה נותן לו.

R. Abraham Ibn Ezra: The reason for the harvest laws being set down immediately following the law concerning the peace-offering is to teach us that just as one offers the sacrificial limbs to God, so should one give to the poor and the stranger from the harvest of his field for the glory of God.

R. Mosheh Alshekh: That you should not wholly reap the corner of the field, take the gleanings of the field and distribute them to the poor, for they will, in this way, be put to shame. Instead, you must leave the corners and the gleanings untouched. The poor will then be able to act with all due dignity as their own harvesters. This conception is conveyed by the statement: "I am *Hashem,* your God — the God of the poor and the stranger as well as your God. Therefore give him what belongs to Me with all due dignity. He might, however, similarly have wanted to teach how worthy it is to give gifts secretly, to avoid causing the recipient to suffer any humiliation. So He, may He be blessed, stated it: "See, I have given you your grain without you being made to feel that it is a gift. You, therefore, take care not to make yourself appear as his benefactor."

Sifra 21:

לגר — יכול לגר תושב ? ת״ל : ללוי, מה לוי בן ברית אף גר בן ברית. אי ללוי ולגר יכול בין חסרים ובין שאינם חסרים ? ת״ל : לעני, מה עני מחוסר ובן ברית אף כולם מחוסרים ובני ברית.

תעזוב — הנח לפניהם והם יבזבזו.

תעזוב לפניהם — הנח תבואה בקשה, תלתן בעמיריו, תמרים במכבדות. מנין שספק לקט לקט ? ספק שכחה שכחה ? ספק פאה פאה ? ת״ל : לעני ולגר תעזוב אותם אני ה׳ אלוהיכם. אני איני גובה מכם אלא נפשות, שנאמר : **אל תגזול דל כי דל הוא ואל תדכא עני בשער.**

וכה״א : **כי ה׳ יריב ריבם וקבע את קובעיהם נפש. (משלי כב)**

"To the stranger" — One might take this term to refer to a resident alien, hence Scripture states "to the Levite" — to inform that just as the Levite is an Israelite, so too is the stranger mentioned here. Since, however, a Levite and a stranger are placed in juxtaposition, one might be led to think that the law applies whether they are needy or not, hence Scripture adds "to the poor." "The poor" obviously refers to someone in need and an Israelite; so all mentioned have to be in need and Israelites to be eligible for these gifts.

"You shall leave" — leave the grain before them and they shall despoil it.

"You shall leave" — leave the grain in its stalks, the fenogrec in the stem, the dates on their twigs.

From where does it follow that doubtful gleanings must be treated as definite gleanings, a sheaf possibly forgotten as one definitely forgotten, doubtful peah (corner leaving) as definite *peah?*—Scripture states: "you shall leave them for the poor and the stranger, I am *Hashem,* your God." I shall exact nothing less than your souls, as it says: "Rob not the weak because he is weak, neither crush the poor in the gate; for *Hashem* will plead their cause and despoil the life of those that despoil them." (Prov. 22.22-23)

Yerushalmi, Peah, end of Chap. 4:

כך היה ר"מ משיב את החכמים : אין אתם מודים לי שספק לקט לקט ? ומנין שספק לקט לקט ? ר"ש ב"ר נחמן בש"ר יונתן : עני ורש הצדיקו (תהלים פב) הצדיקוהו במתנותיו.

ר"ש בן לקיש בשם בר קפרא : לא תטה משפט אביונך בריבו (שמות כג). בריבו אין אתה מטהו אבל מטהו אתה במתנותיו.

א"ר יוחנן : וכה הוא מה ששנה לנו רבי : **תעזוב** — **הנח לפניהם משלך. אמר** רבי : לא כתיב לגר ליתום ולאלמנה יהיה ? — בין מדידך בין מדידיה הב לו. (ירושלמי פאה סוף פ' ד)

So R. Meir would retort to the Sages: Do you not concede that doubtful gleanings are treated as definite gleanings? And from where is it deduced that doubtful gleanings are to be treated as definite gleanings? R. Samuel b. Naḥman in the name of R. Jonathan: "Be just to the afflicted and destitute" (Ps. 82.3) — justify him as being the righteous in his claim for gifts.

R. Shimon b. Lakish in the name of Bar Kappara: "Neither shall you favor the poor man in his litigation" — in his litigation, you must not favor him, but you must favor him in respect to his gifts.

Said R. Johanan: And so Rabbi [Judah the Prince] succeeded in teaching us: "You shall leave" (repeated for emphasis) — leave of your own before them. Rabbi [Judah the Prince] said: Is it not written: "it shall be for the stranger, the orphan and the widow". Give him both from his and from yours.

Sefer Haḥinukh, The Law of Peah 213-2 (216).

The "stranger" here signifies a proselyte. So similarly does every reference to the "stranger" in respect of gifts to the poor. In connection with the tithe of the poor, Scripture states "for the stranger, the orphan and the widow." Here the reference is obviously to a righteous proselyte, the proof lying in the context. The same, therefore, applies to all gifts to the poor. Nevertheless our Rabbis of blessed memory enjoined that, to promote peaceful relations, we do not withhold these from the gentile poor (see Maimonides, Laws of Gifts to the Poor, 1.9).

The underlying reason for this mitzvah is that *Hashem,* be He blessed, desired His people to be crowned with every precious virtue, that they be good natured and generous. As I have stated previously, one's actions affect and improve one's nature, and thereby cause the Divine blessing to be vouchsafed upon it.

Sefer Haḥinukh, The Law to Leave the Forgotten Sheave (552.21).

One of the underlying reasons for this commandment is that the needy and destitute, in their poverty and sin, look enviously on their neighbors' grain. When the poor see the owners, in so far as God has blessed them, binding their sheaves in their fields, the poor think to themselves: Would that we had the good fortune to gather sheaves and bring them to our home — If I had but one sheaf to bring home, I would be happy. In His kindness to His creatures, God, blessed be He, provided for the satisfaction of this craving, on every occasion that an owner forgets one of his sheaves.

Here too, benefit accrues to the owner, for he thereby becomes better natured, even truly generous and blessed, by his having no regrets at losing the sheaf, but leaving it for the poor instead. And *Hashem's* blessing will rest forever on the good of heart.

*

"And when you reap the harvest of your land, you shall not wholly reap the corner of your field, neither shall you gather the gleanings of your harvest; you shall leave them for the poor and the stranger, I am *Hashem* your God." (Lev. 23.22)

רש״י : **ובקצרכם** — חזר ושנה לעבור עליהם בשני לאווין.
אמר רבי אורדימוס ברבי יוסי : מה ראה הכתוב ליתנה באמצע הרגלים ; פסח ועצרת מכאן וראש השנה ויום הכיפורים מכאן ? ללמדך, שכל הנותן לקט שכחה ופאה לעני כראוי, מעלין עליו כאילו בנה בית המקדש והקריב עליו קרבנותיו בתוכו. [הספרא : כאילו ביהמ״ק קיים והוא מקריב קרבנותיו לתוכו.]
ספורנו : **אני ה׳ אלהיכם, אלהי הקוצרים ואהלי המלקטים,** הלקט והפיאה לעניים, ואיטיב למטיבים להם כדי לעשות רצוני.

Rashi: Scripture repeats the prohibition here in order to make the one transgressing this law infringe two negative commandments. R. Urdimos son of R. Jose said: What reason had Scripture to place it (this law) amidst those relating to the festival sacrifices — those of Pesach and Shavuoth before it and those of Rosh Hashanah, Yom Kippur and Sukkoth after it? To teach you that he who properly leaves the gleanings, the forgotten sheaf and the corner of the field to the poor as it ought to be, is regarded as if he had built the Temple and offered sacrifices there.
[Sifra: As if the Temple were in existence, and he had offered his sacrifices there.]

Seforno: I am *Hashem,* your God — the God of the harvesters and of the gatherers who collect the gleanings, the corners reserved for the poor, and I shall do good to those who are beneficent to the poor and obey My will.

ש כ ח ה

כי תקצור קצירך בשדך ושכחת עמר בשדה לא־תשוב לקחתו
לגר ליתום ולאלמנה יהיה,
למען יברכך יי אלהיך בכל מעשה ידיך.

כי תחבט זיתך לא תפאר אחריך
לגר ליתום ולאלמנה יהיה.

כי תבצור כרמך לא תעולל אחריך
לגר ליתום ולאלמנה יהיה.

וזכרת כי־עבד היית בארץ מצרים
על־כן אנכי מצוך לעשות את־הדבר הזה. (דברים כד, יט—כא)

נשים לבנו על החזרה הסוגרת כל פסוק : ״לגר ליתום ולאלמנה יהיה״. והמשמעות רבה גם לענייננו. כי רוח הולכת היום מכוח שלשתם.

The Forgotten Sheaf:

> "When you reap your harvest in your field, and have forgotten a sheaf in the field, you shall not go back to fetch it; It shall be for the stranger, the fatherless and for the widow; That *Hashem,* your God, may bless you in all the work of your hands.
> When you beat your olive tree, you shall not go over your boughs again.
> It shall be for the stranger, for the fatherless and for the widow.
> When you gather the grapes of your vineyard, you shall not glean it after you,
> It shall be for the stranger, for the fatherless and for the widow.
> And you shall remember that you were a bondman in the land of Egypt.
> Therefore I command you to do all this thing." (Deut. 24.19-21)

It has considerable significance for our study.
Due note should be taken of the refrain ending each sentence: "It shall be for the stranger, for the fatherless and for the widow." It has considerable significance for our subject, because Ruth is going today to glean in the role of all three of them.

[B]
ON RIGHTEOUS PROSELYTES

שלושה גרים הם. יש גר שנתגייר לשם אכילה. אמר לו הקב"ה: נתגיירת בשביל הנבלה, הרי היא נתונה לך! שנאמר (דברים יד) לא תאכלו כל נבלה לגר אשר בשעריך תתננה ואכלה.

הגר השני — להיות מתפרנס כעני, הרי הם נתונים לו, שנאמר: (ויקרא כג) ובקצרכם את קציר ארצכם וכו'.

הגר השלישי — גר שנתגייר **לשמו של הקב"ה**. אמר לו הקב"ה: הרי הוא שקול עלי כאחד מכם. שנאמר: הקהל חקה אחת לכם ולגר הגר חקת עולם לדרתיכם **ככם כגר יהיה לפני ה'**. תורה אחת ומשפט אחד יהיה לכם ולגר הגר אתכם. (במדבר טו)
ולא עוד, אלא שהוא שקול עלי כלוי. שנאמר: ובא הלוי כי אין לו חלק ונחלה עמך והגר. (דברים יד, כט)

אמר משה לפני הקב"ה: רבונו של עולם, הגר הזה כלוי לפניך? אמר לו: גדול הוא לפני — **שנתגייר לשמי!** משל לצבי שגדל במדבר ובא מעצמו ונתערב בצאן. היה הרועה מאכילו ומשקו ומחבבו יותר מצאנו.

אמרו לו: לצבי זה אתה מחבב יותר מן הצאן? אמר להם: כמה יגיעות יגעתי בצאני, מוציאן בבוקר ומכניסן בערב, עד שלא גדלו. וזה, שגדל במדבריות וביערים ובא מעצמו לתוך צאני — לכן אני מחבבו.

כך אמר הקב"ה: כמה יגעתי בישראל, הוצאתים ממצרים והארתי לפניהם, הורדתי להם את המן, הגזתי את השלו, העליתי להם את הבאר, הקפתים ענני כבוד עד שקיבלו תורתי — וזה בא מעצמו, לפיכך שקול עלי כישראל וכלוי. (ילקוט שמעוני אמר, תרמ"ה; אלה הדברים זוטא)

There are three types of proselytes: The one who converted on account of food. To him God says: You have converted for the sake of carrion. Here, take it, as it is said (Deut. 14.21): "You shall not eat anything that dies of itself. You may give it to the stranger that is within your gates, that he may eat it."

The second type converts to obtain support, like the poor. These gifts are given to him, as it is said (Lev. 23): "And when you reap the harvest of your land..."

> The third type converts for the sake of the Holy One, blessed be He. To him, God says: "For my part, He is considered just as one of you," as it is said: "As for the congregation, there shall be one statute for you and for the stranger that sojourns with you, a statute for ever through your generations; as you are, so shall the stranger be before *Hashem*. One law and one ordinance shall be for both you and for the stranger that sojourns with you." (Num. 15)
> Furthermore, to Me, he is also the equal of a Levite, as it is said: "And the Levite because he was no portion and no inheritance with you, and the stranger." (Deut. 14.29)
>
> Moses said before the Holy One, blessed be He: Master of the universe, is the stranger the equal of a Levite to You? He (God) said: To me he is greater — since he converted for My Name's sake. He may be compared to a deer that grew up in the desert, yet came of itself and mingled with the sheep. The shepherd would give it better food and drink, favor it more, than his own sheep.
>
> They said to him: Do you favor this deer more than your sheep? He answered: What trouble have I gone to on behalf of my sheep? Until they grew up I had to lead them out in the morning and gather them towards evening.
> This deer grew up in deserts and forests and came, on its own, to join my sheep — for this reason, I favor him.
>
> So the Holy One. blessed be He, said: To how much trouble did I go on behalf of My people Israel! I led them out of Egypt, I lighted their way, I brought down the manna for them and made the quail fly to them, I brought up the well for them, I surrounded them with clouds of glory, before they accepted My Torah. — This one came on his own. For Me, then, he is the equal of an Israelite and a Levite. (Yalkut Shim'oni, *Emor* 645; Deut. Zuta)

Possibly, their study of the Book of Ruth inspired our Sages of blessed memory to compose this paean of praise and love to the proselyte.

> [He is comparable] to the deer that grew up in deserts and forests and came of his own and mingled with My sheep — therefore I favor him.

The Torah has admonished thirty-six times that the proselyte is to be loved and not to be oppressed.
[Others say: forty-six times. (Cf. Bava Metzia 59b)]
And the Holy One, blessed be He, included this trait of loving the stranger among His Divine attributes.

> "For *Hashem,* your God, He is the God of gods, Lord of lords, the great God, the mighty, the awful, Who does not regard persons nor take rewards.
>
> He executes justice for the fatherless and the widow, and loves the stranger in giving him food and clothing.
>
> Therefore love the stranger, for you were strangers in the land of Egypt." (Deut. 10.17-19)

"Therefore love the stranger":

> I therefore command you to love the stranger so that you should imitate My attributes, for this is how I behaved towards you when you were strangers in the land of Egypt. (Malbim)
>
> "For you were strangers" — nevertheless your worth is great, for who can know what strength lies hidden in the lowly stranger and his descendants for days yet to come? (Ha'amek Davar)

ב ד. וְהִנֵּה־בֹעַז בָּא מִבֵּית לֶחֶם
וַיֹּאמֶר לַקּוֹצְרִים יְיָ עִמָּכֶם וַיֹּאמְרוּ לוֹ יְבָרֶכְךָ יְיָ:

2.4 **"AND BEHOLD BOAZ CAME FROM BETH-LEHEM, AND HE SAID UNTO HIS REAPERS: '*HASHEM* BE WITH YOU.' AND THEY ANSWERED HIM: *HASHEM* BLESS YOU."**

This is a preparation for what is to follow. "And behold Boaz came." Apparently his coming created some stir among the reapers. The greeting is in the Name of God.*

Was Boaz accustomed to tour his fields every day?

Or did he come specially then to supervise the harvest, to check whether the reapers were doing their work diligently?

Or else, did he only come that day to greet them?

Or did he come to oversee the proper fulfillment of the commandments pertaining to the gleanings, the forgotten sheaves and the corners of the fields?

We have, after all, learned to appreciate the overriding importance of these commandments.

Benefit accrues to the owner of the field, for he thereby becomes better natured. (Sefer Haḥinukh)
Just as one offers the sacrificial limbs to God, so should one give to the poor and the stranger from the harvest of his field for the glory of God. (Ibn Ezra)
As if the Temple were in existence, and he had offered his sacrifices there. (Sifra)

For Boaz was an outstanding figure in his generation, a prince in Israel.

"A mighty man of valor" is rendered by the Targum as: a mighty man, firm in the observance of the Torah.

Did he not derive enjoyment from the *mitzvah* that day, the mitzvah he was also obliged to impart to his reapers?

Indeed, they had not been able to fulfill the commandment for a considerable time. Now, however, God had remembered them and blessed them with an abundant harvest.*

"For the poor and the stranger you shall leave them, I am *Hashem*, your God."
The God of the reapers and of the gatherers (Seforno).

The law states:

The owner shows himself three times during the day; in the morning, at midday and in the afternoon. (Peah 4.5)

The owner presents himself and is visible in his field, so that the poor should come and take their *Peah* (R. Obadiah Bertinoro, following the Yerushalmi.)

To allow the poor to enter with his approval and gather their share from the corners, for at those times three categories of poor, weak persons are present and, as it concludes, that is why the owner should be there, to guard their rights, to prevent their colleagues from doing them harm. (Tifereth Israel)

ב ה. וַיֹּאמֶר בֹּעַז לְנַעֲרוֹ הַנִּצָּב עַל־הַקּוֹצְרִים
לְמִי הַנַּעֲרָה הַזֹּאת:

2.5 "THEN SAID BOAZ TO HIS SERVANT THAT WAS SET OVER THE REAPERS: 'WHOSE DAMSEL IS THIS?' "

Was Boaz, then, accustomed to inquire about women? (Rashi, Shabbath 113a)

"They shall be for the fatherless and for the widow" — And who have any better right to the gleanings, than this poor woman, a proselyte and a widow?

Now Boaz was perfectly well aware that Naomi and her daughter-in-law were back from the field of Moab. What enjoyment could he have derived from his harvest that day, and what mitzvah could he have performed for the poor, if the poor and widowed of his own family sat at home with nothing to eat?

Nor had he sent them anything. And we still have no explanation for this conduct.

Did he expect them to come to his field to gather?*

> [Therefore let them take their share with all due dignity.] (Alshekh)

Apparently Boaz was happy to see Ruth gathering in his field. He knew who she was. He was not, however, aware of her status in the city, and why or on what grounds the reapers had allowed her to gather corn. Was she not a Moabitess, shunned by the entire population of Beth-lehem? He, therefore, addressed his question to the servant in charge of the harvesters, asking "Whose?" rather than "Who?"

> The Halakhah enjoins us to go forth and see how the public are accustomed to act. (Berakhoth 45a)

What depths lie in the observations of our Rabbis! They have discovered glimpses of far-reaching consequences between the lines of Scripture.

"WHOSE DAMASEL IS THIS?"

— בן מי זה הנער ? — בן מי זה העלם ?— (ש״א יז, נה)
למי הנערה הזאת ? — וכי לא היה מכירה ? אלא כיון שראה אותה נעימה ומעשיה נאים, התחיל שואל עליה. כל הנשים שוחחות ומלקטות, וזו יושבת ומלקטת. כל הנשים מסלקות כליהן, וזו משלשלת כליה.
כל הנשים משחקות עם הקוצרים וזו מצנעת עצמה. כל הנשים מלקטות בין העמרים, וזו מלקטת מן ההפקר.

ודכוותיה (ש״א יז) וכראות שאול את דוד יוצא לקראת הפלשתי וכו׳ ויאמר המלך שאל אתה בן מי זה העלם ! (נה, נו)
ולא הווה חכים ליה ? אתמול היה משלח לומר לישי : ״יעמוד נא דוד לפני כי מצא חן בעיני״ ועכשיו שואל עליו ?
אלא כיון שראה שאול את ראש הפלישתי בידו התחיל שואל עליו אם מפרץ הוא — מלך הוא ! (יבמות עו ; רות רבה, ד, ח)

"Whose son is this youth? Whose son is this stripling?" (1 Sam. 17.55-56)
"Whose damsel is this?" — Did he not recognize her? — When he saw, however, that she was pleasing and her conduct was pleasing, he began to inquire about her. All the other women bent over to gather; she sat down to gather. All the other women tucked up their clothes, she let hers hang down. All the other women flirted with the reapers, she acted modestly. All the other women gathered between the sheaves; but she only gathered from the discarded grain.

In the same way, one must understand the verse (1 Sam. 17.55): "And when Saul saw David go forth against the Philistines, he said unto Abner... 'Whose son is this youth?'" Did he not then recognize him? Just yesterday he sent to Jesse saying: "Let David, I pray thee, stand before me; for he has found favor in my eyes" (*Ibid.* 16.22) and now he inquired concerning him.
However, when Saul saw the head of the Philistine (Goliath) in David's hand, he began to ask: Is he a descendant of Perez, — a king? (Yevamoth 76b; Ruth Rabba 4.5)

The two incidents are compared, not merely for the sake of discovering word meanings, but to convey some much more significant idea.

The servant in charge of the reapers, too, did not know what to answer Boaz. The question took him by surprise. He knew that Naomi was a relative of Boaz. Everybody knew that. Everyone kept on talking against this Moabitess who had spoiled the family's record. Because of her, the rest of the family had maintained this distance from them, and so had Boaz.

And so, at first, the servant feigned innocence in his answer.

ב ו. וַיַּעַן הַנַּעַר הַנִּצָּב עַל־הַקּוֹצְרִים וַיֹּאמַר
נַעֲרָה מוֹאֲבִיָּה הִיא הַשָּׁבָה עִם־נָעֳמִי מִשְּׂדֵי מוֹאָב׃

2.6 "AND THE SERVANT THAT WAS SET OVER THE REAPERS ANSWERED AND SAID:
'IT IS A MOABITISH DAMSEL THAT CAME WITH NAOMI OUT OF THE FIELDS OF MOAB.'"

The servant had no idea what Boaz really thought about Ruth. Hence, he continued to speak, but as if confused. His remarks were verbose and vague and did not answer the question.*

ז. וַתֹּאמֶר אֲלַקֳטָה־נָּא וְאָסַפְתִּי בָעֳמָרִים
אַחֲרֵי הַקּוֹצְרִים
וַתָּבוֹא וַתַּעֲמוֹד מֵאָז הַבֹּקֶר וְעַד־עַתָּה
זֶה שִׁבְתָּהּ הַבַּיִת מְעָט׃

"AND SHE SAID: LET ME GLEAN, I PRAY YOU, AND GATHER AFTER THE REAPERS AMONG THE SHEAVES; SO SHE CAME AND HAS CONTINUED EVEN FROM THE MORNING UNTIL NOW, SAVE THAT SHE TARRIED A LITTLE IN THE HOUSE."

The servant began by recounting her virtue and modesty. For all the days she has been here, she has never exposed a finger or a toe — and we do not know whether she is reserved or talkative. (Ruth Zuta 2.7)

Boaz now realized that the time had come for him to proclaim publicly the law, in all its goodness and righteousness, pertaining to Ruth's status. And he would do so with public assent and approval.* He, as it were, continued where the servant had left off.

ח. וַיֹּאמֶר בֹּעַז אֶל־רוּת
הֲלוֹא שָׁמַעַתְּ בִּתִּי! אַל־תֵּלְכִי לִלְקֹט בְּשָׂדֶה אַחֵר
וְגַם לֹא־תַעֲבוּרִי מִזֶּה וְכֹה תִדְבָּקִין עִם־נַעֲרֹתָי:

2.8 "THEN SAID BOAZ TO RUTH: HEAR YOU NOT MY DAUGHTER?
GO NOT TO GLEAN IN ANOTHER FIELD,
NEITHER PASS FROM HERE, BUT ABIDE FAST BY MY MAIDENS.' "

Ruth might have been taken aback at the sight of men talking about her. Boaz, therefore, spoke to her directly to calm and comfort her.

We can sense the joy dwelling in his heart, now that the time had finally arrived for his doubts and his hesitations regarding Naomi to be resolved. For the duty to care and provide for his brother's family fell on him.

ט. עֵינַיִךְ בַּשָּׂדֶה אֲשֶׁר־יִקְצֹרוּן וְהָלַכְתְּ אַחֲרֵיהֶן
הֲלוֹא צִוִּיתִי אֶת־הַנְּעָרִים לְבִלְתִּי נָגְעֵךְ
וְצָמִת וְהָלַכְתְּ אֶל־הַכֵּלִים
וְשָׁתִית מֵאֲשֶׁר יִשְׁאֲבוּן הַנְּעָרִים׃

י. וַתִּפֹּל עַל־פָּנֶיהָ וַתִּשְׁתַּחוּ אָרְצָה
וַתֹּאמֶר אֵלָיו מַדּוּעַ מָצָאתִי חֵן בְּעֵינֶיךָ לְהַכִּירֵנִי
וְאָנֹכִי נָכְרִיָּה׃

9 "LET YOUR EYES BE ON THE FIELD THAT THEY DO REAP, AND GO AFTER THEM;
HAVE I NOT CHARGED THE YOUNG MEN THAT THEY SHALL NOT TOUCH YOU?
AND WHEN YOU ARE THIRSTY, GO TO THE VESSELS,
AND DRINK OF THAT WHICH THE YOUNG MEN HAVE DRAWN.

10 THEN SHE FELL ON HER FACE, AND BOWED DOWN TO THE GROUND, AND SAID UNTO HIM: 'WHY HAVE I FOUND FAVOR IN YOUR SIGHT, THAT YOU SHOULD TAKE COGNIZANCE OF ME,
FOR I AM FOREIGNER.' "

How astonished she was! From the time of her arrival there, she had never been treated with any consideration or favor. She still vividly recalled the shocked stares she had encountered when they first returned. Suddenly words of kindness were addressed to her in public by a distinguished, noble man:

"MY DAUGHTER!"

And she could not believe it was true. She was not sure of their gratuitous kindness.

"I AM A FOREIGNER."

CONSOLATION

Ruth's remarks contained an unintentional reproach — a rebuke to the kinsman, the redeemer, who had ignored his own relatives and had allowed Naomi to sit at home, alone and hungry. Here was Naomi's daughter-in-law. She had come to gather food for her aged mother-in-law. Ruth — she was all that was left to Naomi; the rest had died. Here she was, the widow of Mahlon, falling at his feet in submission, thanking him for a morsel of bread.
Was she not instead crying out in protest at all the humiliation inflicted on the entire house of Elimelech, so cruelly treated in Beth-lehem?

"AND I AM A FOREIGNER!"

Boaz was deeply moved by this confrontation. He addressed her with words of consolation and blessing. Publicly paying tribute to her, he also clarified her status, stating the ruling he had suppressed so far. He reaffirmed the law, not fully known in that generation, that it was permissible for Ruth to enter the community of Israel— this same Ruth, so steeped in kindness and compassion, who had converted for the sake of Heaven.

> "And I am a foreigner" — I am of an alien people, a daughter of Moab — the people unworthy to enter the congregation of *Hashem.** "And he answered" — Boaz answered and said : No! The declaration of the Sages has been intimated to me, viz., that when God issued the decree, it applied only to the males and not to the females. And it has been prophetically revealed to me that kings and prophets are destined to issue forth from you in consequence of the good that you have extended to your mother-in-law... (Targum Jonathan)

ב יא. וַיַּעַן בֹּעַז וַיֹּאמֶר לָהּ
הֻגֵּד הֻגַּד לִי כֹּל אֲשֶׁר־עָשִׂית אֶת־חֲמוֹתֵךְ
אַחֲרֵי מוֹת אִישֵׁךְ:
וַתַּעַזְבִי אָבִיךְ וְאִמֵּךְ וְאֶרֶץ מוֹלַדְתֵּךְ
וַתֵּלְכִי אֶל־עַם אֲשֶׁר לֹא־יָדַעַתְּ תְּמוֹל שִׁלְשֹׁם:

2.1 "AND BOAZ ANSWERED AND SAID TO HER:
IT HAS FULLY BEEN TOLD TO ME, ALL THAT YOU HAVE DONE TO YOUR MOTHER-IN-LAW,
SINCE THE DEATH OF YOUR HUSBAND;
AND HOW YOU HAVE LEFT YOUR FATHER AND MOTHER AND THE LAND OF YOUR NATIVITY,
AND ARE COME TO A PEOPLE THAT YOU KNEW NOT HERETOFORE."

There is a distinct resemblance between this verse and one referring to an experience of our forefather Abraham, which was regarded, in his case, as a trial.

> "Get you out of your country and from your kindred, and from your father's house, unto the land that I will show you." (Gen. 12.1)

> Heretofore — (lit. yesterday and the day before) —

> Had you come here yesterday or the day before we would not have accepted you,
> Since the halakhah had not yet been reaffirmed, stating: A male and not a female Ammonite; a male and not a female Moabite. (Yerushalmi Yevamoth 8.3; Pesikta deR. Kahana 124)

יב. יְשַׁלֵּם יְיָ פָּעֳלֵךְ
וּתְהִי מַשְׂכֻּרְתֵּךְ שְׁלֵמָה מֵעִם יְיָ אֱלֹהֵי יִשְׂרָאֵל
אֲשֶׁר־בָּאת לַחֲסוֹת תַּחַת־כְּנָפָיו:

2.12 "MAY GOD RECOMPENSE YOUR WORK,
AND BE YOUR REWARD COMPLETE FROM *HASHEM*,
THE GOD OF ISRAEL,
UNDER WHOSE WINGS YOU HAVE COME TO TAKE REFUGE."

"May God recompense your work" —

The One Who is destined to grant the righteous their reward, will recompense you, (Pesikta deR. Kahana *Ibid.*)
For no human act is capable of granting you reward commensurate with your deed. (Akedath Yitzḥak)

אשר באת לחסות תחת כנפיו —

אמר ר' אבין :

כנפים לארץ — **מכנף הארץ זמירות שמענו.** (ישע' כד)

כנפים לשחר — **אשא כנפי שחר.** (תהלים קלט)

כנפים לשמש — **שמש צדקה ומרפא בכנפיה.** (מלאכי ג)

כנפים לכרובים — **וקול כנפי הכרובים.** (יחזקאל י)

כנפים לשרפים — **שש כנפים לאחד.** (ישעיהו ו)

אמר ר אבין : גדול כוחן של גומלי חסדים שאין חסין לא בצל כנפי הארץ, ולא בצל כנפי השחר, ולא בצל כנפי השמש, ולא בצל כנפי הכרובים, ולא בצל כנפי החיות — אלא בצילו של מי שאמר והיה העולם, שנאמר : (תהלים לו) **מה יקר חסדך אלהים ובני אדם בצל כנפיך יחסיון.** (ילק"ש תרב ; רו"ר ה, ד ; פסדר"כ קכד)

"That you came to take refuge under His wings" —

R. Avin said:

The earth has wings — "From the wings of the earth we heard songs" (Isa. 24).

The morning has wings — If I take the wings of the morning" (Ps. 139.9).

The sun has wings — "The sun of righteousness shall arise with healing in its wings" (Mal. 3.30).

The cherubim have wings — "And the sound of the wings of the cherubim" (Ezek. 10.5).

The Hayyoth have wings — "Also the noise of the wings of the Hayyoth" (Ezek. 3.13).

The Seraphim have wings — "Each one (seraph) had six wings" (Isa. 6.12).

Said R. Avin: Great is the power of those who act benevolently, for they shelter, neither in the shadow of the wings of the earth, nor in the shadows of the wings of the morning, nor in the shadow of the wings of the sun, nor in the shadow of the wings of the Cherubim, nor in the shadow of the wings of the Hayyoth, but in the shadow of Him at whose word the world was created, as it is said (Ps. 36.8): "How precious is Your loving-kindness O God and the children of the world take refuge in Your wings." (Yalkut Shim'oni 602; Ruth Rabba 5.4; Pesikta deR. Kahana 124)

יג. וַתֹּאמֶר אֶמְצָא־חֵן בְּעֵינֶיךָ אֲדֹנִי כִּי נִחַמְתָּנִי
וְכִי דִבַּרְתָּ עַל־לֵב שִׁפְחָתֶךָ
וְאָנֹכִי לֹא אֶהְיֶה כְּאַחַת שִׁפְחֹתֶיךָ׃

13 "THEN SHE SAID: 'LET ME FIND FAVOR IN YOUR SIGHT, MY LORD; THAT YOU HAVE COMFORTED ME,
AND FOR THAT YOU HAVE SPOKEN TO THE HEART OF YOUR HANDMAID,
THOUGH I BE NOT AS ONE OF YOUR HANDMAIDENS.'"

"For that you have comforted me" —
and declared me fit to enter the congregation of *Hashem*. (Targum Jonathan)

SUFFICIENT FOOD AND MORE

ב יד. וַיֹּאמֶר לָה בֹעַז לְעֵת הָאֹכֶל גֹּשִׁי הֲלֹם
וְאָכַלְתְּ מִן־הַלֶּחֶם וְטָבַלְתְּ פִּתֵּךְ בַּחֹמֶץ
וַתֵּשֶׁב מִצַּד הַקֹּצְרִים וַיִּצְבָּט־לָהּ קָלִי
וַתֹּאכַל וַתִּשְׂבַּע וַתֹּתַר:

2.14 "AND BOAZ SAID TO HER AT MEAL TIME: 'COME HITHER AND EAT OF THE BREAD AND DIP YOUR MORSEL IN VINEGAR.'
AND SHE SAT DOWN BESIDE THE REAPERS; AND HE REACHED HER PARCHED CORN
AND SHE ATE AND WAS SATISFIED AND LEFT OVER THEREOF."

The plain meaning of the verse seems to convey that Boaz was continually drawing her nearer, making her feel more and more secure. At first, he invited her to drink from the reapers' vessels, and now to partake of the food.
Our Sages, however, have deduced from here, that he also gave his reply to the remarks she had just made (v. 13):

> "And Boaz said to her: God forbid! Don't say so.
> You do not belong among the handmaidens (*amahoth*) — but among the matriarchs (*imahoth*). (Pesikta deR. Kahana)
> *Lah,* to her, being taken as *Lo,* not, since the *Heh* is silent here and not consonantal.

Remarkably, our Rabbis have beckoned to us here to listen to the prophetic echo predicting that Ruth was destined to play a significant role in Israel.

Did her heart not beat with joyous hope at that time, too?

> R. Johanan said: It alludes to David, "Come hither" — draw nigh to royalty.
>
> Said R. Eleazar: He intimated to her: The royal house of David is destined to come forth from you, as it is written (2 Sam. 7.18): "Then David the king went in, and sat before the Lord; and he said, 'Who am I, O Lord, God, and what is my house that you have brought me hither?' " (Shabbat 113b; Ruth Rabba 5.6; Yalkut Shim'oni 632)

Our Rabbis have likewise taught us to regard the deed of Boaz as a great mitzvah. Apparently, for that occasion and those circumstances, the event was truly extraordinary.

> Had Boaz known that the Holy One, blessed be He, would have it recorded of him that "he reached her parched corn and she ate" — he would have fed her fatted calves. (*Ibid.*)

How much care is exercised in choosing words in holy writings! "The Holy One, blessed be He, would have it recorded!"*

"And she ate and was satisfied and left over..."

Ruth was sitting at the side of the reapers, eating. She had not eaten for some time — since the morning. Yet, certainly, no one paid attention to the fact or even cared that she left over and hid more than she ate.

> It seems probable that the food in her stomach was blessed (i.e. satisfied her). (Ruth Rabba *Ibid.*)

Was this not the 'blessing' viz. that she ate to satiety and so was able to hide and take back baked bread to her mother-in-law who was waiting for her at home?

טו. וַתָּקָם לְלַקֵּט
וַיְצַו בֹּעַז אֶת־נְעָרָיו לֵאמֹר גַּם בֵּין הָעֳמָרִים תְּלַקֵּט
וְלֹא תַכְלִימוּהָ׃

טז. וְגַם שֹׁל־תָּשֹׁלּוּ לָהּ מִן־הַצְּבָתִים וַעֲזַבְתֶּם וְלִקְּטָה
וְלֹא תִגְעֲרוּ בָהּ׃

2.15 "AND WHEN SHE WAS RISEN UP TO GLEAN
BOAZ COMMANDED HIS YOUNG MEN, SAYING: 'LET
HER GLEAN EVEN AMONG THE SHEAVES,
AND PUT HER NOT TO SHAME.

16 AND ALSO PULL OUT SOME FOR HER ON PURPOSE FROM
THE BUNDLES,
AND LEAVE IT, AND LET HER GLEAN,
AND REBUKE HER NOT.' "

"And also pull out" — pretend that you forgot them.
"Bundles" (*tzevatim*) — small sheaves. (Rashi)

"And rebuke her not —"
No sooner had she gone away somewhat, than Boaz said to his servants: Neither put her to shame nor rebuke her, nor shall you make any difficulties for her, since she is a royal daughter. (Yalkut Shim'oni 604)

יז. וַתְּלַקֵּט בַּשָּׂדֶה עַד־הָעָרֶב וַתַּחְבֹּט אֵת אֲשֶׁר־לִקֵּטָה
וַיְהִי כְּאֵיפָה שְׂעֹרִים׃

יח. וַתִּשָּׂא וַתָּבוֹא הָעִיר
וַתֵּרֶא חֲמוֹתָהּ אֵת אֲשֶׁר־לִקֵּטָה
וַתּוֹצֵא וַתִּתֶּן־לָהּ אֵת אֲשֶׁר־הוֹתִרָה מִשָּׂבְעָהּ׃

17 "AND SHE GATHERED IN THE FIELD UNTIL EVEN; AND
SHE BEAT OUT THAT WHICH SHE HAD GLEANED,
AND IT WAS ABOUT AN EPHAH OF BARLEY.

18 AND SHE TOOK IT UP, AND WENT INTO THE CITY; AND
HER MOTHER-IN-LAW SAW WHAT SHE HAD GLEANED;
AND SHE BROUGHT FORTH AND GAVE TO HER THAT
WHICH SHE HAD LEFT AFTER SHE WAS SATISFIED."

The verse draws a portrait. How beautiful and exact is every detail.

The mother-in-law gazing at what she had brought, and wondering. But before Naomi could open her mouth to speak, Ruth was hastening to bring out what she had so lovingly and carefully hidden away for Naomi.*

"THAT WHICH SHE HAD LEFT OVER AFTER SHE WAS SATISFIED."

In the events of that day, all our concern was for Ruth, we neglected Naomi. Yet we can appreciate her feelings, too, as she remained home alone, waiting in trepidation for Ruth to return, praying that Ruth suffer no humiliation. For who appreciated Ruth's precious qualities more than she, and who was responsible to, owed more to, Ruth than she?

ב יט. וַתֹּאמֶר לָהּ חֲמוֹתָהּ
אֵיפֹה לִקַּטְתְּ הַיּוֹם וְאָנָה עָשִׂית יְהִי מַכִּירֵךְ בָּרוּךְ:

2.19 "AND HER MOTHER-IN-LAW SAID UNTO HER: 'WHERE DID YOU GLEAN TODAY? AND WHERE HAVE YOU WROUGHT?
BLESSED BE HE THAT TOOK KNOWLEDGE OF YOU!' "

Her remarks are comprised of three brief questions, in rapid succession. She expressed surprise, excitement, and a joy that called for explanation.

וַתַּגֵּד לַחֲמוֹתָהּ אֵת אֲשֶׁר־עָשְׂתָה עִמּוֹ
וַתֹּאמֶר שֵׁם הָאִישׁ אֲשֶׁר עָשִׂיתִי עִמּוֹ הַיּוֹם בֹּעַז:

"AND SHE TOLD HER MOTHER-IN-LAW WITH WHOM SHE HAD WROUGHT,
AND SAID: THE MAN'S NAME WITH WHOM I WROUGHT TODAY IS BOAZ."

Boaz! —

Ruth could hardly have felt the tremor that shook Naomi at the sound of that name!

אשר עשיתי עמו —
תני בשם ר׳ יהושע: יותר ממה שבעל הבית עושה עם העני, העני עושה עם בעל הבית. שכן אמרה רות לנעמי; שם האיש אשר **עשיתי עמו** ולא אמרה אשר עשה עמי, אלא אשר עשיתי עמו — הרבה פעולות והרבה טובות עשיתי עמו בפרוסה שהאכילני. (רו״ר ה, ט; ילק״ש תרד)

"The man with whom I wrought."

It was taught in the name of R. Joshua: More than the householder does for the poor man, the poor man does for the householder, for so Ruth said to Naomi: "The man's name for whom I wrought." She did not say "who wrought for me," but "for whom I wrought." I wrought him many benefits in return for the one morsel of food which he gave me. (Ruth Rabba 5.9; Yalkut Shim'oni 604)

The whole episode unfolded itself before Ruth as illustrating one aspect of the purpose of giving gifts to the poor — she could not have missed noticing Boaz's delight. She could not have had any inkling how great was the kindness she had extended to Boaz by coming to his field to glean. — It was there that Boaz relieved himself of the burden oppressing his soul. The opportunity was finally granted to him to do what had been impossible for him before — to comfort Naomi, the widow of his friend and kinsman (see the beginning of Chapter 2).

Perhaps Ruth had said so merely to placate Naomi, seeing how difficult Naomi had found sending Ruth to collect charity.

כ. וַתֹּאמֶר נָעֳמִי לְכַלָּתָהּ
בָּרוּךְ הוּא לַיְיָ אֲשֶׁר לֹא־עָזַב חַסְדּוֹ
אֶת־הַחַיִּים וְאֶת־הַמֵּתִים

2.20 "AND NAOMI SAID TO RUTH, HER DAUGHTER-IN-LAW: 'BLESSED BE HE OF THE LORD, WHO HAS NOT LEFT OFF HIS KINDNESS TO THE LIVING AND THE DEAD.'"

It was a happy day for Naomi — a day of atonement for, a day of hope for the survival of, her family. Boaz had inquired after her. It was a happy day, not only for her, but for her daughter-in-law, Ruth, as well, who had insisted so strongly on accompanying her. It was good that Ruth had come, for now the first ray of hope that the name of her dead son would be perpetuated had shone through the darkness. Perhaps her family would, after all, be rebuilt through Ruth.

[We have to develop a sensitivity to the veiled hints of the verses, and not only in respect of the actual words spoken, but even in respect of modifiers, titles, etc., being omitted. Here is a striking example. There reawakens in Naomi the awareness of her relationship — Naomi "the mother-in-law" begins to talk — to Ruth, "her daughter-in-law." (v. 22)
And, similarly, here (v. 20): "And Naomi said to Ruth, her daughter-in-law."]

Yet Naomi still repressed her exultation; she, as it were, prayed inwardly.

The entire verse reads as if Naomi were merely thinking aloud. Ostensibly she was talking to Ruth; in reality to herself.

Then she stopped — unable for a moment to decide whether to reveal, or not to reveal, her innermost thoughts to Ruth.

וַתֹּאמֶר לָהּ נָעֳמִי קָרוֹב לָנוּ הָאִישׁ מִגֹּאֲלֵנוּ הוּא:

"AND NAOMI SAID UNTO HER: 'THE MAN IS NIGH OF KIN UNTO US, ONE OF OUR NEAR KINSMEN.'"

R. Samuel b. Naḥman said: Boaz was one of the notables of the generation, and yet the woman called him her relative. (Ruth Rabba 5.10)

And Ruth?

The person preoccupied with earning his daily bread concentrates his prayers on trivial matters alone. His soul cannot discern the angels on high, appointed by God to bring him good tidings, that stand above his head.* Ruth was exulting over her achievement. She had entered a field owned by an Israelite and had been permitted to glean. She would go tomorrow too, calmly and confidently, for Boaz had admonished them not to hinder her.

Possibly she did not, on this account, grasp Naomi's far-reaching designs, nor had she any remark to offer in reply.
Or else she recoiled, disqualifying herself, since she realized how high Boaz's station was among his people, while she was but a foreigner.

כא. וַתֹּאמֶר רוּת הַמּוֹאֲבִיָּה
גַּם כִּי־אָמַר אֵלַי עִם הַנְּעָרִים אֲשֶׁר לִי תִּדְבָּקִין
עַד־אִם כִּלּוּ אֵת כָּל־הַקָּצִיר אֲשֶׁר־לִי׃

2.21 "AND RUTH, THE MOABITESS SAID: 'YEA, HE SAID UNTO ME: YOU SHALL KEEP FAST BY MY YOUNG MEN, UNTIL THEY HAVE ENDED ALL MY HARVEST.' "

Said R. Johanan: A Moabitess indeed was she, to utter such slander against that righteous man.
He said to her: "Abide here fast by my maidens."
And she said to her mother-in-law: You shall keep fast by my young men. (Yalkut Shim'oni 603)

Naomi was somewhat aggrieved. She trembled in doubt, like any person whose hopes have been roused, but is still unsure. She certainly expected Ruth to encourage and reassure her, for Ruth was her partner in this venture and the peg on which she was pinning her hope.

Had Ruth forgotten her oath?
But she had set her heart on her gleaning, and so she paid no particular attention to Boaz's exact wording.

Naomi did not remonstrate with Ruth. With all the circumspection of an understanding mother, Naomi not only corrected Ruth's remark, but set her thoughts right as well.*

כב. וַתֹּאמֶר נָעֳמִי אֶל־רוּת כַּלָּתָהּ
טוֹב בִּתִּי כִּי תֵצְאִי עִם נַעֲרוֹתָיו
וְלֹא יִפְגְּעוּ־בָךְ בְּשָׂדֶה אַחֵר׃
כג. וַתִּדְבַּק בְּנַעֲרוֹת בֹּעַז
לְלַקֵּט עַד־כְּלוֹת קְצִיר־הַשְּׂעֹרִים וּקְצִיר הַחִטִּים
וַתֵּשֶׁב אֶת־חֲמוֹתָהּ׃

22 "AND NAOMI SAID UNTO RUTH, HER DAUGHTER-IN-LAW:
IT IS GOOD, MY DAUGHTER, THAT YOU GO OUT WITH HIS MAIDENS,
AND THAT YOU BE MET NOT IN ANY OTHER FIELD."
23 SO SHE KEPT FAST BY THE MAIDENS OF BOAZ
TO GLEAN TO THE END OF THE BARLEY HARVEST AND WHEAT HARVEST,
AND SHE DWELT WITH HER MOTHER-IN-LAW."

Did Ruth have any inkling of Naomi's innermost reflections?

LEVIRATE MARRIAGE

"If brethren shall dwell together, and one of them die, and have no child,
The wife of the dead shall not be married abroad unto one not of his kin,
Her husband's brother shall go in unto her, and take her to him to wife and perform the duty of a husband's brother to her.

And it shall be, that the firstborn that she bears, shall succeed in the name of his brother that is dead,
that his name not be blotted out from Israel.

And if the man like not to take his brother's wife,
Then his brother's wife shall go up into the gate unto the elders and say:
My husband's brother refuses to raise up unto his brother a name in Israel; he will not perform the levirate duty unto me.

Then the elders of the city shall call him and speak unto him;
And if he stand and say: 'I like not to take her,';

Then shall his brother's wife draw nigh unto him in the presence of the elders and loose his shoe from off his foot,
And she shall spit in his presence and say:
So shall it be done unto the man that does not build up his brother's house.

And his name shall be called in Israel, 'The house of him that had his shoe loosed.'" (Deut. 25.5-10)

Maimonides, Laws of Levirate Marriage and Chalitza 1.5:

According to Scriptural law, there need be no marriage ceremony, since she is his wife already, married to him by Heaven.

Sefer Haḥinukh. Mitzvah 598 (554):

משורשי המצוה, לפי שהאשה אחר שנשאת לאיש הרי היא אחד מאבריו, שכן יחייב הטבע מפני מעשה האב הראשון שלוקחה אחת מצלעותיו וממנה בנה לו האל אשה.
והאיש הזה שמת בלא בנים שיהיה חלק ממנה לזכרון לו ולמלאות מקומו בעולם לעבודת בוראו, ועוד אין זכר לו בעולם הגופני זולתי זאת האשה שהיא עצם מעצמיו ובשר מבשרו, היה מחסדי האל עליו להקים לו זרע על ידי אחיו שהוא גם כן כחצי בשרו. כדי שיהיה אותו הזרע ממלא מקומו ועובד בוראו תחתיו ויזכה על ידו בעולם הנשמות אשר הוא שם. כמו שידוע, דברא מזכה אבא. (ספר החינוך מצוה תקצח)

Among the underlying reasons for this commandment is this: After a woman is married to a man, she becomes as one of his limbs, for so nature has ordained through the experience of the first father, one of whose ribs was taken by God and fashioned into a woman. As for the man who dies childless, in order to allow part of him to survive as his memorial and take his place in serving his Creator — since he has no other memorial in this physical world except for this woman, bone of his bone and flesh of his flesh — it is a Divine act of mercy to allow him to reproduce children through his brother, who is also like part of himself. In this way the children will take his place and serve his Creator in his stead. He will therefore derive merit in the world of souls where he remains, as it is said: A son acquires merit for his father.

אבל הענין [יבום] סוד גדול מסודות התורה בתולדות האדם. וניכר הוא לעיני רואים, אשר נתן להם השם עיניים לראות ואזניים לשמוע.

והיו החכמים הקדמונים קודם התורה [מתן-תורה] יודעים כי יש תועלת גדולה ביבום האח והוא הראוי להיות קודם בו ואחריו הקרוב במשפחה, כי כל שארו הקרוב אליו ממשפחתו אשר הוא יורש נחלה יגיע ממנו תועלת. והיו נוהגים לישא אשת המת. האח או האב או הקרוב מן המשפחה.

ולא היינו יודעים אם היה המנהג קדמון לפני יהודה.

ובב"ר אמרו, כי יהודה התחיל במצות יבום תחילה, כי כאשר קיבל הסוד מאבותיו נזדרז להקים אותו.

וכאשר באת התורה ואסרה אשת קצת הקרובים, רצה הקב"ה להתיר איסור אשת האח מפני היבום, ולא רצה שידחה מפני איסור אשת אחי האב והבן וזולתם, כי באח הרגל הדבר ותועלת קרובה ולא בהם. כמו שהזכרתי.

והנה נחשב לאכזריות גדולה באח כאשר לא יחפוץ ליבם, וקוראים אותו בית־חלוץ־הנעל כי עתה חלץ מהם, וראוי הוא שתעשה המצוה הזאת בחליצת הנעל.

וחכמי ישראל הקדמונים מדעתם העניין הנכבד הזה הנהיגו לפנים בישראל לעשות המעשה הזה בכל יורשי הנחלה באותם שלא היה בהם איסור השאר, וקראו אותו גאולה. וזהו עניין בועז, וטעם נעמי והשכנות. והמשכיל יבין.
(רמב"ן בראשית לח, ח.)

Nahmanides, Genesis 38.8:

But this matter (levirate marriage) is one of the great, hidden secrets of the Torah and it possesses a great significance for the generations of man. This is evident to those whom God has given eyes to see and ears to hear.

The sages of old, even before the revelation of Torah, knew that considerable benefit accrues through the brother performing the levirate duty, and he, therefore, takes precedence over all the others. After him, comes the next kin, for every one of the close relatives who is an heir would produce benefit. And so either the brother, father, or another relative would customarily marry the widow.

But we do not know whether the practice obtained prior to the time of Judah.

The Sages have asserted in Genesis Rabba that Judah was the first to fulfill this mitzvah of levirate marriage, for when this hidden knowledge was imparted to him by his fathers, he hastened to observe the commandment.

Now the Torah forbids certain relatives to marry one another. Nevertheless, the Holy One, blessed be He, desired to exclude the prohibition of marrying a brother's wife because of the mitzvah of levirate marriage. He did not, however, wish to abrogate the prohibition against marrying an aunt, a daughter-in-law, etc., since the performance of this duty usually devolved upon the brother and greater benefit accrues through him, as I have stated.

Now, it is considered exceedingly cruel for the brother to refuse to perform this duty. He is called the "house of him that had the shoe loosed," now he loosed himself from them, and it is fit for this mitzvah to be performed by removing the shoe.

> Now the sages of Israel of old appreciated the great worth of this mitzvah and involved the other relatives who would be heirs, in this duty, as long as the laws of incest would not be infringed. They referred to the act as "redemption." This is the explanation for the act of Boaz, and this explains Naomi's and the neighbor's behavior. The intelligent person will understand.

Malbim offers an explanation for the removal of the shoe. Here is an abridgment of his remarks:

> The shoe is an expression of human dignity and the assertion of a person's will, "This was the attestation in Israel to confirm every transaction," as if expressing that the party to the transaction was pledging all his human worth as surety for the keeping of his word. He also gave expression to his determination (will) — that nothing would prevent him from fulfilling his undertaking.
>
> As for the commandment regarding levirate marriage, the Torah ordered the setting aside of one of its prohibitions, viz. the marrying of a brother's widow, in order to perpetuate the name of the dead.
>
> Whoever refuses to take his childless brother's widow and does not understand that the Torah ordained this practice, in violation of one of its laws, as it were, makes it appear as if he is deficient in will-power. The widow therefore removes his shoe, thereby indicating that he is not fit to wear it.

> "Mercy and truth are met together; righteousness and peace have kissed each other,
>
> Truth springs out of the earth; and righteousness has looked down from heaven." (Ps. 85.11-18)

The mitzvah strikes us as strange. The Torah has set aside one of its most stringent prohibitions — the one forbidding incest, prohibiting the taking of a "brother's wife" — and has transformed the act into a religious duty.

Accordingly, the reasons underlying this mitzvah must be exceedingly profound and lie at the very basis of the existence of the world. They must be of the secrets of creation revealed to us by the Giver of the Torah, Who hallows the people of Israel through betrothal and marriage.

For so God willed — He Who made man in His image after His likeness and prepared unto him out of his very self a perpetual fabric. Its basis is love, brotherhood, peace and fellowship. Its basis is holiness which has been imprinted upon family life in Israel. Man and woman, parenthood, brotherhood, inheritance and possession — and all of these attributes form the cornerstone on which the glorious Jewish home is constructed, and they constitute the Torah of life.*

> Rabbi Akiva expounded: Husband and wife — if they are worthy, the *Shekhinah* dwells between them. (Sotah 17a)

> "If brothers dwell together and one of them dies and has no children."

The Rock, His work is perfect, for all His ways are just!
Blessed be the true Judge and blessed be He "Who has not left off his kindness to the living and the dead."
The laws of mourning are set down in detail in our Code of Torah life:
The rending of the garments for the dead, the eulogy, the funeral service, the comforting for the benefit of the mourners, the kaddish — the sanctification of His great Name according to His will in the world which He created.
And this great mitzvah of levirate marriage extends itself over all these practices.
How careful, how anxious was the Torah to preserve the name of the dead, "that his name not be blotted out from Israel."
Have not mercy and truth met together here?

> I consider this reference to her as the wife of the dead an intimation that she should still be called his wife, even after his death, for his spirit still resides in her. (Alshekh)

> "The wife of the dead shall not be married abroad to one not of his kin."

The "wife of the dead" — leaves her mourning and goes up to the gate, to the elders, to demand the satisfaction for the shame of her husband's childless death — she makes the demand, as the one obliged to perpetuate his house and to preserve his name in his father's family.

> "And if the man like not to take his brother's wife . . .
> Then shall his brother's wife draw nigh unto him in the presence of the elders, and loose his shoe from off his foot,
> And spit in his presence and answer and say:
> 'So shall it be done to the man that does not build up his brother's house.' "

What boldness did the Torah impart to this widow, in assigning her the duty to demand justice for her deceased husband in the gate of Israel.
This is the *ḥesed* she is to extend to him, after becoming his betrothed, in accordance with the law of Moses and Israel.

[The halakhah designates this woman by the appellation of *shomereth yavam*, explained by Rashi as signifying one waiting expectantly (*shomereth*) for the brother-in-law.* Cf. Yevamoth 38a.]

Here we are able to appreciate what great honor and glory the Torah has accorded Jewish family life. "Who hallowed us with His commandments."

How strikingly true is the above-mentioned observation of Nahmanides:

> It is evident to all to whom God has given eyes to see and ears to hear.

NAOMI'S PLAN

"UNTO THE END OF THE BARLEY HARVEST AND OF THE WHEAT HARVEST."

Rabbi Samuel b. Naḥmeni said: Wherever "until the end of the barley harvest and the wheat harvest" is mentioned — a period of three months is indicated. (Yalkut Shim'oni 604)

Three months!

Every morning Ruth would leave to gather in Boaz's field, and every evening she would return home to Naomi.
All that time, Naomi sat and waited. Perhaps Ruth would bring the good tidings of the fulfillment of her dreams — that Boaz would finally bestir himself and extend the full measure of kindness — the rebuilding of her deceased son's family.
But Boaz made no move to fulfill the mitzvah.

Was it that he was still preoccupied with his mourning?

Rabbi Yitzḥak said: On the day that Ruth the Moabitess came to Eretz Israel, the wife of Boaz died. (Bava Bathra 91a)

Or did he believe that this mitzvah no longer devolved upon him, since he was advanced in years and had endured a plentitude of suffering; all his sons died in his lifetime?

Rav said: Ibzan is Boaz. What does this come to teach us? The same that Rabbah son of Rav Huna taught elsewhere: Boaz made a hundred and twenty wedding feasts for his sons, as it is said: "And he (Ibzan) had thirty sons and thirty daughters he sent abroad, and thirty daughters he brought in from abroad for his sons" — all these died in his lifetime. (*Ibid.*)

Could he have dared to hope that he would reestablish his family? Was such a person as he fit and worthy to establish a new family?

When harvest had passed by and they had not been rescued; Ruth returned to sit with Naomi. During all that time they never discussed the future with each other. Naomi had no idea what thoughts were passing in Ruth's heart.

Finally, on that day, she decided to break the silence, to put Ruth's thoughts to the test. Was Ruth still true to the oath she had sworn to Naomi on the way?

Carefully, Naomi began to broach the subject. Every sentence was weighed and measured, worded in good taste, as befitted a deeply concerned mother.

> She began to lead Ruth on with words, till she could state bluntly what she wanted. (Ruth Zuta 3.1)

ג א. וַתֹּאמֶר לָהּ נָעֳמִי חֲמוֹתָהּ
בִּתִּי!
הֲלֹא אֲבַקֶּשׁ־לָךְ מָנוֹחַ אֲשֶׁר יִיטַב לָךְ׃

3.2 "AND NAOMI, HER MOTHER-IN-LAW SAID TO HER:
'MY DAUGHTER!
SHALL I NOT SEEK REST FOR YOU, THAT IT MAY BE WELL WITH YOU.'"

Naomi knew that she was demanding a great sacrifice of Ruth. Boaz, the relative-redeemer, was, indeed, rich and respected, but he was very old.*
If Ruth the Moabitess was indeed permitted to marry an Israelite would it not have been better for her to seek a younger man, whether poor or rich? (See below v. 10).

Moreover, Boaz had not taken any step to fulfill his duty. Yet here Naomi was placing the responsibility on Ruth to remind, to beg, or to reprove him.

We have indeed learned that the widow should also request the perpetuation of the deceased's name.

> "And his wife shall go up to the gate, to the elders." (Deut. 25)

Although Boaz was not actually the brother of the deceased, he was, nevertheless, fit to perform this duty (Cf. Nahmanides above). He had begun by recounting her praises in the presence of the inhabitants of Beth-lehem. He had declared her fit to enter the community of God. Was his awakening merely temporary? Was he prepared to give them just bread, and nothing more?

ב. וְעַתָּה, הֲלֹא בֹעַז מֹדַעְתָּנוּ
אֲשֶׁר הָיִית אֶת־נַעֲרוֹתָיו
הִנֵּה־הוּא זֹרֶה אֶת־גֹּרֶן הַשְּׂעֹרִים הַלָּיְלָה:

2 "AND NOW IS THERE NOT BOAZ OUR KINSMAN,
WITH WHOSE MAIDENS YOU WERE,
BEHOLD HE IS WINNOWING BARLEY TONIGHT IN THE THRESHING FLOOR."

"With whose maidens you were"—a hint to Ruth, a reference to verses 22 and 23 of the preceding chapter.

ג. וְרָחַצְתְּ וָסַכְתְּ וְשַׂמְתְּ שִׂמְלֹתַיִךְ עָלַיִךְ
וְיָרַדְתִּי (וירדת קרי) הַגֹּרֶן
אַל תִּוָּדְעִי לָאִישׁ עַד כַּלֹּתוֹ לֶאֱכֹל וְלִשְׁתּוֹת:

ד. וִיהִי בְשָׁכְבוֹ וְיָדַעַתְּ אֶת־הַמָּקוֹם אֲשֶׁר יִשְׁכַּב שָׁם
וּבָאת וְגִלִּית מַרְגְּלֹתָיו וְשָׁכָבְתְּי (ושכבת קרי)
וְהוּא יַגִּיד לָךְ אֵת אֲשֶׁר תַּעֲשִׂין:

3 "AND WASH YOURSELF THEREFORE, AND ANOINT YOURSELF, AND PUT YOUR RAIMENT ON YOU,
AND GO DOWN TO THE THRESHING FLOOR;
BUT MAKE NOT YOURSELF KNOWN UNTO THE MAN,
UNTIL HE HAS DONE EATING AND DRINKING.

4 AND IT SHALL BE WHEN HE LIES DOWN, THAT YOU SHALL MARK THE PLACE WHERE HE LIES DOWN,
AND YOU SHALL GO IN AND UNCOVER HIS FEET AND LIE DOWN
AND HE WILL TELL YOU WHAT YOU SHALL DO."

You will ask his advice and he, in his wisdom, will tell you what to do. (Targum Jonathan)

Read as imperatives, the verbs: "go down", "lie down", are spelled as if they were first person future verbs, as if to say: I shall go down, I shall lie down.

From the spelling (*kethiv*) our Rabbis have sensed Naomi's trepidation at sending off Ruth on such a mission.

She sympathized with Ruth, who might not have had the temerity for, or might have doubted the propriety of, such an act.

Naomi therefore identified herself with the deed. Similarly Rebeccah, when she sent Jacob to deceive Isaac, said: "Upon me be your curse, my son."

"And you shall to down to the barn"—the *kethiv*: I shall go down. She said: May my merit go down with you. (Yerushalmi Peah 8.7; Yalkut Shim'oni 604)

ה. וַתֹּאמֶר אֵלֶיהָ
כֹּל אֲשֶׁר־תֹּאמְרִי ـ ـ אֶעֱשֶׂה:

5 "AND SHE SAID UNTO HER
'ALL THAT YOU SAY (to me) I SHALL DO.'"

Ruth replied calmly, as if obeying an order. Perhaps the Massoretic text indicated this fact by omitting the words "to me"—as if she had effaced herself before Naomi, who had issued the command.

> "To me"—is read, but not transcribed in the text, to convey that although the advice seemed improper to her, nevertheless since she (Naomi) had given it, Ruth would not do otherwise. (Akedath Yitzḥak)

> "That you say" is written; "That you say unto me" is read. This is handed down by tradition (by the law of Moses handed down from Sinai).
> [R. Nissim: So Moses received it at Sinai and handed it down to Israel*] (Nedarim 37b)

ON THE THRESHING FLOOR

ג ו. וַתֵּרֶד הַגֹּרֶן וַתַּעַשׂ כְּכֹל אֲשֶׁר־צִוַּתָּה חֲמוֹתָהּ׃

3.6 "AND SHE WENT DOWN UNTO THE THRESHING FLOOR, AND DID ACCORDING TO ALL THAT HER MOTHER-IN-LAW BADE HER."

Of Moab it is written (Jeremiah 48.30): "I know his arrogancy, says the Lord, that it is illfounded."
R. Simon said: Moab was first conceived not out of noble motives, but in a spirit of immorality, as it is said (Num. 25.1): "And Israel dwelt in Shittim..."
His scions did not act thus, but with a noble motive, as it says "And she went down unto the threshing floor, and did according to all her mother-in-law bade her." (Ruth Rabba 5.14; Gen. Rabba 51; Yalkut Shim'oni 331)

"AND SHE WENT DOWN TO THE THRESHING FLOOR."

Ruth's shock, as she went out to fulfill this noble assignment, is quite understandable.

She was going at night, to a strange threshing floor, to a strange man.

Would Boaz realize what she was doing, and not deem her deed wicked? Would he understand her pure intentions, since she had come to seek the fulfillment of the mitzvah of levirate marriage, for the sake of Heaven?

The man was a notable of Beth-lehem. He was an old man!

We may possibly believe, however, that she stepped out confidently, securely, since she knew that her soul was pure. Was this not essentially her vow? It was for this reason that she had left her people and the home of her mother and had come from the fields of Moab to the land of Israel and Judah!

Was her trembling not calmed by an inner exultation at going to perform a mitzvah — the performance of kindness and truth, the perpetuation of a name in Israel?

It may be difficult for us to comprehend fully the purity and holiness of this idea. It is therefore incumbent upon us to attune our minds to its purity and innocence, in the manner that our Rabbis have understood its import.

> Two women sacrificed themselves for the sake of the tribe of Judah: Tamar and Ruth. (Yalkut Shim'oni 601)

Of Tamar it is written:

ותשב בפתח עינים אשר על דרך תמנתה. (בראשית לח, יד)

א"ר אמי: חזרנו על כל המקרא ולא מצאנו מקום ששמו פתח־עינים — אלא מלמד שתלתה עיניה בפתח שכל העיניים תלויות בו ואמרה:
יהי רצון מלפניך ה' אלוקי שלא אצא מן הבית הזה ריקנית. (ב"ר וישב, פ"ה)

> "And she sat in Petah Enayim which is by the way to Timnah." (Genesis 38.14)
> R. Ammi said: We have searched through the whole of Scripture and found no place called Petah Enayim. What then is the purport of Petah Enayim? It teaches us that she lifted her eyes to the gate (*petah*) to which all eyes (*enayim*) are directed, and prayed: "May it be Your will that I do not leave this house emptyhanded." (Gen. Rabba 85)

And Ruth prayed similarly:

> "And I came to seek from God that He give me a share in your family." (Ruth Zuta 3.8)

Both supplications were richly rewarded, for they were as genuine and sincere as the souls of the two who uttered the prayers.

Here the merits of the two righteous and genuine proselytes reached their culmination — the two proselytes who had clung to the Shechinah and bound themselves up in the eternity of Israel, to become illuminated by the light of the Messiah.

ג ז. וַיֹּאכַל בֹּעַז וַיֵּשְׁתְּ וַיִּיטַב לִבּוֹ
וַיָּבֹא לִשְׁכַּב בִּקְצֵה הָעֲרֵמָה
וַתָּבֹא בַלָּט וַתְּגַל מַרְגְּלֹתָיו וַתִּשְׁכָּב׃

3.7 "AND WHEN BOAZ HAD EATEN AND DRUNK, AND HIS HEART WAS MERRY,
HE WENT TO LIE DOWN AT THE END OF THE HEAP OF CORN;
AND SHE CAME SOFTLY, AND UNCOVERED HIS FEET, AND LAID HER DOWN."

And when Boaz had eaten and drunk, and his heart was happy and he blessed the Name of *Hashem,* Who had accepted their prayers and banished hunger from the land of Israel... (Targum Jonathan)

ח. וַיְהִי בַּחֲצִי הַלַּיְלָה וַיֶּחֱרַד הָאִישׁ וַיִּלָּפֵת
וְהִנֵּה אִשָּׁה שֹׁכֶבֶת מַרְגְּלֹתָיו׃

8 "AND IT WAS AT MIDNIGHT, THAT THE MAN WAS STARTLED, AND TURNED HIMSELF;
AND BEHOLD A WOMAN LAY AT HIS FEET."

(that "the man" was startled — In describing a sudden surprise, one has no time to go into detail concerning the name of the person involved).

זה שאמר הכתוב (תהלים קיט, סב) **חצות לילה אקום להודות לך על משפטי** צדקך. כך אמר דוד: חייב אני לקום להודות לך על מה שעשית לזקני ולזקנתי בחצי הלילה. שנאמר: ויהי בחצי הלילה ויחרד האיש וילפת, **שאילו השחיל** לה קללה אחת — מהיכן הייתי **עומד?**
נתן בלבו לברכה וברכה: ברוכה את לה' בתי (ילק"ש תרו)

דאמר ר' אחא בר ביזנא, א"ר שמעון חסידא:
כינור היה תלוי למעלה ממיטתו של דוד וכיוון שהגיע חצות לילה, **באה** רוח צפונית ונושבת בו ומנגן מאליו. (ברכות ג: רו"ר ו, א)

This is what Scripture has stated (Ps. 119.62): "At midnight I will rise to give thanks unto You, because of Your righteous ordinances." So said David: I am obliged to arise to give thanks unto You for what You have done for my grandfather and grandmother in the middle of the night, as it is said: "And it was at midnight, that the man was startled and turned himself." Had he hurled a single curse-word at her, from where would I have arisen?
He put it into his heart to bless. And he blessed her: "Blessed be You of the Lord, my daughter." (Yalkut Shim'oni 606)

For so said R. Aha bar Bizana in the name of R. Shimon the Pious:
A harp was hanging above David's bed. As soon as midnight arrived, a North wind came and blew upon it and it played of itself. (Berakoth 3b; Ruth Rabba 6.1)

ט. וַיֹּאמֶר: מִי אָתְּ?
וַתֹּאמֶר: אָנֹכִי רוּת אֲמָתֶךָ
וּפָרַשְׂתָּ כְנָפֶךָ עַל־אֲמָתְךָ כִּי גֹאֵל אָתָּה:

9 "AND HE SAID: 'WHO ARE YOU?'
AND SHE SAID: "I AM RUTH YOUR HANDMAID,
SPREAD THEREFORE YOUR SKIRT OVER YOUR HANDMAID; FOR YOU ARE A NEAR KINSMAN."

R. Abraham Ibn Ezra: Naomi had told her that such was the rule in Israel....

Had Naomi also put these words, chosen with such delicate discrimination, into Ruth's mouth?

Or had Ruth expressed herself so on her own, her words thereby according her grace and humility, the modesty commensurate with the performance of a mitzvah? * (Cf. vv. 12-13 in Chap. 2)

Now Boaz, too, saw and realized that Ruth had come within the borders of the land of Israel with pure intentions, something he may not have been disposed to concede till now. For since the time that Naomi and Ruth had arrived, and during the past three months that Ruth had been gleaning in his field, he certainly knew that the obligation of redemption devolved upon him. Yet could he have dared to approach her and broach the subject of levirate marriage? Would this foreign woman understand the hidden significance of this mitzvah and its underlying reasons? How would she receive this "proposal" — she a young woman from an old man?

Instead, however, she had taken the initiative toward fulfilling the mitzvah.

י. וַיֹּאמֶר בְּרוּכָה אַתְּ לַיְיָ בִּתִּי
הֵיטַבְתְּ חַסְדֵּךְ הָאַחֲרוֹן מִן הָרִאשׁוֹן
לְבִלְתִּי־לֶכֶת אַחֲרֵי הַבַּחוּרִים אִם־דַּל וְאִם עָשִׁיר׃

3.10 "AND HE SAID: 'BLESSED BE YOU OF THE LORD, MY DAUGHTER,
YOU HAVE SHOWN MORE KINDNESS IN THE END, THAN AT THE BEGINNING,
INASMUCH AS YOU DID NOT FOLLOW THE YOUNG MEN, WHETHER POOR OR RICH."

You have shown more kindness in the end, than at the beginning: Rabbi Shmuel the son of Rabbi Yitzchak says:
A woman loves a young man though he be poor more than an old man though he be wealthy. (Ruth Rabba 6.4)
R. Abraham Ibn Ezra: Since all are attracted to you on account of your beauty.

Boaz tried to comfort and encourage her. After all, was it not he who was responsible for her lot, by having neglected her till now, to the extent that she had become constrained to undertake this bold act, to go down to the threshing floor this night?

יא. וְעַתָּה בִּתִּי אַל־תִּירְאִי כֹּל אֲשֶׁר־תֹּאמְרִי אֶעֱשֶׂה־לָּךְ
כִּי יוֹדֵעַ כָּל שַׁעַר עַמִּי כִּי אֵשֶׁת חַיִל אָתְּ:

11 "AND NOW MY DAUGHTER FEAR NOT; I WILL DO TO YOU ALL THAT YOU SAY;
FOR ALL THE MEN IN THE GATE OF MY PEOPLE DO KNOW THAT YOU ARE A VIRTUOUS WOMAN.'"

"I will do to you all that you say" —
So too Ruth had expressed herself to Naomi (v. 5), and the reward for one promise is another. Here Boaz added the word "to you" — in recompense and in compensation for her self-effacement in omitting the word "to me".
By beginning with praise for her, Boaz intended to console her; but by his broad promise at the same time he also apologized to her and admitted to her that she had been more righteous than he.

יב. וְעַתָּה כִּי אָמְנָם כִּי אם גֹאֵל אָנֹכִי
וְגַם יֵשׁ גֹּאֵל קָרוֹב מִמֶּנִּי:

12 "AND NOW IT IS TRUE THAT I AM A NEAR KINSMAN, HOWBEIT THERE IS A KINSMAN NEARER THAN I."

The obligation of "redemption" in those days first devolved upon the nearest of kin, but that relative was quite unconcerned for the sufferings of the house of Avimelech. Boaz knew and had certainly seen that kinsman more than once. Yet people refrained from discussing among themselves the plight of their relative Naomi who had returned from Moab, since this was a painful matter in Beth-lehem and a blot on the family.

Even though Boaz did not believe that the other kinsman would perform the act of "redemption", he was obliged by law to clear the matter with that relative first, and only thereafter to acquire from him the rights and obligations the "redemption" entailed.

He would no longer delay her future. As soon as morning would come, he would rise and go up to the gate to the elders and seek out the kinsman. He took an oath.

יג. לִינִי הַלַּיְלָה וְהָיָה בַבֹּקֶר אִם־יִגְאָלֵךְ טוֹב יִגְאָל
וְאִם לֹא יַחְפֹּץ לְגָאֳלֵךְ וּגְאַלְתִּיךְ אָנֹכִי
חַי יְיָ שִׁכְבִי עַד־הַבֹּקֶר׃

3.13 "TARRY THIS NIGHT, AND IT SHALL BE IN THE MORNING, THAT IF HE WILL PERFORM UNTO YOU THE PART OF A KINSMAN, WELL; LET HIM DO THE KINSMAN'S PART;
BUT IF HE IS NOT WILLING TO DO THE PART OF A KINSMAN TO YOU,
THEN I WILL DO THE PART OF THE KINSMAN TO YOU,
AS THE LORD LIVES; LIE DOWN UNTIL THE MORNING.'"

As the Lord lives! He swore to her by the Name of *Hashem*, in a spirit of holy exaltation. For this was a great hour in his life, when Ruth had undertaken to make him a part of her fervent, sincere and devoted prayer to establish a name in Judah.

יד. וַתִּשְׁכַּב מַרְגְּלוֹתָו עַד־הַבֹּקֶר (מרגלותיו קרי)
וַתָּקָם בְּטֶרֶם יַכִּיר אִישׁ אֶת־רֵעֵהוּ
וַיֹּאמֶר אַל יִוָּדַע כִּי בָאָה הָאִשָּׁה הַגֹּרֶן:

14 "AND SHE LAY AT HIS FEET UNTIL THE MORNING (the spelling — "his foot")
AND SHE ROSE UP BEFORE ONE COULD DISCERN ANOTHER.
FOR HE SAID: 'LET IT NOT BE KNOWN THAT THE WOMAN CAME TO THE THRESHING FLOOR.'"

There they stood at the threshing floor, as the morning star rose. Before men could discern one another, Boaz discerned and realized what a great privilege had been accorded him, the merit of being the ancestor of royalty, through the loving-kindness that would lead to the perpetuation of Israel and its anointed king.
For so his heart prophesied to him, and so he prophesied and hinted to her as well:

"I WILL DO THE PART OF THE KINSMAN"
(lit. "I shall redeem you") —

וגאלתיך אנכי.
ועל דא אמר לה הקב"ה (לכנסת־ישראל) הטבת חסדך האחרון מן הראשון. דאתקיימת בקיומא לגבאי, ולא חיישת לחרופא וגדופא דשאר עממין. אבל ליני הלילה — הוי השתא בגלותא ואנהיגי לבניך תמן באוריתא ובעובדין טבין, ואם יסהדון עליך עובדין טבין למפרק לך יפרוק. ואם לאו וגאלתיך אנכי חי ד' שכבי עד הבוקר — עד דייתי צפרא ונהירו דפורקנא. (זהר חדש רות, פ"ח)

In reference to this, the Holy One, blessed be He, said to her (the congregation of Israel): "You have shown more kindness in the end than at the beginning.
That you have remained faithful to Me, and that you paid no heed to the reviling and mocking of the rest of the peoples, 'Tarry here for the night' — remain in exile as of now, and lead

> your sons there by means of the Torah and good deeds. And if your good deeds will testify on your behalf, they will redeem you. And if not, then I shall redeem you, as the Lord lives, 'Lie down until the morning' — until the morning comes and the light of redemption shines forth." (Zohar Ḥadash, Ruth, 8)

At the time Boaz reiterated the expression signifying redemption. he certainly had its plain meaning in mind, the redemption of Ruth, the widow of Mahlon the son of his relative and kinsman. The prophetic spirit, however, ranging from the past to the future, from beginning to end, caught the echo of the promise of redemption of the entire nation and a glimpse of the dawn that would rise some morning in the distant future.

טו. וַיֹּאמֶר: הָבִי הַמִּטְפַּחַת אֲשֶׁר־עָלַיִךְ וְאֶחֳזִי־בָהּ
וַתֹּאחֶז בָּהּ
וַיָּמָד שֵׁשׁ־שְׂעֹרִים וַיָּשֶׁת עָלֶיהָ
וַיָּבֹא הָעִיר׃

3.15 "AND HE SAID: 'BRING THE MANTLE THAT IS UPON YOU, AND HOLD IT';
AND SHE HELD IT;
AND HE MEASURED SIX SHEAVES OF BARLEY, AND HE LAID IT ON HER.
AND HE WENT INTO THE CITY."

Six sheaves of barley.

The commentators are put to some strain to discover the meaning of this particular quantity. Before we clarify the matter, let us pay attention to the verse as a whole, which takes such pains to describe every item in detail. We shall of necessity have to rely upon this striking thought of the Midrash to cast light upon this remarkable confrontation.

וכי דרכו של בועז ליתן שש שעורים מתנה?

אלא רמז לה, שעתידים לצאת ממנה, שישה בנים שמתברכים בשש ברכות ואלו הם: דוד ומשיח, דניאל וחנניה, מישאל ועזריה.

דוד: יודע נגן, גבור חיל, איש מלחמה, ונבון דבר, ואיש תואר, וה׳ עמו. (ש״א טז)

משיח: ונחה עליו רוח ה׳; רוח חכמה ובינה, רוח עצה וגבורה, רוח דעת, ויראת ה׳. (ישעיה יא — סנהדרין צג.)

But was it Boaz's practice to give gifts of six sheaves of barley?

He intimated to her that six sons were destined to issue from her, each of whom would be blessed with six blessings, namely; David, the Messiah, Daniel, Hananiah, Mishael, and Azariah.

David, in that he was a musician, a mighty man of valor, a warrior, wise in affairs, handsome and that the Lord was with him. (1 Sam. 16)

Messiah: "And the spirit of the Lord shall rest upon him, the spirit of wisdom and understanding, the spirit of counsel and might, the spirit of knowledge and of the fear of God." (Isa. 11 — Sanhedrin 93a)

WHO ARE YOU, MY DAUGHTER?

ג טז. וַתָּבוֹא אֶל־חֲמוֹתָהּ...

3.16 "AND WHEN SHE CAME UNTO HER MOTHER-IN-LAW..."

As for the mother-in-law, she had remained awake all night. Her heart trembled expectantly as she waited for her daughter-in-law, in effect her daughter.
Had she done right in sending Ruth thus? Did Boaz recognize and appreciate Ruth's initiative for what it was and not humiliate her?
Was there any hope still left for her, for Naomi?

Suddenly, Ruth was back.
Naomi discerned her from afar, as she was approaching nearer with the first light of the morning.
Naomi was bracing herself to meet Ruth. And now Ruth entered very slowly and came to Naomi.

At that moment Naomi was curious to know all. If only she could pour out all the thoughts and feelings of her heart in the question she wanted to ask. But she restrained herself, and kept silent. She looked with compassion upon her daughter.
Only one short and modest question, phrased with utmost care and with true motherly wisdom:

וַתֹּאמֶר מִי אַתְּ בִּתִּי?

"AND SHE SAID: 'WHO ARE YOU, MY DAUGHTER?'"

Could Ruth really have told Naomi everything that had occurred, what had welled up in her heart that time?

וַתַּגֶּד לָהּ אֵת כָּל־אֲשֶׁר עָשָׂה־לָהּ הָאִישׁ׃

"AND SHE TOLD HER ALL THAT THE MAN HAD DONE TO HER."

Through her soft and quiet answer, she replied to, and calmed, her mother-in-law. As one interpreting a pleasant dream in which dormant hopes rise up, she handed over the evidence and reported the implications of what Boaz had done to her.

יז. וַתֹּאמֶר שֵׁשׁ־הַשְּׂעֹרִים הָאֵלֶּה נָתַן לִי
כִּי אָמַר ‗ ‥ אַל־תָּבוֹאִי רֵיקָם אֶל־חֲמוֹתֵךְ׃

"AND SHE SAID : 'HE GAVE ME THESE SIX SHEAVES OF BARLEY, FOR HE SAID (to me): GO NOT EMPTY TO YOUR MOTHER-IN-LAW.'"

Did Boaz really say that to her? Or had Ruth on her own added some embellishment to placate Naomi, for Ruth realized how great was Naomi's share in what had happened.

(It is written: "And I shall go down" — the signification being: "My merit shall go down with you.")

And perhaps this is hinted at in the text, as here also "to me" is not written, for here too Ruth had effaced her own self and had transferred all her rights to Naomi.

"GO NOT EMPTY TO YOUR MOTHER-IN-LAW."

It was a consolation gift that he had sent to Naomi, the Naomi who had stood on that previous day in the gates of Beth-lehem and had declared: "I went out full and the Lord has brought me back empty."

גיח. וַתֹּאמֶר שְׁבִי בִתִּי עַד אֲשֶׁר תֵּדְעִין אֵיךְ יִפֹּל דָּבָר
כִּי לֹא יִשְׁקֹט הָאִישׁ כִּי אִם־כִּלָּה הַדָּבָר הַיּוֹם׃

3.18 "THEN SHE SAID: 'SIT STILL MY DAUGHTER, UNTIL YOU KNOW HOW THE MATTER WILL FALL:
FOR THE MAN WILL NOT REST UNTIL HE HAS FINISHED THE THING THIS DAY.'"

"How the matter will fall" — Since decrees issue from Heaven. (Ibn Ezra)

R. Huna said in the name of R. Samuel b. Isaac: The yes of the righteous is yes, and their no, no — as it is said: For the man will not rest until he has finished the thing this day. (Ruth Rabba 7.6)

THE UNNAMED RELATIVE

ד א. וּבֹעַז עָלָה הַשַּׁעַר וַיֵּשֶׁב שָׁם
וְהִנֵּה הַגֹּאֵל עֹבֵר אֲשֶׁר דִּבֶּר־בֹּעַז

4.1 "NOW BOAZ WENT UP TO THE GATE, AND SAT HIMSELF DOWN THERE;
AND BEHOLD THE NEAR KINSMAN OF WHOM BOAZ SPOKE CAME BY."

Was the relative waiting in readiness behind the gate? Said R. Berekhia: So the two pillars of the world, R. Eliezer and R. Joshua expounded: R. Eliezer stated: Ruth played her part, Boaz played his. The Holy One, blessed be He said: I will play Mine.
The Rabbis stated: Even had he (the relative) been at the uttermost ends of the earth, the Holy One blessed be He would have flown him and brought him back there, to prevent that righteous person (Boaz) from grieving while sitting there (Yalkut Shim'oni 606: Ruth Rabba 7).

וַיֹּאמֶר סוּרָה שְׁבָה־פֹּה פְּלֹנִי אַלְמֹנִי
וַיָּסַר וַיֵּשֵׁב׃

"AND HE SAID: HO, YOU THERE! TURN ASIDE, SIT DOWN HERE. AND HE TURNED ASIDE AND SAT DOWN."

Some maintain that the name of this anonymous person was *Tov* ("If Tov will perform the part of the kinsman"). It was therefore only proper for Boaz not to have addressed him by his name; for he did not deserve to be called *Tov*— good. Boaz referred to him as *Peloni Almoni* ("such a one"—"you there"), for that person had ignored his family obligation, deliberately overlooking the mitzvah of "redemption in Israel."

Almoni — R. Shim'on b. Nahmani said: He was silent (*Ilem — Almoni*) in affairs of Torah, since he thought: The earlier ones died only because they married her, shall I go and take her to me? Shall I mix pollution with my seed?

Yet he did not know that the law had already been reinstated An Ammonite is unfit but not an Ammonitess; a Moabite, but not a Moabitess. (Yalkut Shim'oni 606).

"TURN ASIDE, SIT DOWN HERE. AND HE TURNED ASIDE AND SAT DOWN."

Boaz gave the order, but did not begin speaking to the relative before he had summoned the elders.

ב. וַיִּקַּח עֲשָׂרָה אֲנָשִׁים מִזִּקְנֵי הָעִיר
וַיֹּאמֶר שְׁבוּ־פֹה, וַיֵּשֵׁבוּ:

2 "AND HE TOOK TEN MEN OF THE ELDERS OF THE CITY, AND SAID: 'SIT DOWN HERE', AND THEY SAT DOWN."

He spoke in the imperative to the elders as well, for Boaz was distinguished and respected among his people. He was a leader and one of the judges.*

Or else his abruptness might indicate his firm resolve. He was also urging himself on, since he had decided to make amends for his dilatory behavior in fulfilling the mitzvah till then.

ג. וַיֹּאמֶר לַגֹּאֵל
חֶלְקַת הַשָּׂדֶה אֲשֶׁר לְאָחִינוּ לֶאֱלִימֶלֶךְ מָכְרָה נָעֳמִי
הַשָּׁבָה מִשְּׂדֵה מוֹאָב:

ד. וַאֲנִי אָמַרְתִּי אֶגְלֶה אָזְנְךָ לֵאמֹר
קְנֵה נֶגֶד הַיֹּשְׁבִים וְנֶגֶד זִקְנֵי עַמִּי
אִם־תִּגְאַל גְּאָל וְאִם־לֹא יִגְאַל הַגִּידָה־לִּי וְאֵדְעָ
כִּי אֵין זוּלָתְךָ לִגְאוֹל וְאָנֹכִי אַחֲרֶיךָ.

3 "AND HE SAID TO THE NEAR KINSMAN:
'NAOMI, WHO HAS COME BACK OUT OF THE FIELD OF
MOAB, IS SELLING HER PARCEL OF LAND.

4 AND I THOUGHT TO DISCLOSE IT UNTO YOU, SAYING:
BUY IT BEFORE THEM THAT SIT HERE AND BEFORE
THE ELDERS OF MY PEOPLE.
IF YOU WILL REDEEM IT, REDEEM IT; BUT IF HE WILL
NOT REDEEM IT, THEN TELL ME THAT I MAY KNOW;
FOR THERE IS NONE TO REDEEM IT BESIDE YOU; AND
I AM AFTER YOU.'"

The verse is rather long. The words seem to have been uttered with deliberation and dignity. Yet they also betray excitement. For Boaz had come to reinstate and reinforce a law in the minds of his people, one that had faded and lapsed into oblivion.

The remark may also have been a reproof to the kinsman and himself for having delayed the performance of the deed till then.

"But if he will not redeem it" — the third person is used.

And I am after you — but Boaz did not state the implication explicitly.

וַיֹּאמֶר אָנֹכִי אֶגְאָל.

"AND HE SAID: 'I WILL REDEEM IT.'"

Did the relative feel compelled to give this answer?

Perhaps the emotional words of Boaz made an impression.

ה. וַיֹּאמֶר בֹּעַז
בְּיוֹם־קְנוֹתְךָ הַשָּׂדֶה מִיַּד נָעֳמִי
וּמֵאֵת רוּת הַמּוֹאֲבִיָּה אֵשֶׁת־הַמֵּת
קָנִיתָ (קניתי כתיב!) לְהָקִים שֵׁם־הַמֵּת עַל נַחֲלָתוֹ:

5 "THEN BOAZ SAID:
'ON THE DAY THAT YOU BUY THE FIELD OF THE HAND OF NAOMI — YOU HAVE ALSO BOUGHT IT (the *kethiv* is 'I have bought') OF RUTH THE MOABITESS, THE WIFE OF THE DEAD, TO RAISE UP THE NAME OF THE DEAD ON HIS INHERITANCE.' "

Legal usage would have required him to state of Ruth too "of the hand". But apparently the text wanted to include Ruth, too, as being acquired.

"And of Ruth you have acquired" — you have also acquired Ruth the Moabitess herself.

Note! Here Boaz gives her the same designation as Scripture itself: the wife of the dead. "The wife of the dead shall not be married abroad!"

ו. וַיֹּאמֶר הַגֹּאֵל לֹא אוּכַל לִגְאוֹל־לִי
פֶּן־אַשְׁחִית אֶת־נַחֲלָתִי
גְּאַל־לְךָ אַתָּה אֶת־גְּאֻלָּתִי כִּי לֹא־אוּכַל לִגְאוֹל:

6 "AND THE NEAR KINSMAN SAID: 'I CANNOT REDEEM IT FOR MYSELF,
LEST I MAR MY OWN INHERITANCE,
TAKE YOU MY RIGHT OF REDEMPTION UPON YOURSELF; FOR I CANNOT REDEEM IT.' "

He thought: The former ones (Mahlon and Chilion) died only because they married them (Ruth and Orpah). Shall I go and take her? (Ruth Rabba 7.9)
I cannot, I cannot!

How foolish was this anonymous individual — "silent in Torah" — in his anxiety to preserve his property.
Deaf and dumb he was in his refusal to listen to the law that had been reinstated, that Ruth was permitted to enter the community of Israel. So too was his heart insensitive to the greatness of the inheritance of Ruth and the greatness of the reward stored up for her in Israel.

ז. וְזֹאת לְפָנִים בְּיִשְׂרָאֵל עַל־הַגְּאֻלָּה וְעַל־הַתְּמוּרָה
לְקַיֵּם כָּל־דָּבָר
שָׁלַף אִישׁ נַעֲלוֹ וְנָתַן לְרֵעֵהוּ
וְזֹאת הַתְּעוּדָה בְּיִשְׂרָאֵל׃

ח. וַיֹּאמֶר הַגֹּאֵל לְבֹעַז קְנֵה־לָךְ וַיִּשְׁלֹף נַעֲלוֹ׃

7 "NOW THIS WAS THE CUSTOM IN FORMER TIME IN ISRAEL CONCERNING REDEEMING AND EXCHANGING, TO CONFIRM ALL THINGS:
A MAN DREW OFF HIS SHOE, AND GAVE IT TO HIS NEIGHBOR
AND THIS WAS THE ATTESTATION IN ISRAEL.

8 SO THE NEAR KINSMAN SAID TO BOAZ: 'BUY IT FOR YOURSELF.'
AND HE DREW OFF HIS SHOE."

> Who gave (the shoe) to whom? Boaz gave his shoe to the redeemer.
> R. Judah said: The kinsman gave his shoe to Boaz (Bava Metzia 47a)

The Gemara cites this conflict of opinion on the law of conveyance by exchange,* for all agree that a legal transfer of property was effected here. *Geulah* ('redemption') — designates sale; *temurah* — ('exchange') — refers to the transfer of property by symbolic exchange. The ruling follows the opinion of Rav, that the transfer is effected by handing over an article belonging to the purchaser.

The scene portrayed here in these verses, and the opinion of R. Judah in the Tannaitic disagreement, allows us to view the redeemer here, the unnamed individual, standing shoe-less, as being reminded of the Biblical *chalitzah*, the removal of the shoe of the man who "does not build up his brother's house." —

"And his name shall be called in Israel: 'The house of him that had the shoe loosed.' " *

ד ט. וַיֹּאמֶר בֹּעַז לַזְּקֵנִים וְכָל־הָעָם
עֵדִים אַתֶּם הַיּוֹם כִּי קָנִיתִי אֶת־כָּל־אֲשֶׁר לֶאֱלִימֶלֶךְ
וְאֵת כָּל־אֲשֶׁר לְכִלְיוֹן וּמַחְלוֹן מִיַּד נָעֳמִי:

י. וְגַם אֶת־רוּת הַמֹּאֲבִיָּה אֵשֶׁת מַחְלוֹן
קָנִיתִי לִי לְאִשָּׁה לְהָקִים שֵׁם־הַמֵּת עַל־נַחֲלָתוֹ
וְלֹא־יִכָּרֵת שֵׁם־הַמֵּת מֵעִם אֶחָיו וּמִשַּׁעַר מְקוֹמוֹ
עֵדִים אַתֶּם הַיּוֹם:

4.9 "AND BOAZ SAID UNTO THE ELDERS, AND UNTO ALL THE PEOPLE:
'YOU ARE WITNESSES THIS DAY, THAT I HAVE BOUGHT ALL THAT WAS ELIMELECH'S,
AND ALL THAT WAS CHILION'S AND MAHLON'S, OF THE HAND OF NAOMI.

10 MOREOVER, RUTH THE MOABITESS, THE WIFE OF MAHLON,
HAVE I ACQUIRED TO BE MY WIFE, TO RAISE UP THE NAME OF THE DEAD UPON HIS INHERITANCE,
THAT THE NAME OF THE DEAD BE NOT CUT OFF FROM AMONG HIS BRETHREN,
AND FROM THE GATE OF HIS PLACE,
YOU ARE WITNESSES THIS DAY.' "

Boaz had proclaimed this fulfillment of the mitzvah of redemption in the presence of the elders and all the people.

And so he had removed the shame from that family.
He mentioned the names of all the dead that day so as to achieve atonement for them. And Mahlon he mentioned last, because "Mahlon is an expression of *meḥilah*—forgiveness." (Yalkut Shim'oni 600).

You are witnesses!

For all the people and the elders of Beth-lehem would acknowledge this forgiveness—for they, too, had to forgive.
And all of them acknowledged, gave witness, and pronounced their blessing!

יא. וַיֹּאמְרוּ כָּל הָעָם אֲשֶׁר־בַּשַּׁעַר וְהַזְּקֵנִים עֵדִים
יִתֵּן ה׳ אֶת־הָאִשָּׁה הַבָּאָה אֶל־בֵּיתֶךָ
כְּרָחֵל וּכְלֵאָה אֲשֶׁר בָּנוּ שְׁתֵּיהֶם אֶת־בֵּית יִשְׂרָאֵל
וַעֲשֵׂה־חַיִל בְּאֶפְרָתָה וּקְרָא־שֵׁם בְּבֵית לָחֶם׃

11 "AND ALL THE PEOPLE THAT WERE IN THE GATE, AND THE ELDERS, SAID: 'WE ARE WITNESSES.
THE LORD MAKE THE WOMAN THAT IS COME INTO YOUR HOUSE,
LIKE RACHEL AND LIKE LEAH, WHICH TWO DID BUILD THE HOUSE OF ISRAEL;
AND DO WORTHILY IN EPHRATH AND BE FAMOUS IN BETH-LEHEM."

Scripture should have stated "like Leah and Rachel." However, although Boaz and all his Beth Din were descended from Leah, they acknowledged that the preeminence belonged to Rachel, since Jacob had only become indentured in the house of Laban for the sake of Rachel.* (Tanhuma, Yalkut Shim'oni)

Now that Boaz upheld the ruling they had rejected, by performing this demonstrative act*, his Beth Din, too, acknowledged its validity.

To all the people, this confrontation brought joy and gladness, as they expressed their complete forgiveness of the house of Elimelech in terms of the blessing conferred on Ruth that day.*

Like Rachel and Leah!

Boaz, too, performed this great and worthy act, not fearing lest his stock be considered defiled, and rejoiced that day (not like the anonymous kinsman who objected: Lest I mar my inheritance).

Boaz, too, deserved encouragement — blessing and confidence — this day. As if all of those present wanted to share in the mitzvah he had performed, they bestowed their blessing upon him, the blessing of a royal posterity and of the Messiah. For this idea had been preserved in the tribe of Judah from the day that Tamar had sent her father-in-law the seal, the fringes and the staff.*

חותמך — זו מלכות ; (שה״ש ח. ו — ירמיהו כב, כד)

ופתילך — זו סנהדרין ; (שמות לט, לא)

מטך — זה מלך המשיח. (ישעיהו יא, תהלים קי) (בראשית רבה פה:)

Your signet — this signifies royalty. (Cant. 8.6 — Jer. 22.24)

Your fringes — the Sanhedrin. (Exod. 39.31)

Your staff — the king-messiah. (Isa. 11 — Ps. 110)
(Gen. Rabba 85.)

יב. וִיהִי בֵיתְךָ כְּבֵית פֶּרֶץ אֲשֶׁר־יָלְדָה תָמָר לִיהוּדָה
מִן־הַזֶּרַע אֲשֶׁר יִתֵּן יְיָ לְךָ מִן־הַנַּעֲרָה הַזֹּאת׃

4.12 "AND LET YOUR HOUSE BE LIKE THE HOUSE OF PERETZ, WHOM TAMAR BORE UNTO JUDAH,
OF THE SEED WHICH THE LORD SHALL GIVE YOU FROM THIS YOUNG WOMAN."

How lofty was this blessing. It was as if all felt that they had witnessed a great event occurring in Israel that day. Hovering over it were the spirit and holiness of the people joined together.

Like Rachel and Leah both of whom had built the house of Israel.

And similar to Tamar and Ruth both of whom had built the house of Judah.

This was the acclamation of Israelite royalty, the threads of which were spun together from the strands of loving-kindness of the original matriarchs.

Rachel and Leah — they too had purified themselves of the defilements of Aram, and had dedicated themselves to Israel through the power of their prayers and entreaties in their craving to cleave to this people — to be the matriarchs of the tribes of God. "Heavenly struggles have I struggled with my sister."

Like them too, Tamar coming from the Timnah road and Ruth from the field of Moab had given their lives for the sake of the tribe of Judah. They, too, had entered the community of Israel and had set in its crown the precious and durable pearls which they had brought up from the depths of the souls of the nations.

Hence they clung to the eternity of the people of Israel until the end of days.

THE MESSIANIC LIGHT

שמואל בר נחמן פתח:
כי אנכי ידעתי את המחשבות (ירמיהו כט)

שבטים היו עסוקים במכירתו של יוסף.
ויוסף היה עסוק בשקו ובתעניתו.
ראובן היה עסוק בשקו ובתעניתו.
ויעקב היה עסוק בשקו ובתעניתו.
ויהודה היה עסוק ליקח לו אשה.

והקב"ה היה עוסק, בורא אורו של משיח. (ב"ר פה)

Samuel b. Nahman commenced his discourse:
"For I know the thoughts..." (Jer. 29.11).

The tribal ancestors were engaged in selling Joseph.
Joseph was occupied with his sackcloth and ashes.
Reuben was occupied with his sackcloth and ashes.
Jacob was occupied with his sackcloth and ashes.
Judah was occupied in taking a wife.

The Holy One, blessed be He, was engaged in creating the light of the messiah. (Gen. Rabba 85.1).

The Messianic light breaks through and rises in the world unexpectedly.*

"He peers through the lattice." (Song of Songs 2.9)

At that time the attention of the fathers of that people, from whom and on behalf of whom that light had been prepared, was also distracted.
They were all preoccupied. Israel their father was also preoccupied with his mourning for someone still alive, and the Holy Spirit departed from him.

It is only that this light is too great and too wonderful for human conception, since men have not the capacity to absorb it before its appointed time — the end of days.

Jacob desired to reveal the end of days to his children and it was hidden from him. (Pesaḥim 56; Gen. Rabba 96)

The Zohar teaches: R. Judah said:
From the effrontery of one righteous woman many benefits accrued to the world.

Who was she? — Tamar, of whom it is written: She sat at Petach Enayim.*

R. Abba said:
This passage proves that the Torah consists of hidden and revealed (meanings). (Zohar, *Aḥarei,* 71).

All the Biblical narratives of the patriarchs and their descendants appear beautiful even when understood in their plain sense, but it is nevertheless incumbent upon us to realize that there is a deeper hidden meaning. The more we learn, standing far removed in awed contemplation of the holy, the more shall we understand that the Torah bears the imprint of the wisdom of Divine intelligence.

"I said: 'I will get wisdom'; but it was far from me.' " * (Eccl. 7.23)

> "Behold I was brought forth in iniquity,
> And in sin did my mother conceive me,
> Behold You desire truth in the inward parts; Make me, therefore, to know wisdom in my inmost heart."

How remarkable!

Here it is, the light of the Messiah breaking forth and rising aloft in stories completely at variance with the rulings of the Torah, and deviating from its ethic.
This light rises from an obscure cave near Sodom, from Petach Enayim on the way to Timnah, and from the threshing floor of Boaz. And so it continues to radiate, for *Hashem's* sake, towards David and towards Solomon whose name was Yedidiah (beloved of God).
Even the tribes of Israel seem to have been conceived in sin, for Jacob had married two sisters.*

So in the bypaths, where acts of loving-kindness, which to us seem sinful, were performed, did the daughters of foreign nations cross the borders into Israel.
These are the two "good shoots" that were merited to join with the root of Jesse, so as to bring benefit to the world with the light of the end of days.

אור עולם באוצר חיים
אורות מאופל אמר ויהי.

In God's life treasure there is eternal light
He spoke, and from darkness came light.*

THE NAME THE NEIGHBORS GAVE HIM

ד יג. וַיִּקַּח בֹּעַז אֶת־רוּת וַתְּהִי־לוֹ לְאִשָּׁה וַיָּבֹא אֵלֶיהָ
וַיִּתֵּן יְיָ לָהּ הֵרָיוֹן וַתֵּלֶד בֵּן:

4.13 "SO BOAZ TOOK RUTH, AND SHE BECAME HIS WIFE;
AND HE WENT IN UNTO HER,
AND THE LORD GAVE HER CONCEPTION AND SHE BORE A SON."

Of all the Biblical heroines whom God had remembered by giving them sons, not a single one besides Ruth was described in this manner by Scripture.

This is the last verse to mention Ruth. Her task was accomplished. What more by way of happiness, joy, and rest in the home of her wealthy and distinguished husband could we wish for her? She herself, after all, had not even asked for so much. For here was rest and tranquility for her. And she bore a son! — For his sake she had come from the field of Moab to Beth-lehem in Judah.

> "And it shall be, that the firstborn that she bears shall succeed in the name of the brother that is dead, that his name be not blotted out of Israel." (Deut. 25.6)

This wonderful truth is indicated in the commentary of the Rabbis on this verse.

> "And Boaz took Ruth." They said: The very night that he cohabited with her, he died. (Yalkut Shim'oni 608).

And this truth is hidden in the treasure that is life.

יד. וַתֹּאמַרְנָה הַנָּשִׁים אֶל־נָעֳמִי
בָּרוּךְ יְיָ אֲשֶׁר לֹא הִשְׁבִּית לָךְ גֹּאֵל הַיּוֹם
וְיִקָּרֵא שְׁמוֹ בְּיִשְׂרָאֵל:

טו. וְהָיָה לָךְ לְמֵשִׁיב נֶפֶשׁ וּלְכַלְכֵּל אֶת שֵׂיבָתֵךְ
כִּי כַלָּתֵךְ אֲשֶׁר אֲהֵבָתֶךְ יְלָדַתּוּ
אֲשֶׁר־הִיא טוֹבָה לָךְ מִשִּׁבְעָה בָּנִים:

14 "AND THE WOMEN SAID UNTO NAOMI:
'BLESSED BE THE LORD, WHO HAS NOT LEFT YOU THIS DAY WITHOUT A NEAR KINSMAN,
AND HIS NAME SHALL BE CALLED IN ISRAEL.

AND HE SHALL BE UNTO YOU A RESTORER OF LIFE
AND A NOURISHER OF YOUR OLD AGE,
FOR YOUR DAUGHTER-IN-LAW WHO LOVES YOU,
WHO IS BETTER TO YOU THAN SEVEN SONS, HAS BORNE HIM.' "

Here the women were speaking — the very women who had been resentful against Naomi when she had entered Beth-lehem accompanied by Ruth, the Moabitess.

They had ostracized her. They had despised her at the time. Now they comforted and placated her, and bestowed their love, consolation and forgiveness upon her.

Now they all acknowledged and understood that the kindness and love Ruth had accorded to Naomi and the oath she had sworn to her mother-in-law had been responsible for rebuilding Boaz's family and had restored blessing to him.

טז. וַתִּקַּח נָעֳמִי אֶת־הַיֶּלֶד וַתְּשִׁתֵהוּ בְחֵיקָהּ
וַתְּהִי לוֹ לְאֹמֶנֶת׃

16 "AND NAOMI TOOK THE CHILD AND LAID HIM IN HER BOSOM AND BECAME NURSE TO HIM."

Joy in recompense for all her suffering. Was it not she who had accompanied Ruth constantly until now?

יז. וַתִּקְרֶאנָה לוֹ הַשְּׁכֵנוֹת שֵׁם
לֵאמֹר יֻלַּד־בֵּן לְנָעֳמִי
וַתִּקְרֶאנָה שְׁמוֹ עוֹבֵד
הוּא אֲבִי־יִשַׁי אֲבִי דָוִד׃

17 "AND THE WOMEN, HER NEIGHBORS, GAVE HIM A NAME,
SAYING: THERE IS A SON BORN TO NAOMI,
AND THEY CALLED HIS NAME OBED;
HE IS THE FATHER OF JESSE, THE FATHER OF DAVID."

And they called — and they called —

One verse calls another to mind, connecting the end of the book with its beginning.
As if the author wanted to appease Naomi: and to comfort her upon her troubles which she expressed in saying: "Do not *call* me Naomi, *call* me Marah."

"HE IS THE FATHER OF JESSE, THE FATHER OF DAVID."

דרש רבא: מאי דכתיב: פתחת למוסרי. (תהלים קטז)
שתי מוסרות — רות המואביה ונעמה העמונית.
[רש"י: מוסרות הן רצועות שקושרין בהן העול.]

דרש רבא: מאי דכתיב · רבות עשית אתה ה׳ אלוהי נפלאותיך ומחשבותיך אלינו (תהלים מ) ״אלי״ לא נאמר אלא ״אלינו״,
מלמד שהיה רחבעם יושב בחיקו של דוד, אמר לו: עלי ועליך נאמרו שני מקראות הללו.
[רש״י: עלי ועל רחבעם בן בני חשבת לטובה כשהתרת את הנקבות.] (יבמות עז)

Rava gave this exposition:
What is meant by "You have loosened my bonds"? (Ps. 116)
Two bonds — Ruth the Moabitess and Na'amah the Ammonitess.
(Rashi: bonds are the straps with which the yoke is tied.)

Rava gave the following exposition:
What is the meaning of: "Many things you have done, O Lord, my God, Your wondrous works and Your thoughts towards us" (Ps. 40).
Not "towards *me*" but "towards *us*" is written here.
This teaches that Rehoboam sat on David's lap, and he (David) said to him:
These two Scriptural statements refer to me and to you.
Rashi: You thought of my grandson Rehoboam's and my welfare when You declared the (Moabite and Ammonite) females permissible. (Yevamoth 77)

רבי יצחק פתח: (תהלים מ) **אז אמרתי הנה באתי.**
שירה הייתי צריך לומר שבאתי.
ואין אז אלא שירה שנאמר: (שמות טו) אז ישיר משה.
— מכלל ״לא יבוא״ הייתי ובאתי.

במגילת ספר כתוב עלי. (תהלים, שם)
במגילה — אשר צוית לא יבואו בקהל לך. (איכה א)
בספר — לא יבוא עמוני ומואבי. (דברים, תצא)
ולא די שבאתי, אלא במגילה ובספר כתוב עלי.
במגילה (כאן) — **פרץ חצרון רם עמינדב נחשון דוד.**
ובספר (ש״א טז) — **ויאמר ה׳ קום משחהו כי זה הוא.** (רות רבה ח, ג)

Rabbi Isaac opened his exposition with (Ps. 40.8); "Then I said: Lo, I am come."
I ought to have sung a song telling of my coming,
since the word "then" (*az*) refers to a song, as it is said (Exod. 15.1) "Then (*az*) sang Moses."

I was included in the prohibition against (a Moabitess) coming, yet I came.

In the scroll that is prescribed for me." (Ps. *ibid.*)
In the scroll — where You commanded that they should not enter into Your community. (Lam. 1.10)
In the Book — "An Ammonite and a Moabite shall not enter into the community of the Lord." (Deut. 23.4)
And not only did I come, but it is written down in a book and scroll concerning me.
In the scroll — (here in the Book of Ruth) — "Perez, Hezron, Ram, Amminadab, Nachshon, David."
In the Book — "And the Lord said: Arise, anoint him, for this is he." (1 Sam. 16.12) (Ruth Rabba 8.3)

יח. וְאֵלֶּה תּוֹלְדוֹת פָּרֶץ פֶּרֶץ הוֹלִיד אֶת־חֶצְרוֹן:
יט. וְחֶצְרוֹן הוֹלִיד אֶת־רָם וְרָם הוֹלִיד אֶת־עַמִּינָדָב:
כ. וְעַמִּינָדָב הוֹלִיד אֶת־נַחְשׁוֹן
וְנַחְשׁוֹן הוֹלִיד אֶת־שַׂלְמָה:

כא. וְשַׂלְמוֹן הוֹלִיד אֶת־בֹּעַז וּבֹעַז הוֹלִיד אֶת עוֹבֵד:
כב. וְעֹבֵד הוֹלִיד אֶת־יִשָׁי וְיִשַׁי הוֹלִיד אֶת דָּוִד:

4.18 NOW THESE ARE THE GENERATIONS OF PERETZ: PERETZ BEGOT HEZRON;
19 AND HEZRON BEGOT RAM AND RAM BEGOT AMMINADAB;
20 AND AMMINADAB BEGOT NAHSHON, AND NAHSHON BEGOT SALMAH,

21 AND SALMON BEGOT BOAZ, AND BOAZ BEGOT OBED;
22 AND OBED BEGOT JESSE, AND JESSE BEGOT DAVID."

ר׳ ברכיה ור״ס: משל למלך שהיה עובר ממקום למקום ונפלה מרגלית מעל ראשו. עמד המלך וכל פמליא שלו שם. והיו עוברים ושבים אומרים מה טיבו של מלך וכל פמליא שלו כאן? אמרו: ראו, נפלה מרגלית מעל ראשו. מה עשה? צבר את העפר והביא הכברות וכבר את הצבור האחד ולא מצאה. והשני ולא מצאה והשלישי ומצאה, אמרו: מצא המלך את מרגליתו!

כך הקב״ה אמר אל אברהם לך לך. לך הייתי מצפה.
מה צורך היה לי לייחס שם, ארפכשד, שלח, עבר, פלג, נחור, תרח? אלא בשבילך: אברהם הוא אברהם. (דהי״א א, כו)
ומצאת את לבבו נאמן לפניך. (נחמיה ט)

כך אמר הקב״ה לדוד. מה צורך היה לי לייחס פרץ, חצרון, רם, עמינדב, נחשון, שלמון, בועז, עובד, ישי? לא בשבילך?
מצאתי דוד עבדי בשמן קדשי משחתיו! (תהלים פט: רות רבה ח)

R. Berekhia and R. Simon said: This may be illustrated by a story: A king was travelling from one locality to another. A precious pearl fell from his head. The king and his entire retinue stopped. All the passers by asked: "Why are the king and his retinue staying here?" They said: a precious pearl has fallen from his head. What did he do? He gathered all the soil in heaps — and brought sieves. He sifted the first heap, but did not find it; the second, and still did not find it; the third, and found it. They said: "The king has found his pearl."

So the Holy One, blessed be He, said (Gen. 12.1): "Get you out."
It was for you that I was waiting.
What need was there for Me to recount the genealogy of Shem, Arpachshad, Shelah, Eber, Peleg, Nahor and Terah?
It was only for your sake, Abram who is Abraham. (1 Chron. 1.26)
"And you found his heart faithful before You" (Neh. 9)

So the Holy One, blessed be He, said to David:
What need was there for Me to recount the genealogy of Perez, Hezron, Ram, Amminadab, Nahshon, Salmah, Boaz, Obed, Jesse? Was it not for your sake? "I have found My servant David, with My holy oil have I anointed him." (Ps. 89; Ruth Rabba 8)

MOTHER OF ROYALTY

אמר ר׳ זעירא: מגילה זו אין בה לא טומאה ולא טהרה, לא איסור ולא היתר. ולמה נכתבה? ללמדך, כמה שכר טוב לגומלי חסדים. (רות רבה ב, טו)

R. Zeira said: This scroll tells us nothing of ritual purity or defilement, of prohibition or permission. For what purpose was it written? To teach you how great is the reward of those who dispense *ḥesed*. (Ruth Rabba 2.15)

The Book of Ruth is beautiful in its tranquility, even though its events often stir up turbulent and stormy emotions.

Apparently, Ruth herself sheds this grace upon the entire narrative in her kindness and modesty. Here too lay her strength in suppressing all feelings of grief and in impressing the narrative with her sense of gratification.

At the very end of the Book, at the very time when the good tidings that her descendants would ascend the throne was first hinted at, she stood aside and was not mentioned at all. For she had sought no reward for her deed.

And her reward was complete from *Hashem*, the God of Israel. For so Boaz had blessed her in the field:

ישלם ה׳ פעלך, אמר לה: מי שעתיד לשלם שכר לצדיקים הוא יתן שכרך. ותהי משכרתך שלֵמה — שלמה כתיב, רמז לה: שלמה יעמוד ממך. (ילק״ש תרב)

"The Lord recompense your work." — He said to her: He, Who will recompense the righteous in the future, will give your reward. "And be your reward complete" (*shelemah*) — The spelling is *Shelomo* — Solomon. He indicated to her: King Solomon will emerge from you. (Yalkut Shim'oni 602)

And the Rabbis also envisioned her enjoying a good old age and years of life, seeing her grandchildren wearing the royal crown of Israel — the kingdom of peace at the end of days.

וישם כסא לאם המלך ותשב לימינו (מ״א ב. יט)
אמר ר׳ אלעזר: זו רות המואביה, שהיא אמה של מלכות. (בבא בתרא צא:)

"And caused a throne to be set for the king's mother: and she sat on his right hand."

R. Eliezer said: This was Ruth the Moabitess, the queen mother, mother of the royal house of Israel. (Bava Bathra 91b)

THE "SCROLL" OF OBED

ויהי־לי שור וחמור צאן ועבד ושפחה.

ועבד — זה דוד.

ושפחה — זו רות שעתיד דוד לצאת ממנה.

וכתיב עליו : אני עבדך בן־אמתך.

(ב"ר עה; תנחומא, וישלח א)

"And I have ox, ass, sheep, servant and maid."

Servant — refers to David.

Maid — to Ruth from whom David was destined to come forth.

Of him it is written: "I am Your servant, the son of Your handmaid." (Gen Rabba 78.; Tanhuma, *Vayishlaḥ* 1)

Dedicated
to the blessed memory of
my brother

SHMUEL BACHRACH

THE SCROLL OF OBED

Chapter 1

AND THEY CALLED HIS NAME OBED

The "Scroll" of Obed — is named after the son Ruth bore to Naomi, to restore her spirit and to sustain her in her old age. Because nothing was written of him in this Book, except that his name was given him by the women neighbors.

> "AND THE WOMEN HER NEIGHBORS GAVE HIM A NAME,
> SAYING, 'THERE IS A SON BORN TO NAOMI';
> AND THEY CALLED HIS NAME OBED."

It is difficult for us to understand why precisely the women neighbors gave the child his name. Why not Ruth, his own mother, or else Naomi who laid him in her bosom and was a nurse to him?

"Saying" — and this does not at all explain why they called him this particular name — "Obed."

> Cf. "And she called his name Joseph, saying: 'The Lord add (*yosef*) to me another son." (Gen. 30.24)
> "And she named the child Ichabod, saying: 'The glory (*kavod*) is departed from Israel.' " (1 Sam. 4.21)

> "AND THEY CALLED HIS NAME OBED;
> HE IS THE FATHER OF JESSE, THE FATHER OF DAVID."

His entire lineage is in his descendants.
R. Abraham Ibn Ezra has noted the ambiguity of the text:

> The father of David — may possibly refer to Jesse and also to Obed, as in "The God of my father Abraham and the God of my father Isaac."

That is to say that Obed, too, was the father of David.

And his name shall be called in Israel — his name shall be called among the righteous of Israel.

And Boaz begot Obed — because he served (*avad*) the Master of the universe with a perfect heart. (Targum)

The Rabbis too have interpreted Obed as referring to the service of God (*avodath Hashem*), thereby stating the praise of Ruth and Boaz, his progenitors.

על שם אביו שהיה זקן ונשא אשה לשם שמים ונקרא **עובד אלהים.**
ועל שם אמו דכתיב (מלאכי ג, יח) ושבתם וראיתם בין צדיק לרשע בין עובד אלהים לאשר לא עבדו — בין רות לערפה, ערפה היתה לחרפה ורות דבקה ביחוד — לכן נקרא שמו עובד. צדיק נשא צדקת והבן צדיק גמור, שלישי לו בחר הקב"ה דכתיב: (תהלים עח) ויבחר בדוד עבדו. (מדרש לקח טוב)

Named for his father who was a notable and who had married a wife for the sake of Heaven, and was therefore called the servant (*obed*) of God.
Also named for his mother, as it is written (Mal. 3.18): "Then shall you discern between the righteous and the wicked,
Between him that serves God, and him that serves Him not" — between Ruth and Orpah. Orpah disgraced herself, but Ruth clung to the Oneness of God — Hence his name was called Obed. A righteous man married a righteous woman and their son was a completely righteous person. The third generation was chosen by the Holy One, blessed be He, as it is said (Ps. 78.70): "He chose also David His servant." (Midrash Lekaḥ Tov)

This excerpt has been illuminatingly explained by R. Lipowitz, of blessed memory, in his commentary on Ruth.

To understand this Midrash we must quote the Gemara:
Bar He-He said to Hillel: What does this (Mal. 3) mean: "Then shall you discern between the righteous and the wicked, between him that serves God and him that serves Him not"?
Is not the righteous identical with him that serves God, and the wicked with him that does not serve God?

He (Hillel) answered: He that serves God and he that does not serve God both refer to perfectly righteous men — but the one who reviewed his chapter 100 times cannot be compared to one who reviewed 101 times. (Ḥagigah 9b)

It follows, then, that the *oved Elokim,* the one who serves the Lord, has reached the highest level of perfection. A person can be completely righteous, yet if he flagged in his efforts to reach the very highest stage in his Torah learning and good deeds, he has failed to attain the state of *oved Elokim,* the highest goal of man. Hence it is written of the revelation at Sinai (Exod. 3.12): "You shall serve (*ta'avdun*) God upon this mountain."

The Midrash cites the example of Orpah and Ruth. At first, both seemed properly imbued with dedication. Naomi's evaluation: "May God give you" remained directed, in the book, at both of them. But Orpah failed to cope with the very last test, one beyond all reason. Finally the two drifted so far apart that the one became the mother of David and the other of — Goliath. This is a striking example. "Then shall you discern."

The servants of *Hashem!*

Not everyone who wishes to assume this title may do so. Very few Biblical personalities had the merit of being called by that name.

"The first ones in the land" — our forefathers and the other shepherds who strengthened themselves and were victorious and purified their hearts before Him (Mesillath Yesharim — The Path of the Just, Chap. 16 — The Trait of Purity.)

There were some who called themselves "servant" and the Holy One blessed be He called them "servant".

There were some who called themselves "servant" and the Holy One blessed be He did not call them "servant".

There were some who did not call themselves "servant" and the Holy One, blessed be He, called them "servant".

Abraham called himself servant, as it is said (Gen. 18.3): "Pass not away, I pray you, from your servant." The Holy One, blessed be He, called him "servant" (Ibid. 26.4): "For the sake of Abraham, My servant."

> Jacob called himself "servant", as it is said (Ibid. 32.11): "I am not worthy of all the mercies and all the truth, which you have shown to Your servant," and the Holy One, blessed be He, called him "servant", as it is said (Isa. 41.8): But you Israel, My servant, whom I have chosen."
>
> Moses called himself "servant," as it is said (Deut. 3.24): "You have begun to show Your servant Your greatness," and the Holy One, blessed be He, called him servant (Num. 12.7): "My servant Moses is not so."
>
> David called himself servant, as it is said (Ps. 116.16): "I am Your servant the son of Your handmaid," and the Holy One, blessed be He, called him servant at it is said (1 Kings 11.13): "For David, My servant's sake," and (Ezek. 37.25): "And David My servant shall be their prince for ever." (Sifrei, *Vaethḥanan*)

And so David achieved greatness and, attaining that same state as the patriarchs and Moses, was merited to be called "My servant" by the Holy One, blessed be He, tens of times in the Books of the Earlier and Later Prophets and in the Hagiographa. And he lovingly described himself as "Your servant" in his many prayers and supplications.

Certainly many sought after this name, but not many were able to pronounce themselves so. And of these, but few were found worthy to be called so by *Hashem*.

For this service is performed in the heart, and is to stand the test of the purest love.

> "To love the Lord your God, and to serve Him with all your heart and all your soul" (Deut. 11.13).
>
> And just as it is not permissible to offer up upon the earthly altar any but the cleanest flour, sifted through thirteen sieves and therefore entirely free of any impurity, so is it impossible to offer up upon the Heavenly altar so that they will be accepted as representing perfect, choice, Divine service, any but the choicest of actions, entirely free of imperfections.

What I am saying is that perfect Divine service, the type which should be characteristic of all those who love God in truth, is that which is entirely pure, that which is directed to the Blessed One and to nothing else besides. Anything which falls short of this standard, to the extent that it falls short, is lacking in perfection.
As King David, may Peace be upon him, said:
"Who is mine in Heaven and I want none beside You on earth." (Psalms 73:25)
And the Scripture states in the same vein: (*Ibid.* 119:140) "Your word is very pure and Your servant loves it." (Mesillath Yesharim — The Path of the Just — *ibid.*)

*

The elders in the gate of Beth-lehem and all the populace were witnesses to the great act of Boaz, who, serving God with the purest motives, stood the test. Hence the blessing, which derived from the roots of the people and led to the throne of the Messiah, was bestowed on him.

"AND LET YOUR HOUSE BE LIKE THE HOUSE OF PERETZ,
WHOM TAMAR BORE UNTO JUDAH,
OF THE SEED WHICH THE LORD SHALL GIVE YOU OF
THIS WOMAN."

וממנו השתיל שיצא זרע דוד.
שנאמר (תהלים כב, לא) זרע יעבדנו יספר לד' לדור.
הוא שנאמר (שם פט, לז) זרעו לעולם יהיה וכסאו כשמש נגדי.
(זהר חדש רות, פה)

And from there emerged the shoot which was the seed of David, as it is said (Ps. 22.31): "A seed shall serve him; it shall be told to the Lord of the next generation."

This is what Scripture states (Ibid. 89.37): "His seed shall endure forever, and his throne as the sun before Me."

Also the women who came to placate Naomi on the day that Ruth had given birth to her son, blessed God for not having left her without a redeemer.

For they knew how great a share Naomi had played, since it was to her that Ruth had clung in love, and the two together had constructed this Book of *ḥesed*. Hence she too was rebuilt through Ruth.

"FOR YOUR DAUGHTER-IN-LAW WHO LOVES YOU HAS BORNE HIM."

And the women neighbors called her happy for all the service that she had rendered, and they named the baby accordingly, the child which had come as her reward.

"SAYING: 'THERE IS A SON BORN TO NAOMI':
AND THEY CALLED HIS NAME OBED."

(From the Hebrew root "avod" — "to serve".)

Extending loving-kindness and bearing suffering in love — are these not the purest forms of serving God with one's heart?

Chapter 2

KINDNESS

למה קוראים ספר רות בעצרת, בזמן מתן תורה ?

לפי שמגילה זו כולה חסד והתורה כולה חסד

שנאמר (משלי לא, כו) ותורת חסד על לשונה. (מדרש לקח טוב)

Why is the Book of Ruth read on Shavuoth, on the anniversary of the giving of the Torah? —

Because this Book is permeated with *ḥesed,* and the Torah is permeated with *ḥesed,*

As it is said (Prov. 31.26): "The Torah of *ḥesed* is on her tongue." (Midrash Lekaḥ Tov)

This Book is permeated throughout with kindness.
First, the story of Elimelech, the evader, who did not remember to do kindness and, in his sin, went down with his family to the territory of Moab, to the people which had withheld kindness from the children of Israel:

"Because they met you not with bread and water in the way... You shall not seek their peace nor their prosperity all your days for ever." (Deut. 23.4-7)

And there, in that very darkness brought on by sin and the retribution of death and childlessness, the light of kindness radiated upon her, upon Naomi, the remnant, as she arose to return from the field of Moab, and as her two daughters-in-law arose with her to go on the journey back to the land of Judah.

"THE LORD DEAL KINDLY WITH YOU, AS YOU HAVE DEALT WITH THE DEAD AND WITH ME."

Traversing the hidden paths of repentance, which belong to the God of kindness and mercy, the two nations met and merged. It was the young Moabite woman "who returned with Naomi from the field of Moab," who sang her great hymn of lovingkindness:

> "WHITHER YOU GO, I WILL GO; WHERE YOU LODGE, I WILL LODGE;
> YOUR PEOPLE SHALL BE MY PEOPLE, AND YOUR GOD, MY GOD."

And in the fields of Israel in Beth-lehem, in the tribe of Judah, a hymn of *ḥesed* answered her, as she came to glean among the ears after the reapers.

> "Neither shall you gather the gleaning of your harvest, you shall leave them for the poor and for the stranger: I am the Lord your God." (Lev. 23.22)

> The God of the reapers and the God of the gleaners — (Seforno *ibid.*)

> "AND BOAZ ANSWERED AND SAID UNTO HER:
> 'IT HAS FULLY BEEN TOLD UNTO ME ALL THAT YOU HAVE DONE UNTO YOUR MOTHER-IN-LAW...
>
> THE LORD RECOMPENSE YOUR WORK AND BE YOUR REWARD COMPLETE FROM THE LORD THE GOD OF ISRAEL
> UNDER WHOSE WINGS YOU ARE COME TO TAKE REFUGE!' "

> R. Avin said: Great is the power of those who perform acts of *ḥesed* for they shelter neither in the shadow of the wings of the earth nor in the shadow of the wings of the morning... but in the shadow of the Holy One, blessed be He, as it is said: "How precious is Your lovingkindness (*ḥesed*), O God, and the children of man take refuge in Your wings." (Ruth Rabba 5,4)

"AND HE REACHED HER PARCHED CORN, AND SHE ATE AND WAS SATISFIED AND LEFT THEREOF..."

AND SHE SAID: "THE MAN'S NAME WITH WHOM I WROUGHT TODAY IS BOAZ."

The poor does more for the householder, than the householder does for the poor. (Ruth Rabba, *ibid.*)

"AND NAOMI SAID UNTO HER DAUGHTER-IN-LAW: 'BLESSED BE HE OF THE LORD,
WHO HAS NOT LEFT OFF HIS KINDNESS TO THE LIVING AND TO THE DEAD.'"

This too was a song of kindness which Naomi had directed at Boaz:

"THE MAN IS NIGH OF KIN UNTO US, ONE OF OUR NEAR KINSMEN" ("redeemers").

And from here the narrative proceeds to the consummating kindness, the levirate marriage.

"SPREAD THEREFORE YOUR SKIRT OVER YOUR HANDMAID, FOR YOU ARE A NEAR KINSMAN."

AND HE SAID: 'BLESSED BE YOU OF THE LORD, MY DAUGHTER;

YOU HAVE SHOWN MORE KINDNESS AT THE END THAN IN THE BEGINNING.'"

And the Torah too is completely pervaded by *ḥesed.*

At first sight the Torah seems based entirely on strict justice. Commandments, statutes, laws. Meticulous attention is paid to a pennysworth and less. Fines, stripes, exile. Capital punishment executed by the court and by Heaven.
Indeed, there are many negative commandments to prevent man from doing harm by encroaching upon his neighbor's rights. Yet the Torah has not explicitly enjoined the positive commandment to extend kindness. That is because *ḥesed* transcends all the mitzvot and is involved in them.

"You shall diligently keep the commandments of the Lord your God, and His testimonies and His statutes which He has commanded you.
And you shall do that which is right and good in the sight of the Lord; that it may be well with you."... (Deut. 6.17-18)

The plain sense conveys: You shall observe the mitzvoth of *Hashem* and His testimonies and statutes and you shall have in mind that you are performing them to do what is right and good in His eyes alone.

"That it may be well with you" — is a promise. (Scripture) states that by your doing what is good in His eyes, good will accrue to you. For God does good to the good and upright in their hearts.

And our Rabbis offer a beautiful, Midrashic interpretation of this teaching. (Bava Metzia 35a, 108a): That which is right and good refers to compromise — and to acting beyond the requirement of the law. First Scripture requires that you guard the statutes and testimonies which God commanded you — then it states, in reference to that which you have not been commanded: Set your mind to do what is right and good in His eyes, for He loves what is right and good. (Nahmanides)

(Nahmanides regards this commandment as the equivalent of the injunction "You shall be holy" [Lev. 19.1]. Cf. *ibid.*)

R. Moses Haim Luzzatto has given a similar exposition:

> The root of Saintliness is epitomized in the statement of our Sages:
> "Fortunate is the man whose toil is in the Torah and gives pleasure to his Creator."
> The underlying idea is this: It is known which mitzvoth are binding on all Israel and to what extent one is bound by them.
> However, one who truly loves the Creator, may his Name be blessed, will not endeavor and intend to fulfill his obligations by means of the duty which is acknowledged by all Israel in general, but will act very much in the same manner as a son who loves his father, who, even if his father gives only a slight indication of desiring something, undertakes to satisfy this desire as completely as he can. And even though the father may air his desire only once, and even then, incompletely, it is enough for such a son just to understand the inclination of his father's mind to do for him even what has not been expressly requested...
> Such a person may be called "one who gives pleasure to his Creator." So it is, then, that Saintliness entails the comprehensive performance of all the mitzvoth, in all aspects and under all conditions within the realm of the appropriate and possible. (Mesillath Yesharim, The Path of the Just — Chap. 18)

Maimonides has already defined the essential nature of *ḥesed* or kindness:

> כבר בארנו בפרקי אבות, שחסד ענינו הפלגה, באיזה דבר שמפליגים בו, ושמשו בו בהפלגת גמילות הטוב יותר.
> גמילות הטוב כולל שני עניינים.
> האחד מהם, לגמול טוב **למי שאין לו חוק עליך כלל.**
> והשני, להטיב למי שראוי לטובה יותר **ממה שהוא ראוי.** (מו"נ ב, נג)

> In our commentary on the Ethics of the Fathers (5.7) we have explained the expression of *ḥesed* as denoting an excess. It is used especially of extraordinary kindness.
> Loving-kindness is practised in two ways:
> First, we show kindness to those who have no claim whatever upon us;
> Secondly, we are kind to those to whom it is due, in a greater measure than is due to them. (Guide to the Perplexed II, 53)

This virtue, since it goes beyond the requirement of the law, was not confined within the area of a single commandment, but is a requisite in the performance of all mitzvoth. Without its exercise, law itself would not exist, for it is the very foundation of the earth.

> "For I have said: The earth is built on kindness." (Ps. 89.3)

Hence we find the virtue of *ḥesed* pervading all the expressions of the Torah:
In the commandments, in the deeds of the patriarchs, and in God's behavior towards His creatures.

> "The Torah of kindness is upon her tongue." (Prov. 31.26)

And we find all categories of *ḥesed* shedding their light, directly and indirectly, upon the Book of Ruth which is all *ḥesed*.

> "I will sing of the mercies of the Lord for ever.
> To all generations will I make known Your faithfulness with my mouth." (Ps. 89.2)

AS GOD WROTE OF HIMSELF

ואמר רבי חמא בר חנינא: מאי דכתיב אחרי ד׳ אלהיכם תלכו (דברים יג)
— וכי אפשר לו לאדם להלך אחרי שכינה?
והלא כבר נאמר (שם, ד) כי ד׳ אֱלהיך אש אוכלה הוא.
אלא, להלך אחר מידותיו של הקב״ה —
מה הוא מלביש ערומים, דכתיב (בראשית ג, כא) ויעש ד׳ אלהים לאדם ולאשתו
כתנות עור וילבישם, אף אתה הלבש ערומים. (סוטה יד.)

R. Hama b. Hanina said further: What is the meaning of (Deut. 13.): "You shall walk after the Lord, your God"? Is it then possible for a human being to walk after the Shekhinah? Has it not been said: "For the Lord, your God is a consuming fire"?

The meaning is, however, that one should imitate the attributes of God: Just as He clothes the naked, as it is written (Gen. 3.21): "And the Lord God made for Adam and for his wife coats of skin and clothed them," so shall you also clothe the naked. (Sotah 14a)

This happened after Adam and Eve had sinned, and consequently mortality was decreed upon the world. Adam and Eve stood disgraced when their eyes were opened and they realized that they were naked.

And after God had severely reproved them and had notified each of the punishments to be meted out to them forthwith and for all generations to come, and when he was ready to drive them summarily from the Garden of Eden and to install the flaming, turning sword,

At that very time, God Himself came, in all His glory, to comfort them; And He did this after they had sown themselves fig leaves and had made themselves girdles. (Gen. 3.7)

This is the *ḥesed* which God taught us to perform, to do good even in excess, even to the undeserving.

And from here it follows that it is mandatory to become reconciled with the transgressor, once he has suffered his punishment — and his darkness is thereby lightened.

> R. Meir had this notation in his *Ḥumash*: "garments of light" (a play on *or*). (Gen. Rabba 20.29)

*

> The Holy One, blessed be He, buries the dead, as it is said (Deut. 34.6): "And He buried him in the valley." (Sotah, *ibid.*)

> And He buried him in the valley — The Holy One blessed be He, in all His glory. (Sifrei — Rashi)
> He Himself extended *ḥesed* to Moses His servant and buried him with his own hands.
> And had this not been written down, to say so would have been impossible. (Deut. Rabba 1.17)

The Holy One, blessed be He, buries the dead!
He sought to teach us how to bestow true kindness.

> "And deal with me in kindness and truth." (Gen. 47.29)

> The kindness that is extended to the dead is the true *ḥesed* since the benefactor can never expect to be repaid in kind. (Rashi *ibid.*)

We still ask in astonishment: Why did God see fit to do this? Moses our teacher was by no means destitute, without anyone to attend to his burial, to the extent that God had to perform the duty. All of the children of Israel would have been eager to pay this last respect to their teacher. Why, then, did the Holy One, blessed be He, see fit to occupy Himself with this burial, and deprive them of the mitzvah?

Our Rabbis have found that the Holy One, blessed be He, here bestowed kindness upon a person commensurate with his deeds.

> To teach you that man is repaid measure for measure...

Joseph earned the merit of burying his father, since there was no one greater among his brothers than he, as it is said (Gen. 50.7,9): "And Joseph went up to bury his father; and there went up with him... And there went up with him both chariots and horsemen; and it was a very great company."

Who could be greater in our estimation than Joseph? His burial was attended to by none other than Moses. Who was greater than Moses, for only the Holy One, blessed be He, occupied Himself with him? (Mekhilta)

The true kindness which Joseph extended to his father, entailed effort and trouble at first. (See Rashi on the verse [Gen. 50.5]: "My father made me swear ..." — [*ibid.* 6]: "As he made you swear.") And the end was that the funeral was carried out with great honor, with chariots, horsemen and a very large company.

When the kings of Canaan and the princes of Ishmael saw the crown of Joseph hanging on Jacob's coffin, they all stood, hung their crowns on it and surrounded it with crowns like a threshing floor. (Sotah 13a)

Joseph, too, therefore earned an excess of good. For none other than Moses attended to his burial.

ועם יוסף הארון והשכינה והכהנים והלויים וכל ישראל ושבעה ענני כבוד. ולא עוד, אלא שהיה מהלך ארונו של יוסף עד ארון חי העולמים, והיו עוברים ושבים אומרים :מה טיבן של שני ארונות הללו ? והם אומרים להם : זה ארונו של מת וזה ארונו של חי העולמים. ואומרים להם : המונח בארון זה קיים מה שכתוב במונח בארון זה. (מכילתא שם)

With Joseph('s bier) went the ark and the Shekhinah, the priests and Levites and all Israel, and the seven clouds of glory.
And furthermore Joseph's coffin was carried abreast of the ark of the Eternal, and passers-by would ask: What is the nature of these two arks? And they would answer: This is the coffin of a deceased and this is the ark of the Eternal. And they would say: The one in this coffin fulfilled what is written on what reposes in this ark. (Mekhilta ibid.)

Moses, too, had to exert effort at first to extend his *ḥesed* to Joseph. Our Rabbis have elaborated on this in the Midrash:

כאשר הגיעה גאולתן של ישראל, כל ישראל היו עוסקים בכסף וזהב ומשה היה מסבב את העיר שלושה ימים ושלושה לילות למצוא ארונו של יוסף — והיה עיף מן היגיעה — (עד שהעלהו מן התהומות) — — —

לקח אותו (משה) ושם אותו על כתפו והיה סובל אותו. וכל ישראל אחריו. וישראל היו סובלים את הכסף ואת הזהב, שנטלו ממצרים. ומשה סובל ארונו של יוסף.

אמר לו הקב"ה: משה, אתה אומר שדבר קטן עשית, חייך, החסד הזה שעשית גדול הוא ולא השגחת לכסף ולזהב. אף אני אעשה עמך החסד הזה ואתעסק עמך. (דברים רבה יא)

When the time of Israel's redemption drew near, all of Israel were busily occupied with silver and gold. Moses, however, kept going round the city for three days and three nights to find Joseph's coffin. His exertions fatigued him — (finally he raised it from the depths of the Nile) — —

Moses took the coffin, hoisted it on his shoulder and was burdened down by it. All Israel followed him.
They were burdened down by the silver and gold they had taken from Egypt.

Moses was burdened down by Joseph's coffin.

The Holy One, blessed be He, said to him: Moses! You say you did very little. By your life, the kindness you extended is great. You did not pay attention to the silver and gold. I too, will do kindness to you and will attend to your burial Myself. (Deut. Rabba 11.)

From where did our Rabbis deduce that Moses had expended so much effort?

Perhaps from the additional term "with him" which they have already explained to mean (Nazir 45): "With him" — in his domain.
(Note: Joseph only used the word *itkhem,* and we have learned that *immo* denotes a closer relationship than *itto.* [See Malbim, Num. 22.20-21.])

And from where does it follow that Moses himself expended the effort and had to carry Joseph's coffin on his shoulder, while the children of Israel were preoccupied with their own affairs?

The indication is perhaps furnished by the location of the verse which is inserted, in isolation, in the midst of the passage relating the preoccupation of the children of Israel with their journeys.

> "And the children of Israel went up armed out of the land of Egypt.
> And Moses took the bones of Joseph with him;
> For he had straitly sworn the children of Israel..."

And in the Book of Joshua where the mitzvah is credited to them (to the one who completes it — Sota 13b), neither the term *immahem* nor *ittam* (with them) is mentioned.

> "And the bones of Joseph, which the children of Israel brought up out of Egypt, they buried in Shechem..." (Josh. 24.32)

All that remains with us is our astonishment at the starkness of this picture. Moses bore the coffin on his shoulder! Was there no one among all the children of Israel who was willing to assist him in the performance of this mitzvah? It is only that the Sages wished to make us conscious of all the holiness of this mitzvah —
the true loving-kindness!

Whoever has set his heart on himself — his silver and gold — does not deserve to occupy himself with the mitzvah.

Yes! Even when we are performing acts of loving-kindness for the dead, falsehood can creep in.

"And deal kindly and truly with me"
Can there be a false kindness? The common maxim runs:
When your friend's son dies, bear; when your friend dies, cast off. (Gen. Rabba 96.5)
(If the son of your friend dies, then lament for him and shoulder the burden of sorrow and wailing, so as to show your love — perhaps your friend will repay you. But when your friend himself dies, cast off your sorrow since his love is already gone and you can no longer hope for reward and gratification from him. (*Etz Yosef, ad loc.*)

Moses alone was able to perform this mitzvah in all its purity, and *ḥesed* commensurate with his exertion was accounted to him, hence he was called wise of heart.

"And Moses took" — to make known his wisdom and saintliness. All of Israel were occupied with the spoil, and Moses with the mitzvah pertaining to the bones of Joseph. Of him Scripture has declared (Prov. 10.8): "The wise in heart will acquire mitzvoth." (Mekhilta)

Hence he acquired this merit, and when he died the Eternal alone attended to his burial — the Holy One, blessed be He, in all His glory.

R. Simlai expounded: The Torah begins with *ḥesed* and ends with *ḥesed*.

These are the two categories of kindness concerning which the Holy One, blessed be He, wrote of Himself in the Torah: At the beginning — that he clothed the naked; at the end — that he buried the dead. And the two types are hinted at in our Book, in the remarks of Naomi:

"AND NAOMI SAID TO HER DAUGHTER-IN-LAW: BLESSED BE HE TO THE LORD WHO HAS NOT LEFT OFF HIS KINDNESS TO THE LIVING AND THE DEAD."

THE DEEDS OF THE FATHERS

ר׳ סימון בש״ר אליעזר:

מי הוא שעשה חסד עם מי שלא היו צריכין? אברהם עם מלאכי השרת.
כתיב (בראשית יח) והוא עומד עליהם תחת העץ ויאכלו.
וכי אוכלין היו? — אמר ר׳ יודן: — נראים כאוכלים ושותים.
ימה פרע הקב״ה לבניו? המן ירד להן, והבאר עולה להן, והשליו מצוי להם,
וענני כבוד מקיפין אותם, ועמוד הענן נוסע לפניהם.

מי הם שלא עשו חסד עם מי שלא היו צריכין לחסד?
עמוני ומואבי עם ישראל, דכתיב (דברים כג) על אשר לא קדמו אתכם בלחם ובמים.
וכי צריכ־ם היו להם ישראל? והלא כל אותם ארבעים שנה שהיו ישראל במדבר
היה המן יורד להם, והבאר עולה להם, והשליו מצוי להם,
וענני כבוד מקיפים אותם, ועמוד הענן נוסע לפניהם.
אלא דרך ארץ הוא, הבא מן הדרך מקדימים להם במאכל ובמשתה. מה פרע
להן הקב״ה מתוך כך? — לא יבוא עמוני ומואבי בקהל ד׳. (ויק״ר לד, ח)

R. Simon said in the name of R. Eliezer:

Who was it that showed kindness to those not needing it?—Abraham to the angels, as it is said (Gen. 18.8): "And he stood by them under the tree and they ate." Did they really eat? — R. Yudan said: They appeared to be eating and drinking. What reward did the Holy One, blessed be He, give to his children? — The manna fell for them, the well rose up for them, quails were provided for them, clouds of glory encircled them, and the pillar of cloud journeyed before them.

"Who are they that did not show kindness to those who had no need of it? The Ammonites and Moabites to Israel; as it is written (Deut. 23.5): "Because they met you not with bread and with water." Now did Israel need them? Is it not a fact that, during all those forty years that Israel spent in the wilderness, the manna fell for them, the well came up for them, the quails were provided for them, the clouds of glory encircled them and the pillar of cloud journeyed before them?

Nevertheless, courtesy requires that, if people come from a journey, they should be welcomed with food and drink. How did the Holy One, blessed be He, punish them? An Ammonite or a Moabite shall not enter into the assembly of the Lord." (Leviticus Rabbah 34.8)

Abraham's realm was that of *ḥesed.*

"You will show faithfulness to Jacob, kindness (*ḥesed*) to Abraham." (Micah 7.20)

Ḥesed permeates the world because of him. (Gen. Rabba 60.2)

With short but very deep strokes the Torah tells us how Abraham conducted himself with *ḥesed* and helped us discover proper worldly conduct.

Receiving strangers is of greater merit than receiving the presence of the Shechinah. (Shabbat 127a)

And how did he extend goodness beyond what was required?—

He ran towards them, bowed, and invited them, pleading with them to enter:

"... Pass not away, I pray you, from your servant.
Let now a little water be fetched — and I will fetch a morsel of bread —" (Gen. 18.3-5)
It follows from here that the righteous say little and do much. (Bava Metzia 87a)

Whatever he did for them was done with alacrity, and with joy at the performance of a mitzvah.

"And Abraham hastened — And Abraham ran unto the herd —"

And so he also urged on the members of his household:

> "And he said: Make ready quickly three measures of fine flour, knead it and make cakes:
> And he gave it to the lad and he hastened to dress it."

(These remarks are thrown into greater relief as compared with the reception of the guests at Lot's home. There all the sense of urgency is missing. Nor could he involve the members of his household with him, and this was derogatory to him and to them.)

Yet here our Rabbis have made us aware of an especially remarkable episode of *ḥesed.*

> "And he stood by them under the tree and they ate."

Although Abraham sensed that these were not ordinary men but angels who only appeared to be eating, and whatever effort he had expended on their behalf was merely for the benefit of beings who had no need of it, nevertheless he remained standing by them and served them and bestowed his kindness upon them.
And the angels, too, maintained their relationship with him and continued to appear as if they were eating.

> "A person should never act contrary to custom." (Bava Metzia 86a)

If one extends loving-kindness to someone who has no need of the favor, then how much more should he extend *ḥesed* to the one who does need it. And whoever has trained himself to do kindness even to those not needing it will not spend time weighing whether he is or is not obliged in a particular instance. For these calculations can often go awry———

This striking Midrash demonstrates the great *ḥesed* of Abraham our forefather. And by contrast points up the lack of kindness on the part of the children of Moab. It also is intended to afford us an understanding of one of the methods of the Torah in assigning reward and punishment and this extends over nations and generations.

And from the individual, the retribution can overtake an entire nation; and vice versa, from an entire nation it can become concentrated in one individual.

For why had the Torah meted out such severe punishment to the people of Moab that they should not enter the community of *Hashem* forever — and warned us not to seek their peace or their welfare "all your days for ever"? (Deut. 23.4-6)

Similar punishment was not meted out to Egypt "even though they cast your males into the Nile", and not to Edom who threatened "to go out to meet you with the sword." On the contrary, the Torah adopted a conciliatory attitude towards those peoples:

> "You shall not abhor an Edomite for he is your brother.
> You shall not abhor an Egyptian because you were a stranger in his land." (*Ibid.* v. 8)

Is it not that, with every journey of the children of Israel as they went out of Egypt and with all the miracles which God performed on their behalf, he wanted them to catch the echo of the footsteps of the Messiah — in that generation, too, and among all the surrounding nations. Hence, at first, a call to peace was sent out to reinstate the relations of brotherhood which had been torn asunder in earlier generations.*

"And command the people saying:

You are to pass through the border of your brethren the children of Esau that dwell in Seir;

And they will be afraid of you; take good heed unto yourselves therefore;

Contend not with them; for I will not give you of their land, no, not so much as for the sole of the foot to tread on,

Because I have given mount Seir unto Esau for a heritage." (Deut. 2.4-5)

"And the Lord said unto me: 'Be not at enmity with Moab, neither contend with them in battle.

For I will not give you of his land for a possession; because I have given Ar to the children of Lot for a possession." (*Ibid.* v. 9)

"And when you come near over against the children of Ammon, harass them not nor contend with them;

for I will not give you of the land of Ammon for a possession; because I have given it unto the children of Lot for a possession." (*Ibid.* v. 19)

To Sihon, too, Moses sent peace offers. Even though, in reference to Sihon, it was said: "Begin to possess it and contend with him in battle" (*ibid.* vv. 25-27), God told Moses: By your life, you have done right; I agree with what you have done. (Tanhuma end of *Shofetim*)

Even with respect to the seven nations about whom it is said, "Thou shalt leave none alive," the intention was to remove them from idolatry. Even unto them it was commanded to begin with a call to peace.

(See Maimonides, Laws of Idolatry, Chapter 10 Halachah 1; Laws of Kings, Chapter 6, Halakhot 1-5; Yerushalmi Shviith Chapter 6.)

"When you draw near unto a city to fight against it, then proclaim peace unto it." (Deut. 20.10)
This refers to the King Messiah who will begin by offering peace to you — and he will talk peace to all the nations and his dominion will be from sea to sea. (Zechariah 9.10)
"And it will be, if it answer you for peace," — that they restrain themselves, as it is said (Isaiah 2.4): "And they shall beat their swords into ploughshares...." (Tanhuma *ibid.*)

And so too the people of Israel were enjoined when they approached the border of Edom:

"You shall purchase food from them for money; and you shall buy water of them for money that you may drink. For the Lord your God has blessed you in all the work of your hand. He has known your walking through this great wilderness; these forty years the Lord your God has been with you; you have lacked nothing." (Deut. 2:6-7)
Rashi: Show yourselves to be rich.
Seforno: "He has known your walking" — He has provided for you and all that you needed — the expression "knew" (*yada'*) being similar to "And God knew" — "Whom God knew face to face" — (i.e. an expression of affection).
"You have lacked nothing." They should realize that you are not buying for your actual needs, but for their benefit, for goodwill, and so that they should come to you and perceive God's deeds and wonders.

For God wished to arouse among the nations the desire to turn to Israel in repentance, once they had recognized Israel to be the chosen people, to whom God had revealed His *ḥesed* on the way through the desert.

"You in Your *ḥesed* have led the people that You have redeemed." (Exod. 15.13)

וחם השמש ונמס (שמות טז, כא) כיון שהחמה זורחת על המן היה פושר והולך ונחלים היו מושכים ממנו ומוליכים לים הגדול. ובאים אילים וצבאים ויחמורים וכל בהמה ושותים מהם. ואחר כך באים האומות וצדים מהם ואוכלים אותם וטועמים בהם טעם המן שהיה יורד לישראל והיו אומרים: אשרי העם שככה לו. (מכילתא בשלח)

"And the sun was hot and it melted" — (Exod. 16.21) — once the sun shone on the manna it would melt and rivers would flow from it towards the Mediterranean Sea. Harts, gazelles and roebucks and diverse kinds of animals would come and drink of it. Then the nations would come and hunt them, eat of them, and taste the flavor of the manna which had fallen for the children of Israel, and say: "Happy is the people to have it thus." (Mekhilta, *Beshallaḥ*)

"The beasts of the field shall honor Me, the jackals and the ostriches,

Because I give water in the wilderness, and rivers in the desert.
To give drink to My people, My elect;

The people which I have formed for Myself, that they may tell of My praise." (Isa. 43.20-21)

*

But the messianic opportunity was cast away, for that generation was not meritorious, and the nations were undeserving.

'The peoples heard and trembled" — (Exod. 15.14)

Once they heard that the Holy One, blessed be He, had exalted the horn of Israel, they became incensed. (Midrash Hagadol)

"And Edom said unto him: 'You shall not pass through me, lest I come out with the sword against you.'" (Num. 20.18)

I shall come against you with the inheritance bequeathed me by my father: "And you shall live by the sword." (Gen. 27.40 — Rashi)

This is what Scripture avers: (Ps. 120:7): "I am all peace, but when I speak they are for war." (Num. Rabba 19.8)

A more brotherly attitude should have been expected from Moab and Ammon, a renewal, as it were, of the covenant of the patriarchs which had been broken during the course of generations.

> For they are members of your family, and Abraham your forefather loved their father like his own brother, whom one mother had nursed; but they broke the covenant of brotherhood — and so it remains void for ever. (Nahmanides, Deut. 23.7)

> "Because they met you not with bread and water on the way, when you came forth from Egypt."

True, it is by no means easy to supply free bread and water to a people numbering tens of thousands (Cf. Nahmanides, Seforno). Since the Torah required this of them, however, it punished them for not complying, for the Torah knew what to demand of them, and that it was in their power to give at the time — but they did not.

Seforno wanted to reconcile what has been related above with the statement (2.29): "As the sons of Esau and the Moabites did to me." True, the Moabites did supply bread and water, but took money in exchange! The Torah had expected them to go out to meet the children of Israel with bread and water — free. And they marred this unique opportunity to do the kindness they were expected to. (Perhaps that is why the text refers to them as Moabites and not the sons of Moab or the sons of Lot, as they were called in v. 9.)

Bread and water! — Kindness!

(Note — the Torah deliberately specified "bread and water" — and not "food" as in the case of Edom [*ibid.* 2.6,21].)

For in meeting the sons of Abraham, the sons of Lot should have followed the path of *ḥesed,* the path from which they had deviated after the shepherds had quarreled, when the earth could not bear them to dwell together and Lot departed from Abraham's home of kindness and had pitched his tents until Sodom, where the opposite extreme of *ḥesed* prevailed! ("Pride, fullness of bread — but she did not strengthen the hand of the poor" [Ezek. 16.49]). The sons of Abraham, however, expected them now to follow that course which would have been their path of repentance.

As their mode of repentance, the sons of Moab should have practised kindness in the extreme form, as Abraham had taught, to extend it even to those who had no need of it, for the children of Israel did not need their favor.

> "But it is the proper conduct, that one greets wayfarers with food and drink." (*ibid.*)

So the Holy One, blessed be He, required of the children of Lot that they acknowledge the worthiness of the *ḥesed* of Abraham and the reward for his deeds that stood the children of Israel in good stead as they journeyed forth from Egypt.*

> The manna came down for them, the well rose, quails were provided for them, clouds of glory encircled them, and the pillar of cloud journeyed before them (*ibid.*)

Bread and Water!

Members of the same family, the two brothers should have met together in conciliation and affection — but this did not occur.

> R. Johanan said in the name of R. Jose b. Kisma:
> "Great is the power of a mouthful since it alienated two families from Israel, as it is said: 'Because they met you not with bread and water on the way.'" (Sanhedrin 103b).

And since the expected reconciliation did not take place, they drifted even farther apart.

> They broke the covenant of brotherhood, so it remained void for ever (Nahmanides).

If you had a close friend and you expected him to evince some gesture of friendship in the time of your distress, but he remained insensitive to your need, or else he did realize your need but ignored you, that friendship would become transformed into animosity. For the disappointment is as intense as the expectation — and the resulting measure of animosity is as great as the former affection.
And this friend, who would not show you kindness, now continues to sin against you and to move further away from you, for he wishes thereby to rationalize what he first did to you, his improper conduct.

Hence Moab, not satisfied with the first hostile act, went and hired Balaam to curse Israel.

> "AND BECAUSE THEY HIRED BALAAM THE SON OF BEOR FROM PETHOR OF ARAM NEHARAIM,
> TO CURSE YOU,
> NEVERTHELESS, THE LORD YOUR GOD WOULD NOT HEARKEN UNTO BALAAM;
> BUT THE LORD YOUR GOD TURNED THE CURSE INTO A BLESSING UNTO YOU." (Deut. 23.5)

Here it is proper to consider a question that has puzzled us for some time!
What was the nature of the curse which Balak requested Balaam to utter? Do nations who live by the sword conduct themselves in this way?

(We find unacceptable the archaeological explanations, that this was the practice of the times, and that their superstitious belief in witchcraft and curses led the Moabites to act in this manner. For if this were the case, the Torah would not have devoted a single, extra verse to this topic. But, here, a whole section dealing with Moab, Balak and Balaam has been inserted. — It must have some special significance).
And why did precisely Moab choose this procedure? Why not the other peoples? And specifically Moab — the people who had absolutely no reason to fear the children of Israel. As Nahmanides has observed:

> Now Moab knew that the Israelites were not bent on conquering their land, for they too had received the message, as had Sihon, "until I shall cross the Jordan into the land which the Lord our God will give unto us." Or else they must have heard God's injunction: "Do not harass Moab."

If so, why all the confusion and trembling which seized the mighty ones of Moab?

> "And Moab was sore afraid of the people because they were many,
> And Moab was overcome with dread because of the children of Israel.
>
> 'Behold there is a people come out from Egypt; behold they cover the face of the earth,
> And they abide over against me.
>
> Come now, therefore, I pray you and curse for me this people
> Now come curse me them.'" (Numbers Chap. 24)

Is it not, that the Moabites half sensed the greatness of the hour that was approaching them, that was pointing to the latter days, to extract the seeds of the Messiah from them? — — —*
(This is one of the exceptional, few passages of the Torah where the end of days is mentioned! The first was the blessings of Jacob and the last, the reprovings of Moses [Deut. 4.30; 31.29])

Since they were afraid of the Divine good to which they should have dedicated themselves in purity, they sought to exorcise it by witchcraft, through the forces of defilement and curse.

> "Yea he loved cursing, and it came unto him; and he delighted not in blessing,
> and it is far from him." (Ps. 109.17)

And this Balaam of the open eye knew the hidden thoughts of the Most High in regard to the Messiah. Therefore he counselled them through his plotting to constrict the steps of the Messiah.

> "I see him but not now; I behold him but not nigh." (Num. 24.17)
> "I see him but not now"—this refers to David; "I behold him but not nigh"—this is the king-messiah. (Midrash Hagadol; Maimonides, Laws of Kings, 11.1)

> פתח ואמר: (דברים ב, ט) ויאמר ד׳ אלי אל תצר את מואב ואל תתגר בו מלחמה. כל דא אתפקיד למשה, הא לאחרא שרי. ואי תימא ליהושע ולאינון זקנים דהוו דאריכו יומין בתריה שרי, לאו הכי, דכולהו מבי דיניה דמשה הוו ומה דאתסר למשה אתסר להו. ועוד דלא נפקו עדיין אינון מרגלאן טבאן, דהא ביומיהון דשופטים נפקא רות. (זהר, בלק קצ)

> He began by saying (Deut. 2.9): "And the Lord said unto me: 'Be not at enmity with Moab, neither contend with them in battle'"—all this was prohibited to Moses, but permitted to others. But if you would ask: Was this permitted to Joshua and the elders who prolonged their days after him?—It is not so, for they were all of the Beth Din of Moses and whatever was forbidden to Moses was forbidden to them as well. Besides, those two precious stones had not yet emerged, for Ruth only emerged in the days of the Judges. (Zohar, *Balak* 190)

Neverthless the Holy One, blessed be He, dealt generously with Ammon and Moab in that he did not exclude them completely. For He had left a small loophole in the law communicated to Moses, the prohibition "Do not be at enmity with Moab", and in the recesses of the Oral Law: A Moabite male [is prohibited to marry an Israelite] but not a Moabitess; An Ammonite male, but not an Ammonitess.

And after many generations, through that small loophole, Ruth the Moabitess was able to enter and join our people about 300 years after Joshua's conquest of the land.
Along this path of *ḥesed,* all of which is paved with love, faith and attachment to the people which she had not known before, Ruth returned with her mother-in-law from the field of Moab to Beth-lehem in Judah.*

> "But *Hashem* your God turned the curse into a blessing unto you, Because the Lord God loved you." (Deut. 23.6)

*

The blessing of the father of the multitude of nations which had been denied her people since the days of Balak and Balaam now awaited Ruth at the other end of the path of *ḥesed.*
And there glittered forth the crown of peace of future descendants.

> "AND HE SAID: BLESSED BE YOU OF THE LORD MY DAUGHTER
> YOU HAVE SHOWN MORE KINDNESS IN THE END THAN IN THE BEGINNING."

> This is what Scripture has stated (Ps. 119.62): "At midnight I will rise to give thanks unto You, because of Your righteous ordinances." So said David: I must necessarily extend my gratitude to you for what you did to my grandfather and grandmother in the middle of the night. As it is said: "And it happened at midnight that the man was startled and turned himself." Had he hurled a single curse-word at her, from where would I have arisen? He put it in his heart to bless and he blessed her: "Blessed be you of the Lord my daughter." (Yalkut Shim'oni 606)

PUNISHMENT AND REHABILITATION

This Book is completely permeated with *ḥesed* both in respect to its conclusion, and in respect to the people of Beth-lehem. They did so much good, forgave so wholeheartedly and acted so kindly to the remnant of this family who had sinned so grievously against them by begrudging them help.

This kindness, too, is recorded in the Torah:

> If there be a controversy between men and they come unto judgment and the judges judge them,
> by justifying the righteous and condemning the wicked,
>
> Then it shall be, if the wicked man deserves to be beaten,
> That the judge shall cause him to lie down, and to be beaten before him, according to his wickedness by number.
>
> Forty stripes he may give him, he shall not exceed,
> lest, if he should exceed, and beat him above these with many stripes,
> then your brother should be dishonored before your eyes." (Deut. 25.1-3)

This small passage is the only one in the Torah where the main halakhoth pertaining to those liable for stripes are recorded: How to give lashes, with what, and how many.

This is the corporal punishment entrusted to the court to mete out to anyone transgressing a negative commandment of the Torah.

At first sight, this passage is completely dominated by the mood of strict justice — yet it is all *ḥesed.*

Among the reasons for this mitzvah is that Israel are termed sons of the Allpresent, and He, blessed be He, wanted to chastise them for their transgressions, so that they should repent and ultimately merit the world that is completely good. As has been said (Prov. 19.18): "Chasten your son, for there is hope, but set not your heart on his destruction." (Sefer Haḥinuch Mitzvah 553)

In the Gemara, R. Judah cited this verse in support:

"With which I was wounded in the house of friends." (Zech. 13.6; Makkoth 22b)

This too should be marked and noted: the entire intent of the passage is to admonish how *not* to give stripes!

ארבעים יכנו **לא יוסיף**.
וכמה מלקין אותו ? — **ארבעים חסר אחת !**
שנאמר : במספר ארבעים — מניין שהוא סמוך לארבעים.
רש"י : חשבון המשלים סכום ארבעים, שגורם לקרות אחריו ארבעים והיינו שלושים ותשע. (מכות כב :)

"Forty stripes he may give him he shall not exceed."
And how many stripes does he receive? — forty less one!
As it is said: by the number of forty — a number that is near forty.
Rashi: The number that completes the amount of forty, that causes forty to be counted next, i.e. thirty-nine. (Makkoth *ibid.*)

And this is how Maimonides formulates the rule:

שאפילו הבריא ביותר, מכין אותו שלושים ותשע.
שאם יוסיף לו אחת, נמצאת שלא הכהו אלא ארבעים הראויות לו. (הלכות סנהדרין פי"ז, א)

That even the healthiest is only beaten thirty-nine times.
So that if one more stripe were added, the victim would only receive the forty he deserved. (Laws of Sanhedrin 17.1)

The ruling is explained by R. David b. Zimra (Radvaz) to imply:

> According to this approach, if the violator were given forty stripes and died, the executioner would not be liable to exile (as an unwitting murderer), nor did he transgress the prohibition against "adding to the Torah", since the victim had merely received what the Torah had ordained.

According to Maimonides's view, then, the Torah allots all forty, but immediately warns against giving the violator more than thirty-nine.

> פן יוסיף להכותו על אלה מכה רבה ונקלה אחיך לעיניך.
> וטעם ונקלה אחיך, שהוא דבר ידוע וגזירה מהשם להיות ארבעים סובל הסובל כדין שמים ולא בחפץ השופט. (ראב"ע)
>
> Lest if he should exceed, and beat him above these with many stripes, then your brother will be disgraced before your eyes.
> The meaning of "and your brother will be disgraced before your eyes" is that it is the will and desire of *Hashem* that the punished should receive forty stripes according to the law of Heaven but not according to the wishes of the judge. (Ibn Ezra)

> כדי רשעתו במספר — לא יהיה הפקר לשוטרים להכות כמו שחפצים. (העמק דבר)
>
> "According to his wickedness by number" — the judges should not have the license to have him beaten as many times as they deem fit. (*Ha'amek Davar*)

> שהוזהר הדיין מלהכות את החוטא מכות כבדות המחלחלות (הממוטטות) את הגוף. — ואין מלקים שום אדם עד שיאמדו את המכות כפי יכולת הלוקה וגילו ומזגו ובנין גופו. אם יוכל לסבול את עונש המלקות בכללותו — ילקה. ואם לא יוכל לסבול, מלקים אותו כפי מה שיוכל לקבל, לא פחות משלוש מכות. (ספר המצות להרמב"ם מצות לת"ע)
>
> The judge has been admonished against beating the violator hard blows which shatter the body. And no man is given stripes before the number has been adjusted to fit his endurance, his age, tempera-

ment and physical build. If he is able to endure the full measure of corporal punishment — he is beaten accordingly. But if he is unable to bear the stripes, he is given what he can tolerate, although no less than three stripes. (Maimonides, Sefer Hamitzvoth, Negative Commandments 9).

ואם הוסיף רצועה אחת על האומד ומת, הרי החזן (המכה) גולה. ואם לא מת — הרי החזן עבר על לא תעשה, שנאמר לא יוסיף. (רמב"ם הלכות סנהדרין טז, יב)

And if he added one stripe more than the number assessed and the victim died, the sheriff (the executioner) is sentenced to exile; and if the victim did not die, the sheriff has transgressed a negative commandment, since it is said: "He shall not exceed." (Maimonides, Laws of Sanhedrin 16.12)

The prohibition against excessive beating also applies to anyone striking a person without the permission of the court. And this, the commandment (Deut. 25.3) prohibiting the administering of more than the prescribed number of stripes, also implies that no person is to strike another without the permission of the Beth Din. This is deduced by a fortiori reasoning.

"Now when the Torah granted permission to strike this person (the one sentenced to receive stripes), it nevertheless admonished that he was not to be beaten more than for his wickedness. How much more so does this apply to all men. Hence, whoever strikes someone, even where the blow causes less than a *perutah*'s worth of damage, incurs the penalty of stripes." (Rambam *ibid.*)

This, too, is a *mitzvah* rooted in *ḥesed.*

"David exulted in possessing this good trait to the extent that he sought the good even of those who hated him (Ps. 35.13), 'when they were sick, I put on sackcloth; I tortured my soul with fasting'; and (*ibid.* 7.5), 'If I have paid back those who served me ill . . .'

> Included in this category of saintliness is not causing pain to any creature — even animals — and showing mercy and pity towards them. As it is stated (Prov. 12.10): 'The righteous man knows the soul of his beast.' There are those that hold that the Torah itself prohibits the causing of pain to animals, but at any event, it is at least a Rabbinical prohibition." (The Path of the Just, Chap. 19).

Indeed, not for nothing has the Torah placed, immediately following this prohibition, the mitzvah forbidding one to muzzle his ox when it treads out the grain, a mitzvah embodying kindness and compassion.
(From this juxtaposition of the two mitzvoth, many details pertaining to the halachoth governing the administering of stripes are deduced. The Torah must certainly have had this idea in mind.) (See *Sefer Hachinukh,* mitzvah 601)

> R. Chaninah b. Gamliel says: "All day long the Torah refers to him as the wicked, but once he has received his stripes the Torah calls him 'your brother.'" (Sifri *ibid.*)

The Tanna here shows how the Torah is to be read, viz. by paying the closest attention to its choice of language even when a legal case is being described. Every variation, temporary or sustained — is intended to convey meaning.
Twice the text designates the violator as the wicked one; twice it mentions his guilt by declaring him the wicked one and his wickedness as well. — All along he is called wicked by the text.

All this is to justify the penalty he is to suffer, so that we should not fail, out of compassion, to carry out his sentence and give him stripes. This is all before he receives his stripes or while the Beth Din is administering his stripes, for it is a mitzvah to disgrace him. (Sotah 8, Tosafoth s.v. *vehikkahu*)

Yet soon after he receives his stripes, the text refers to him as "your brother."
From now on all has to be forgotten, and the punished, too, must be made to forget, so as to allow him to resume his normal life in society.

ואל ידמה אדם בעל תשובה שהוא מרוחק ממעלת הצדיקים מפני העוונות והחטאות שעשה, אין הדבר כן אלא אהוב ונחמד הוא לפני הבורא כאילו לא חטא מעולם.
התשובה מקרבת את הרחוקים. אמש היה זה שנאוי לפני המקום, משוקץ ומרוחק ותועבה — והיום הוא אהוב ונחמד, קרוב וידיד. (רמב"ם הלכות תשובה פ"ז, ד—ו)

"Let not the penitent suppose that he is kept far away from the degree attained by the righteous, because of the iniquities and sins that he has committed. This is not so. He is beloved by the Creator, desired by Him, as if he had never sinned.
Repentance brings near those who are far away. But yesterday this person was odious before God, abhorred, estranged, an abomination. Today he is beloved, desirable, near, a friend." (Maimonides, Laws of Repentance 7.4-6).

To forget and to restore the self-respect of a person who has been degraded and beaten before your eyes.—
To forgive and to become conciliated with the person who has sinned against you.— We realize how difficult this must be — but it is one of the commandments of *ḥesed.*
And perhaps this will allow us to resolve a puzzling difficulty.
Maimonides enumerates 207 of the 365 negative commandments of the Torah, all of which carry the penalty of stripes. Almost all of these apply to forbidden things. Only a few prohibitions in the area of human relations carry corporal punishment as their penalty; especially in respect to the description used by the Torah to introduce this topic — "If there be a controversy between men" — does this punishment seem inapplicable. For if this involved money matters — restitution could be made,

and there would be no stripes. And if the case be one of torts, the guilty is obliged to make restitution and whoever is required to pay is not liable to the punishment of stripes.

It is only possible in the very rare instance of someone beating another, where the damage inflicted is less than the worth of a *perutah* (Maimonides, Laws of Sanhedrin 15.12), and also in the case of one person cursing another and using the Name of God.

Then why did the Torah see fit to choose this instance in particular when setting down the laws governing punishment by stripes?

Perhaps it is because of what is written at the end of the passage, the requirement to forgive and forget——— for in matters between man and God it is easier for us to forgive, since God Himself forgives. It is much more difficult to forgive someone who quarreled with us, insulted our honor or hurt us physically. Hence the Torah preferred to use this example.*

And so the Torah admonished us: "Lest your brother be dishonored"—once he has been given his stripes, he is your brother!

And perhaps the Torah, by using this term, wished to remind us of an ancient quarrel between brothers, and also to teach us how to act in conformity with the law.

> "If there be a controversy between men"—quarreling never leads to peace. And so Scripture states (Gen. 13.7); "And there was a strife between the herdsmen of Abraham's cattle and between the herdsmen of Lot's cattle."
> What caused Lot to depart from that righteous one?—say: it was quarrelling. (Sifrei)

Here we are to learn how the righteous Abraham conducted himself in respect of his brother who, if offended, would be harder to win back than a fortified city. How did Abraham address Lot so as to avoid a quarrel?

> " 'Let there be no strife, I pray you, between me and you, between my herdsmen and your herdsmen: for we are brethren.' " (Gen. 13.8)

And how Abraham rushed to rescue Lot, even after Lot had departed from him and had pitched his tent as far as Sodom!

> "And when Abraham heard that his brother was taken captive, he led forth his trained men..."

*

And now we return to the Book of Ruth, and realize that in all its essentials it is constructed upon the foundation of *ḥesed.*

> "AND NAOMI SAID TO HER DAUGHTER-IN-LAW:
>
> BLESSED BE HE TO *HASHEM* WHO HAS NOT LEFT OFF HIS KINDNESS TO THE LIVING AND THE DEAD."

Forgiveness was not granted all at once. It was difficult for them to forgive that iniquity, of which Scripture states (Ps. 109.12):

> "Let there be none to extend kindness unto him; neither let there be any to be gracious unto his fatherless children."

And for all this, our ears catch the echo of this willingness to forgive in Ephrath! First, in the field of the reapers in connection with the mitzvah of gleaning, it was given expression by the servant and by Boaz who consoled Ruth and reached her parched corn, which she ate to satiety and left over —— and finally through the performance of the mitzvah of levirate marriage, when Boaz went up to the gate and announced to the elders and all the populace gathered in the gate:

> "THE PARCEL OF LAND WHICH WAS OUR BROTHER ELIMELECH'S."
>
> — Once he has received his punishment he is your brother —
>
> "MOREOVER, RUTH THE MOABITESS, THE WIFE OF MAHLON, HAVE I ACQUIRED TO BE MY WIFE,
> TO RAISE UP THE NAME OF THE DEAD ON HIS INHERITANCE,
> THAT THE NAME OF THE DEAD BE NOT CUT OFF FROM AMONG HIS *BRETHREN*, AND FROM THE GATE OF HIS PLACE,
> YOU ARE MY WITNESSES THIS DAY."
>
> Mahlon — is an expression of forgiveness (*meḥilah*) (Ruth Rabba)

Following Boaz, all the people in the gate and the elders blessed Ruth that she be like Rachel and Leah who built the house of Israel, and that Boaz's house be like that of Peretz whom Tamar had born to Judah.

And last came the women, before whose eyes Naomi had stood at first in her poverty, bitter and unpitied, when God had brought her back empty handed.
Now they all came compassionately to conciliate her.

> "BLESSED BE GOD WHO HAS NOT LEFT YOU THIS DAY WITHOUT A NEAR KINSMAN,
> AND LET HIS NAME BE FAMOUS IN ISRAEL."

And finally, last of all, came the neighbor women.
Perhaps they found it hardest to be forgiving, for they had been the first to come with their alms boxes that morning, knocking at the door of Elimelech, only to find it locked.— —*

So they consummated the process of forgiveness; their merit being their naming the boy that had been born to Naomi.

"AND THEY CALLED HIS NAME OBED."

*

Is it not remarkable! The commandment not to let your brother be dishonored in your presence is inserted, in the Torah, between the commandments pertaining to gleanings on the one hand, and of levirate marriage on the other. — — —

For so the Torah which is permeated throughout with *ḥesed* hints at the Book of Ruth which, too, is all *ḥesed*.

*

And, in its final passages, the Torah also alludes to this future episode when Moses, the servant of God, looked out from the top of the peak in the land of Moab, in accordance with God's command — and died,

"Now Moses went up from the plains of Moab unto Mount Nebo" (Deut. 34.1)
This teaches that God disclosed to him the dynasty of kings that was destined to issue from Ruth the Moabitess, i.e. David and his seed. (Sifrei)

Chapter 3

SUFFERING

למה קורין ספר רות בעצרת, בזמן מתן תורה ?
ללמדך, שלא ניתנה תורה אלא על ידי יסורים ועוני.
וכה"א (תהלים סח) חיתך ישבו בה תכין בטובתך לעני אלהים.
(רות זוטא, ילק"ש תקצ"ו)

Why is the Book of Ruth read on Shavuoth, the anniversary of the giving of the Torah?
To teach you that the Torah is only acquired through suffering and poverty.
And so Scripture asserts (Ps. 68.11): "Your flock settled therein; You prepared in Your goodness for the poor." (Ruth Zuta, Yalkut Shim'oni 596)

Is the Book of Ruth a tale of woe?

We were only conscious of this fact at the beginning of our reading of the Book. The sufferings, however, have been obscured, perhaps, by the mitigating virtue of *ḥesed* that pervades the narrative.
The Rabbis have compared the travail in the Book of Ruth with the woes of Job.
We shall, therefore, repeat the Job's verse spoken by Naomi when she was bereaved and forsaken, exiled, and wandering.

"CALL ME MARAH; FOR THE ALMIGHTY HAS DEALT VERY BITTERLY WITH ME.
I WENT OUT FULL AND GOD HAS BROUGHT ME BACK EMPTY;
WHY CALL ME NAOMI SEEING THAT GOD HAS TESTIFIED AGAINST ME AND THE ALMIGHTY HAS AFFLICTED ME."

And Job said:

> "For the arrows of the Almighty are within me, the poison whereof my spirit drinks up." (Job 6.4)

(We ought to take note that the Divine Name, Sh-d-i, which was used especially in relation to the patriarchs [Cf. "And I appeared to Abraham..." — Exod. 6.3.] appears very infrequently in Scripture, except in the Book of Job where it is repeated thirty-one times.)

The Rabbis discovered similarities and contrasts in the two personalities, teaching us the significance of Scriptural patterns. And we shall accordingly learn how to evaluate these sufferings, their meaning and their recompense.

סידרן של כתובים: רות וספר תהלים, ואיוב, ומשלי, קהלת.
שיר השירים, וקינות (איכה), דניאל, ומגילת אסתר, עזרא ודברי־הימים.
ולמאן דאמר איוב בימי משה היה — ליקדמיה לאיוב ברישא?
— אתחולי בפורענותא לא מתחילין. — רות נמי פורענותא היא?
— פורענות דאית לה אחרית. דאמר רבי יוחנן: למה נקרא שמה רות, שיצא ממנה דוד שריוה להקדוש־ברוך־הוא בשירים ותשבחות. (בבא־בתרא יד:)

The order of the Hagiographa is Ruth, the Book of Psalms, Job, the Proverbs, Ecclesiastes, Song of Songs, Lamentations, Daniel, the Scroll of Esther, Ezra, Chronicles.
As for the view that Job lived at the time of Moses, should not the Book of Job come first?
We do not begin with a record of suffering.
But is not Ruth also a record of suffering?
It is suffering that has a happy ending. For so R. Johanan said: Why was her name called Ruth?
Because David issued from her, who satiated the Holy One, blessed be He, with songs and praises. (Bava Bathra 14b)

The Tosafoth ask:

> [The life of] Job, too, had a happy ending.
> The answer: Ruth's ending had consequences for all Israel.
> Another answer: The Holy One, blessed be He, redoubled Job's reward only to remove him from the world.

Maharsha (elucidating the Tosafoth's answer):

> The happy ending of Job was specious, taking place only in this world.
> Not so the case of Ruth, Its ending was David — a real, complete and enduring ending, since David satiated the Holy One, blessed be He, with songs and praises.

In his commentary on Gemara, Rashi dwelt upon the sufferings themselves:

> Her troubles were ultimately transformed into hope, since David issued from there.

(This agrees with the remark of Eccles. 7.8: "Better is the end of a thing than the beginning thereof.")

And so R. Lipowitz, of blessed memory, explained in his preface to the Book of Ruth:

> Any similarity between Job and Ruth is only superficial. Job's finale was not the direct outcome of the earlier sufferings. The two are separate and distinct. One sees sufferings befalling an individual all of a sudden, and disappearing just as suddenly. Yet one does not find that these sufferings have produced anything of consequence, that would have rendered the endurance worthwhile. This situation might be likened to the horizon. Black, angry clouds cover it. Then, the sky clears and becomes suffused with the radiance of the sun. But the clouds have not brought down any rain to moisten the parched fields.
> The clouds of the Book of Ruth, however, rained down blessing and caused the wondrous plant known as David to sprout forth. This is what is conveyed by R. Johanan's words quoted in the Talmud: Why was her name called Ruth? — because David issued

from her. R. Johanan's contribution to the discussion was to note the inner connection between Ruth and David, David's outpouring of song having its origin in his ancestress Ruth.

The Book of Job has deep meaning; the Rabbis ascribe its authorship to Moses who received the Torah from God himself.

For all his righteousness, Job was weighed and found wanting by the Rabbis. When chastisements came upon him, he began to curse and blaspheme loudly to question the Divine attribute of justice. (Bava Bathra 15a)

They thereby disclosed their intention to compare him with all sufferers and the manner in which the latter accepted the judgment imposed upon them. And all results from the measure of one's faith in, and love of, God.

In one instance Job was placed by our Rabbis on the same level as Abraham: Both Job and Abraham were designated as human beings who feared the Lord. (Sotah 31a)

But here we have to evaluate Job as compared with David, who also endured privation and was subjected to the severest trials, since the Book of Ruth begins and ends with David.

"So God blessed the latter end of Job more than his beginning;
And he had fourteen thousand sheep and six thousand camels,
And a thousand yoke of oxen, and a thousand she asses;
He also had seven (*shiva'na*) sons and three daughters." (42.12-13)

The remarks of the Rabbis seem all too harsh insofar as they regarded Job's rewards as being merely specious.
Yet the evidence is furnished by the detailed enumeration of the sheep and cattle, the exact numbers which are twice as many as he possessed initially.*

So too the *shiv'ana* sons, which number, according to Rashi, signifies twice seven, double the initial number. Similarly the three daughters were doubly as beautiful as the first. — Yet no fame and glory attached to Job on their account.
All the magnificent poetry of Job was rejected in the end. For when Job died the poetry of his life died with him.

"So Job died, being old and full of days." (44.17)

R. Johanan said: When R. Meir finished the Book of Job he used to say: The end of man is to die, and the end of a beast is to be slaughtered, and all are doomed to die. Happy is he who was brought up in the Torah and whose labor was in the Torah and who has given pleasure to his Creator and who grew up with a good name and departed the world with a good name. (Berakhoth 17a)

The end of the Book of Ruth, however, points to new life, for now begins her hymn celebrating her future hope.
In the Talmudic arrangement of the Bible, our Rabbis placed the Book of Psalms immediately after the Book of Ruth.

Ruth — from whom came David, who satiated the Holy One, blessed be He, with songs and praises. (Bava Bathra 17a)

JOYFUL PRAISE

In the following chapters, we shall endeavor to set David's utterances in the Psalms over against the words of Job.

> "O Lord open my lips and my mouth shall declare Your praise" (Ps. 51.17)
> "I have preached righteousness in the great congregation,
> Lo, I did not restrain my lips, O Lord, You know I have not hid Your righteousness within my heart;
> I have declared Your righteousness and Your salvation. (*Ibid.* 10-11)

The Book of Job, on the other hand, states:

> "For all this Job did not sin with his lips." (2.10)
> Said Rava: With his lips he did not sin; but in his heart, he did. (Bava Bathra 16a)
> "After this Job opened his mouth and cursed his day." (Job. 3.1)

Whereas David said:

> "I am dumb; I open not my mouth. Because You have done it." (Ps. 39.10)
> "A Psalm of David, when he was in the wilderness of Judah:
> O God, You are my God, earnestly will I seek You...
> For Your loving-kindness is better than life
> My lips shall praise You.
> So will I bless You as long as I live
> In Your Name will I lift up my hands.
> My soul is satisfied as with marrow and fatness
> And my mouth praises You with joyful lips." (*Ibid.* 63)
> R. Abba began, read the verse and said: "A Psalm of David when he was in the wilderness of Judah..." This comes to show all the world's men the praise of David. Even though he was enduring grave privation and was being hunted down, he endeavored to recite songs and praises to the Holy One, blessed be He. (Zohar Exod. 140)

THE WILL TO LIVE

"Blaspheme God and die," Job's wife said to him. And even though his rejoinder was sharp, in his heart he had already begun singing his dirge.

> "Why died I not from the womb?
> Why did I not perish at birth?" (3.11-12)
> "So that my soul chooses strangling
> And death rather than these my bones." (7.15)

Because Job had become disgusted with his life, he increasingly mocked in his speech those who go down to Sheol, and this became the refrain of all who long for death.

> "There the wicked cease from troubling
> And the weary are at rest." (3.17)
> "Wherefore is light given to the miserable
> And life unto the bitter in soul,
> Who long for death, but it does not come,
> And dig for it more than for hidden treasure?" (*Ibid.* 20-21)

But the song of David in its entirety was directed towards life:

> "I shall not die but I shall live
> And declare the works of the Lord
> The Lord has chastened me more
> But has not given me over unto death." (118.17-18)
> For You have delivered my soul from death
> My eyes from tears...
> I shall walk before the Lord
> In the land of the living." (116.8-9)

For David hated death and feared Sheol, since they could not bring him a single step nearer to eternal life.

"For You will not abandon my soul to the nether world
Neither will You suffer your Godly one to see the pit." (16.10)
"For in death there is no remembrance of You
In the nether world who will give You thanks?" (6.6)
"Shall Your mercy be declared in the grave
Or Your faithfulness in destruction
Shall Your wonders be known in the dark
Your righteousness in the land of forgiveness?" (88.12-13)

Job hoped for the nether world:

"If I look for the nether world as my house;
I have spread my couch in the darkness
If I have said to the pit: You are my father,
To the worm: You are my mother and my sister." (17.13-14)

Job said:

"O that You would hide me in the nether world
That You hide me till Your wrath be passed." (14.13)

In contradistinction David declared:

"For He conceals me in His pavilion in the day of evil,
He hides me in the covert of His tent, He lifts me upon a rock." (27.5)

David prayed for illumination by the light of life, for he knew from where he had come. And he loved life, even as he loved God.

"For with You is the fountain of life
In Your light do we see light." (36.10)
"Even a prayer unto the God of my life." (42.9)

Hence David sought to see in his lifetime the good and the kindness — the graciousness — of *Hashem.* For these combined, for him, with the life of the world to come, and he called them: The land of the living, the courts of God, His house and His temple, live for ever. (133.3)

> "You make me know the path of life
> In Your presence is fulness of joy,
> In Your right hand bliss for evermore." (16.11)

> David said to the Holy One, blessed be He:
> Make known to me which is the open gate leading to the world to come. The Holy One, blessed be He, answered him: If you desire to live in the world to come, you have to suffer, as it is said (Prov. 6.33): "And reproofs of instruction are the way of life." (Lev. Rabba 50.2)

> "That I may walk before God in the light of the living." (56.14)
> King David is alive and present for ever and evermore. (Zohar Gen. 47)

David's life was constantly bound up in God, with his blessing, song and *Hallel* praise.

> "So I will bless You as long as I live" (63.5); "I will sing unto the Lord as long as I live" (104.33); "I will praise the Lord while I live" (146.2); "Let every living soul praise the Lord" 150.6).

> R. Levi in the name of R. Chaninah said:

> Man should praise his creator for every breath he breathes.
> R. Haim b. Abba of Yafo said: The soul within man constantly rises, only to fall back, in its striving to leave the body. How is it kept within the body? The glory of God fills the earth, and when the soul tries to emerge it catches sight of its Creator and drops back.
> Hence every soul, all the time that it rises and falls back, keeps praising God for all the wonders He does to us. (Yalkut Shim'oni 889)

THE FRESHNESS OF YOUTH

> The first topic, to which it is right that you direct your attention, is the origin of a human being and the earliest processes of his development. You will then see that it is the Divine loving-kindness (*ḥesed*) that has brought him into existence out of nought. (Ḥovoth Halevavoth, the Duties of the Heart, *Sha'ar Habeḥinah,* Chap. 5)

As his pains increased in intensity, Job opened his mouth and cursed the day he was born. In so doing, he cursed all the kindness that God had bestowed upon him and with which God had illuminated his early life.

And when he poured out his resentment, he also angrily denounced the compassion of the mother who bore him.

"Because it did not shut the doors of my (mother's) womb,
  nor hid troubles from my eyes.
Why did I not die from the womb?
  Why did I not perish at birth?
Why did the knees receive me?
And wherefore the breasts that I should suck?" (3.10-12)

David, by contrast, fondly recalled his youth, for there at the outset of his life's journey he saw his God, in Whom he could put his trust.

"For You took me out of the womb;
  You were my trust when I was on my mother's breast
Upon You was I cast from birth
  You are my God from my mother's womb." (22.10-11)
"Surely I have stilled and quieted
My soul is like a weaned child with his mother,
My soul is with me like a weaned child." (131.2)

All the wonder of Creation was regarded by Job as an arbitrary act of God. He looked upon himself as some material substance like milk and cheese, made to be swallowed. He was created merely to be crushed back into dust. Hence he quarrelled with his Creator:

"Your hands have framed me and fashioned me
  Together round about; yet You destroy me!
Remember I beseech You, that You have fashioned me as clay
  And will You bring me into dust again?

Have You not poured me out as milk,
  And curdled me as cheese?
You have clothed me with skin and flesh,
  And knit me together with bone and sinews.
You have granted me life and kindness
  And Your providence has preserved my spirit,

Yet You hid these things in Your heart
  I know that this is with You;
If I sin, then You mark me
  And You will not acquit me from my iniquity." (10.8-14)

And David, contemplating the wonder and sublimity of the Creator, bowed in submission to Him, since he was His creature, God's handiwork.

"For there is not a word in my tongue,
  But lo, You O Lord, know it altogether.
You have surrounded me in behind and before,
  And laid Your hand upon me,
Such knowledge is too wonderful for me;
  Too high, I cannot attain unto it.

For You have made my reins;
  You have knit me together in my mother's womb.
I will give thanks to You, for I am fearfully and wonderfully made.
  Wonderful are Your works.
And that my soul knows full well.

My frame was not hidden from You,
When I was made in secret,
  And curiously wrought in the lowest parts of the earth.

Your eyes saw my unformed substance,
  And in Your book they were all written —
Even the days that were fashioned,
  When as yet there were none of them." (Ps. 139)

And Rabbi Abraham Ibn Ezra has testified:

> This Psalm treats the ways of God in the noblest manner. There is no other Psalm comparable to it in all five books. To the extent that man understands the decrees of God and the ways of the soul, he will find deeper meanings in it.

And in concluding his Psalm of praise, David exclaims:

"How weighty also are Your thoughts unto me, O God!
  How great is the sum of them.
If I would count them they are more numerous than the sand;
  When I awake, I am still with You

If You would but slay the wicked, O God —
  Depart from me, therefore, you men of blood.
Who utter Your name with wicked thought
  They take it for falsehood, even Your enemies.

This love must inevitably come to grips with the rebellious, who, like Job, contend:

> "If He slay me, I shall not trust" (the *keri*: "I shall trust in Him") (13)

This, according to the Rabbis, is the only verse Job uttered out of love for God (Sotah 27b), and then only according to the one (*keri*) interpretation and not the other (*kethiv*).

Even in his love for God, Job could not forget to attribute death and evil to Him.* — [The root *ktl* here used to express "kill" always denotes deliberate killing. It should be borne in mind that this appears only rarely in the Bible (see Obadiah, Daniel) and is found in these two verses in Job on the one hand and in the Psalm quoted above (referring to "slaying the wicked").
God, too, is only rarely referred to as Elo-ah (singular) in the Psalms. The form is used, however, with special frequency in the Book of Job, appearing there tens of times.]

David must have felt the urge to demonstrate his superiority to Job in his love for God. Hence he alluded to Job and, as it were, delivered a sharp rejoinder as one distinguishing between friend and foe, between *arekha* (v. 20), your enemies, and *re'ekha* (v. 17) "your friendly thoughts." *

*

David wished to relive the freshness of his youth as he joyfully contemplated God's glorious holiness.

> "Your people offer themselves willingly in the day of Your warfare,
> In adornments of holiness, from the womb of the dawn,
> Yours is the dew of your youth." (110.3)

FRIENDSHIP AND ISOLATION

The most difficult of all privations is loneliness and isolation, the time when all one's friends, acquaintances and relatives abandon him.

Either they are unable to witness his sufferings and are unable to lighten them, or else they themselves are afraid of such sufferings and so attempt to justify his being afflicted.

> "Because of all mine adversaries I am become a reproach;
> Yea unto my neighbors exceedingly, and a dread to my acquaintances,
>
> They that see me without,
> flee from me.
>
> Like the dead, I am forgotten out of mind;
> I am like a useless vessel." (Ps. 31.13)

There were no better friends in the world than Job's (Bava Bathra 16b). When they learned of all the evil that had befallen him, each came from his locality to sympathize with him and to comfort him. Seven days and seven nights they sat by him without uttering a single word, for they saw how great was his anguish.

Yet when they did speak, they soon forgot their words of consolation and began to rebuke him for his sins.

Then Job realized how far removed they were from him, how alien his suffering was to them.

Then it became clear to Job how alone and ashamed he was.

"He has put my brethren far from me,
And my acquaintances are wholly estranged from me.
My kinsfolk have ceased
And my familiar friends have forgotten me.

My breath is abhorred of my wife,
And I am loathesome of the children of my tribe.
Even urchins despise me,
If I arise, they speak against me.
All my intimate friends abhor me;
And they whom I have loved are turned against me." (Job 19.13-19)

"But now they that are younger than me have me in derision...
And now I am become their song,
Yea, I am a byword unto them." (*Ibid.* 30.1,9)

R. Judah said in the name of Rav: David was afflicted with leprosy for six months. The Shekhinah departed from him and the Sanhedrin held aloof from him (Sanhedrin 107a)

David, then, suffered a similar disaster to Job. But his spirit was not broken and he did not become captive to that loneliness and suffering. Instead he strengthened himself through his attachment to God.
Otherwise it is quite incredible how David preserved his equanimity after all he had undergone.

"My friends and my companions stand aloof from my plague;
And my kinsmen stand afar off

For I said: 'Lest they rejoice over me;
When my foot slips, they magnify themselves against me.
For I am ready to halt
And my pain is constantly before me.
Forsake me not, O Lord;
O my God be not far from me.
Make haste to help me, O Lord, my salvation." (Ps. 38)

"I am become a stranger to my brethren
  And an alien unto my mother's children.
They that sit in the gate talk of me;
  And I am the song of the drunkards.

As for me, let my prayer be unto You, O Lord, in an acceptable time,
  O God in the abundance of Your kindness, Answer me with the truth of Your salvation." (69)

"I will say of the Lord, Who is my refuge and my fortress" — Whenever trouble befalls me, I flee to the fortress of the Holy One, blessed be He.* (Yalkut Shim'oni Ps. 882)

David's fortress of refuge was open to everyone, yet closed to Job. For Job looked upon God as his pursuer, hence he appealed to the compassion of his friends, — those whom he had just previously branded as betrayers.

"Have pity upon me, have pity on me, O you my friends
  For the hand of God has touched me.
Why do you persecute me as God,
  Are you not satisfied with my flesh?" (19.21-22)

While David exclaimed:

"Have pity on me God,
  for man would swallow me up. (56.2)
Have pity on me, O God, have pity on me
  For in You has my soul taken refuge." (57.2)

David transcended his loneliness and isolation; even in the valley of deep gloom, his heart teemed with songs of love.

"Yea, though I walk through the valley of deep gloom,
  I shall fear no evil, For You are with me." (23.4)

ACKNOWLEDGING GOD'S JUSTICE

> One is obliged to recite a blessing on evil with full consciousness and willingly, in the same way as one blesses joyfully for the good, for to the servants of God the evil is their joy and good. By accepting in love what God has decreed on him, one serves God through this submission to privation, and this is his joy. (Oraḥ Ḥayim 222.3)

Job was the author of the epitome of faith in God, and the verse has been inserted in our funeral services. But he himself did not maintain his faith from beginning to end.

> "The Lord gave and the Lord took away; Blessed be the Name of the Lord." (1.21)

And even this verse, Job did not utter with perfect heart.

> "For all this Job did not sin with his lips."—
> With his lips he did not, but in his heart he did, sin. (Bava Bathra 16)

As for David, his pain, by contrast, became the source of song:

> "A Psalm of David, when he fled from his son, Absalom." (Ps. 3.1)
> When did David utter this Psalm?—When David went up by the ascent of the Mount of Olives, and wept as he went up. (2 Sam. 16.30)
> If he was weeping, why was he singing; and if singing, why weeping?
> R. Abba bar Kahana said: To whom could he be compared?—To a king who became angry with his son, and the king banished him. He said: I weep for having vexed my father, and I sing, that I have not been sentenced to death but only to banishment.—He began to say (119.52): "I have remembered Your ordinances which are of old, O God, and have become comforted."

David is the one who called chastisements — love!

"Happy is the man whom You chastise, O God, and teach out of Your Torah." (Ps. 94.12)

R. Eliezer b. Jacob said:
One should be grateful to the Holy One, blessed be He, when sufferings befall him. Why? — Because sufferings lead man to the Holy One, blessed be He, as it is said (Prov. 3.12): "For whom God loves, He corrects; even as a father the son in whom he delights," (Tanḥuma, *Tetzeh,* 2)

But Job did not want to admit this fact.

"Whom, though I were righteous, Yet would I not answer;
  I would make supplication to Him that contends with me.
If I had called, and He had answered me;
  Yet would I not believe that He would hearken to my voice —
He that would break me with a tempest,
And multiply my wounds without cause." (9.15-17)

And the love almost became transformed into hate:

"You put my feet also into the stocks
  And look narrowly unto all my paths; (13.27)
As God lives, Who has taken away my right;
  And the Almighty Who has dealt bitterly with me." (27.2)

But what Job asserted in his contention that God regarded him as an enemy, and looked narrowly into all his paths to do evil to him, is utter heresy and blasphemy.
Far be it from the All-merciful Who is full of compassion to hate and despise Job's works and deliberately and wilfully to do him harm for no fault. (Nahmanides)

David, however, said:

"Blessed be God, Who has not turned away my prayer, nor His mercy from me." (66.20)
What are chastenings of love? — All that do not entail the intermission of prayer. (Berakhoth 5a)

> This is the exceedingly desirable trait which the pious of earlier times, the supremely holy, were privileged to attain. As David, may peace be upon him, stated (Ps. 42.2): "As a hart pants for the waterbrooks, so does my soul yearn for You, O God..."
>
> The test of this type of love is in time of adversity and trouble. As our Sages of blessed memory have said (Berakhoth 54a): "And you shall love the Lord, your God, with all your heart and with all your soul" (Deut. 6.5) even if He takes your soul.— "and with all your might" (*meod*) with whatever measure (*middah*) He metes out to you, give thanks (*modeh*) to Him...
>
> If a man will but consider that everything the Holy One, blessed be He, does with Him, both in relation to his body and to his possessions, is for his own good, although he may not be able to perceive or understand its being so, his love will not weaken because of any pressure or pain, but, to the contrary, will grow stronger and steadily increase.
> Those with true understanding, however, do not need even this explanation, for they are entirely unmotivated by self interest, their sole aspiration being to magnify the honor of God and to give Him pleasure.
>
> The more deterrents that cross their path making it necessary for them to give more of themselves to counteract these deterrents, the more will their hearts fortify themselves and rejoice to show the strength of their faith. (*Mesillath Yesharim,* The Path of the Just, Chap. 19, The Divisions of Saintliness)

Placed next to each other, David's and Job's words emphasize each other by their stark contrast.
Job with his accusation, David with his faith.

Job:

> "How many are my iniquities and sins?
> Make me know my transgressions and my sin." (13.23)

David:

> "I acknowledge my sin unto You, and my iniquity have I not hid. I said: 'I will make confession concerning my transgressions unto the Lord', and You, You forgave my sin." (32.5)

Job:

Let Him take his rod away from me
And let not his terror make me afraid; (9.34)

David:

Thy rod and Thy staff,
They comfort me. (23.4)

*

Job:

"If I had called and He had answered me;
  Yet would I not believe that He would hearken unto my voice". (9.16)

David:

"I love that the Lord should hear
  My voice and my supplications.
Because He has inclined His ear unto me
  Therefore I will call on Him all my days." (116.1,2)

*

Job:

"Behold I go forward, but He is not there;
  And backward but I cannot perceive Him;
On the left hand, when He acts, but I cannot behold Him,
  He turns Himself to the right hand, but I cannot see Him." (23.8-9)

David:

"But lo, O Lord, You know it altogether.
  You have surrounded me in behind and before,
Whither shall I go from Your spirit?
  Or whither shall I flee from Your presence?
Even there Your hand would lead me
  And Your right hand hold me." (139.4-10)

*

Job:

"I would order my cause before Him
And fill my mouth with arguments." (23.4)

David:

"My mouth shall be filled with Your praise,
And with Your glory all the day." (71.8)

HOPE

"For him that will be chosen (*keri* — that is joined) for all life, there is hope." (Eccl. 9.4)

The *kethiv* is *will be chosen* — for as long as man is still alive there is hope. (Yerushalmi Berakhoth 9.1)

And this is supported by the verse (Deut. 30.19): "And you shall choose life." (Torah Temimah)

Life breeds hope — as long as man is attached to life by his free-will, his choice and his faith.
And to the extent he hopes, so will God continue to grant His kindness to him from that source.

"For with You is the fountain of life." (Ps. 36)

יי העלית מן שאול נפשי חייתני מירדי בור. (תהלים ל, ד)
השקיעה בשאול, אף־על־פי שהיא עמוקה, מכל מקום יסוד החיים עדיין לא ניטל בה מהאוצר הנפשי החיותי.
המשאל בעצמו, אעפ״י שחסרים לו כל תקיפיו של מלוי המשאל, אעפ״י שהוא מצב אומלל ונורא מאד, כולו אומר בהלות, פחדים, עצבונות ומכאובי נשמה, בכל זאת זיק של חיים יש כאן.
אבל הירידה להבור זוהי כבר שיקוע של נטילת יסוד החיים, אטימת הצינור של השאיפה של הרצון הפנימי, של השאיפה לחיות ולמלאות תפקידי חיים ומציאות, כשדה בור, אשר אין בה אפילו הכנה להוראה של זריעה, המביאה לידי צמיחה.
וחסד עליון חודר הוא למעמקים, להחיות גם את הנשקעים במעמק שכחת החיים, והאורה החיונית האלהית ביסודה. חייתני מירדי בור.
(״עולת ראיה״ להרב קוק זצ״ל)

*

> "O Lord, You have brought up my soul from the nether world (*sheol*).
> Thou didst keep me alive, that I
> should not go down to the pit." (Ps. 30.4)

> Deep as the sinking into *sheol* may be, nevertheless the essence of life has not yet been withdrawn from the store of the living soul.

> Even though desire itself lacks every capacity for fulfillment— and grievous and awful as the circumstances may be, all bespeaking confusion, terror, nerve wracking and agony of the soul— nevertheless a spark of life is still present.

> But the descent into the pit involves the removal of the essence of Life, the stopping up of the channels of striving, of inner will—the striving to live and to fulfill the functions of life and existence. It is like a field lying waste, which has not even been prepared for the planting which will later lead to growth——

> And the Supreme loving-kindness penetrates into the depths, to revive even those sunk in the deep of oblivion to life; and the Divine, life-giving light is its basis. "You kept me alive that I did not go down to the pit." (R. Abraham Kook, *Olath Reiyah*)

Job had eliminated every element of *ḥesed* from his Book, and so erased all hope as well. Hence he cast all prayer, and supplication aside from his heart.

> "To a man whose way is hid,
> And whom God has hedged in (3.23)
>
> My days are swifter than a weaver's shuttle
> And are spent without hope." (7.6)

He even blamed God for having destroyed his hope:

> "My hope He plucked up like a tree" (19.10).
> "So You destroy the hope of man" (14.19).

The companions labored in vain to infuse a breath of hope into Job, each in accordance with his own powers of persuasion. Eliphaz, Bildad, Zophar:

> "And you shall know that your tent is in peace,
> And shall visit your habitation and shall miss nothing . . ." (5.24)
>
> "And though your beginning was small,
> Your end should greatly increase." (8.7)
>
> "And life shall be clearer than noonday
> Though there be darkness, it shall be as the morning,"
> "And you shall be secure because there is hope
> You shall look about you and take your rest in safety." (11.17-18)

For Job had lost all faith in his own powers, for to hope one must have a strong will and a believing heart.

> "What is my strength that I should wait? And what is my end, that I should be patient?" (6.11)

*

David, on the other hand, exclaimed:

> "I wait for the Lord, my soul waits,
> And in his word do I hope." (130.5)
>
> "But as for me, I will hope continually
> And will praise You yet more and more." (71.19)

For David relied in all his prayers on God's sure kindnesses which were revealed to him every day. Through them he became elevated. He became the prototype of all who hope.

> "For You are the God of my salvation
> For You do I wait all the day." (25.5)

למנצח מזמור לדוד: קוה קויתי ד׳ ויט אלי וישמע שועתי
ויעלני מבור שאון מטיט היון ויקם על סלע רגלי כונן אשרי:
ויתן בפי שיר חדש תהלה לאלהינו יראו רבים וייראו ויבטחו בד׳. (מ)

זהו שאמר הכתוב: (ישעיהו כה, ט) ואמר ביום ההוא הנה אלהינו זה קוינו לו ויושיענו.

אם אין ביד ישראל אלא הקיווי, כדאי הם לגאולה, בשכר הקיווי. דכתיב (איכה ג, כה)) **טוב ד׳ לקוויו לנפש תדרשנו.**

ואומר (זכריה ט) **שובו לבצרון אסירי התקוה.**
ואומר: חזקו ויאמץ לבבכם כל המיחלים לד׳ (תהלים לא, כה) — **אם עושים** כן הרי אתם נושעים, שנאמר (ישעיה מט, כג) אשר לא יבושו קווי.

וכתיב (שם מ, לא) **וקוי ד׳ יחליפו כח.**

וכתיב (תהלים לז, ט) **וקוי ד׳ המה ירשו ארץ.**

לכן נאמר קוה קויתי ד׳ ויט אלי וישמע שועתי — **דוד שקיווה לי, עניתיו.**

ויעלני מבור שאון מטיט היון — וכי לבור ירד דוד או לטיט?

אלא אמר דוד: כבר הייתי בדרך שהולכת לגיהינום הנקרא בור שאון וטיט היון. **והתפללתי וקוויתי שכר תפילתי ומצאתי, ולא הניחני הקב״ה לטבע בתוכו,** דכתיב (טז, י׳) כי לא תעזוב נפשי לשאול לא תתן חסידך לראות שחת. ולא דיי שלא הנחני לירד לבור, **אלא שהודיעני באיזה דרך אלך, דכתיב** (שם י״א) הודיעני אורח חיים שובע שמחות את פניך וכו׳ וכל כך למה? **בשביל** תקוותי שקיויתי, **ולא רצה לא עולות ולא שלמים ולא זבחים אלא** לקיווי.

אמרו לו: מנין אנו יודעים שעשה עמך כך? אמר להם: **מן השירה שאני אומר אתם יודעים,** שנאמר: ויתן בפי שיר חדש תהלה לאלהינו. (שו״ט תהלים מ)

"For the leader. A Psalm of David: I hope patiently for the Lord.
And He inclined unto me, and heard my cry.
He brought me up also out of the tumultuous pit, out of the miry clay, and He set my feet upon a rock, He established my goings.
And He put a new song in my mouth, even praise unto our God;
Many shall see, and fear and shall trust in the Lord." (40.1-4)

This is what Scripture states (Isa. 25.9): "And it shall be said in that day:
'Lo, this is our God, For Whom we waited that He might save us.'"

If Israel does no more than hope, that alone renders them worthy of redemption, as it is written (Lam. 3.25): "The Lord is good unto them that hope for Him, to the soul that seeks Him."

And Scripture states further (Zech. 9.12): "Return to the stronghold you prisoners of hope."

And it states further: "Be strong and let your heart take courage, all you that wait for the Lord" (Ps. 31.25) — If you do, you will indeed be saved,
as it says: "For they shall not be ashamed that wait for Me," (Isa. 49.23) and it is written (Ibid 40.31): "But those that hope in the Lord, shall renew their strength."
And it is written (Ps. 37.9): "But those that hope in the Lord, they shall inherit the land."

Therefore it is stated: "I hope patiently for the Lord and He inclined unto me, and heard my cry." — Since David hoped in Me, I answered him.

"And He brought me up from the tumultuous pit from the miry clay" — did then David descend into a pit or into clay?

David, however, said: "I was already on the way leading to Gehenna that is called tumultuous pit and miry clay. And I prayed, and hoped that my prayer would be answered, and it was. The Holy One, blessed be He, did not allow me to sink in the pit, as it is written (Ps. 16.10): "For You will not abandon my soul to the nether world, You will not suffer Your holy one to see the pit." Nor was it sufficient that You did not leave me to see the pit, but You also showed me the path that I should tread, as it is said (16.11): "You make me to know the path of life; in Your presence is fulness of joy..." And why was I thus rewarded? Because of my waiting in hope. God required neither burnt offerings, nor peace offerings, nor sacrifices, but only that I should hope.

They said to David: How do we know that God did this to you? He said to them: You know this from the song I sing, as it is said (Ps. 40.4): "And He has put a new song in my mouth, a praise unto our God." (Midrash Shoḥer Tov, Ps. 40)

David made hope the main theme of his love-song.

"Hope in the Lord, be strong and let your heart take courage;
Yea, hope in the Lord." (27.14)

Hoping, generally, is not an end in itself. One hopes to attain his desire. The end of hoping is that one should not have to hope. — Hoping for God, however, is an end in itself, the end being that one should have his heart take courage and hope once more.
On this is it said: "Hope, take courage and hope in God." (Malbim)

*

Why are you cast down, O my soul? And why do you moan within me? Hope in God.
For I shall yet praise Him, the salvation of my countenance, and my God. (42.12; 43.5)

For You are my hope O Lord God, my trust from my youth. (71.5)

EPILOGUE

There is hope of another type — a great hope relating to the world of the spirit. The pangs of suffering David first endured acted as the immediate stimulus rousing his poetic spirit. But once his spirit had liberated itself from his own private suffering, it elevated itself and expressed itself in a song of its own, exulting in the joy of the totality of existence. It went forth to share in that exultation which has been prepared for the creation as a whole — the hope, the expectation of the ultimate, perfect bliss.

> "If I had not believed to look upon the goodness of the Lord in the land of the living,
> Hope for the Lord; be strong and let your heart take courage and hope for the Lord." (Psalms 27)

> Trusting in the total, Divine salvation which God will grant His world, and which alone makes all of life palatable!
> Nor is this joy by any means impaired by the individual's uncertainty of his own personal fate in relation to that great bliss. He is filled with satisfaction, knowing that the good is sure to come, that the world is gradually being perfected so as to attain that bliss, that the existence of the world is justified in the eyes of its Creator.
> "If I had not believed to look upon the goodness of the Lord in the land of the living" — — The word *lule* (if not) is marked with dots. David said to the Holy One, blessed be He: I certainly rely on You, that You will give good reward to the righteous in the future, but I do not know whether I will have any share of it with them, since my sin might cause me to forfeit it. (Berakhot 4a)
> Nevertheless his rejoicing was genuine, his delight stemming from his aspiration for the spiritual, and this always involves the ability to grasp the existence of the totality. (*Olath Reiyah*)

Job failed to attain this goal.
His companions, too, who spoke to him at such length did not hold out this hope to him. For he had imprisoned himself in his own suffering, and so remained confined, without being able to transcend it. Hence, his end, like his beginning, involved him alone. And such an ending is specious.

Job and his book stand alone and isolated among the other books of the Bible. Without any tie with the history contained in them, the history of a people and of nations.

David, however, succeeded.
For him, the suffering of the individual became the key for him to feel the poetic spirit of all mankind and to sing the song of all its generations. He became the sweet singer of Israel.

> "O Israel, hope in the Lord from this time forth and for ever." (Ps. 131.3)

And David was found worthy to receive an everlasting covenant of royalty.

> "And I will make an everlasting covenant with you, even the sure mercies of David.
> Behold I have given him for a witness to the peoples, a prince and a commander to the peoples.
> Because you will call a nation that you do not know, and a nation that did not know you shall run unto you;
> Because of the Lord your God, and for the Holy One, of Israel, for He had glorified you." (Isa. 55.3-5)
>
> Whoever desires to repent, should take David as his example, as it is written (*ibid.*): "Behold I have given him for a witness to the peoples." (Midrash Shoḥer Tov, Ps. 9)

*

The sufferings recounted in the Book of Ruth have a happy ending, one that involved all of Israel. For these trials led to the emergence of David who sated the Holy One, blessed be He, with songs and praises.
This, too, Boaz prophesied to Ruth, on the very first day that she came to glean in the field of the reapers.

"AND BOAZ SAID UNTO HER AT MEALTIME: COME HITHER AND EAT OF THE BREAD, AND DIP THY MORSEL IN THE VINEGAR." (2.14)

ר׳ יוחנן אומר: מדבר בדוד
גשי הלום — הקרבי למלכות!
ואין הלום אלא מלכות הה״ד (ש״ב ז) כי הביאותני עד הלם.

ואכלת מן הלחם — זו לחמה של מלכות,
וטבלת פתך בחומץ — **אלו היסורים.** (רות רבה ה, ו)

R. Yochanan said: It refers to David.
"Come hither" means approach the royal state,
since "hither" (*halom*) refers to royalty, as it is said (2 Sam. 7.18): "That You have brought me hither (*halom*)."

"And eat of the bread" — refers to the bread of royalty.
"And dip your morsel in vinegar" — to suffering. (Ruth Rabba 5.6)

*

Chapter 4

NAOMI'S RECOMPENSE

"And these are the generations of Perez." (4.18)

Since David was traced back to Ruth, by name, he was again traced back to Judah. (Rashi)

Ruth attained the privilege of having the entire book named after her, since she was the heroine in respect of her *ḥesed,* and the mother of the Israelite monarchy. But Naomi was the heroine in respect of her suffering and of her hope.
Hence the last scene in the book was left over for her — for her alone. Light radiates upon her. A light of comfort, restoring her soul.

"AND NAOMI TOOK THE CHILD AND LAID HIM IN HER BOSOM,
AND BECAME NURSE UNTO HIM."

So she sat embracing life. — — —

"Return O my soul to your rest;
For the Lord has dealt bountifully with you.
For You have delivered my soul from death, My eyes from tears,
And my feet from stumbling.
I shall walk before the Lord
In the land of the living." (Ps. 116.7-9)

*

This was Naomi's recompense of her suffering, her loneliness and her bereavement.

> And all the city was astir concerning them, and the women said: "Is this Naomi?"
> Bar Kappara said: This may be illustrated by the analogy of an inferior ox which the owner had put up for sale in the market place. He said: The animal is well-trained for ploughing and drives a straight furrow.
> The people asked: Then why does it have weals on its back?
> So, too, said Naomi: Why call me Naomi (pleasant). Seeing that the Lord has testified against me by afflicting me? (Ruth Rabba 3.7)

For Naomi displayed heroism in her suffering. She was a saintly woman. Hence God had preserved her alive to bear the yoke of trial.

> "The Lord tries the righteous" (Ps. 11.5) —
>
> R. Elazar said:
> [This may be compared] to a farmer who owned two cows, one strong, one weak. On which did he fasten the yoke? Was it not on the strong? (Gen. Rabba 55.1)

This analogy is one of those used in connection with the Binding of Isaac. The first two, choosing the potter and the flax dealer * as subjects, apply well to Abraham and perhaps to Job as well. The third fits the case of Naomi in our narrative.

The owner must place the yoke on some animal to plough his field. And God needed to leave Naomi to be His witness, to justify His judgments to the people from whom Elimelech had fled.

And she, too, had to lead back Ruth with her so as to bring forth the seed for the Royal House of David.

*

Naomi performed an act of heroism when she arose with her two daughters-in-law to return to the land of Judah, to Beth-lehem. She knew, after all, that humiliation, poverty and loneliness were in store for her. She also performed an act of heroism when she struggled with her own thoughts, doubting and hesitating whether to take them with her or to send them back. And she finally decided to send them back.
Even her standing in the city square of Beth-lehem was a noble act. For there she spoke and answered. And in explicit and dramatic language she exposed the wounds of her heart, as if confessing:

> "I WENT OUT FULL AND THE LORD HAS BROUGHT ME BACK HOME EMPTY."

She did not thrust her bitterness upon others. Even though she told the neighbors to call her Marah, her words, artfully arranged, have a sweetness about them.

Even the harsh sentence which we compared to Job's utterings is altogether different from his. For Job, as it were, turned back the arrows in anger: "For the arrows of the Almighty are within me, the poison whereof my soul drinks up." (6.4)
Naomi, however, as it were, made her peace with, and accepted, her lot: "The Lord has testified against me and the Almighty has afflicted me" (1.21).

Even her terse and incisive argument that there was no hope for her was expressed in terms of "there would be".
Not in respair, but anxiety: "If I should say: there would be hope for me" (1.12).

And she was brave, too, in her silence, while she remained in her own city, Beth-lehem, isolated from her acquaintances, closed up in her house, not venturing out.

These were the pangs of poverty and isolation both of which afflicted her.

> Nothing in the world is more difficult to endure than poverty. It is the most severe of all anguish. (Exod. Rabba 31.11)
>
> "The poor is hated even of his own neighbor, but the rich has many friends." (Prov. 14.20)

In the past, she had possessed many friends; the daughters of Beth-lehem used to adorn themselves with her ornaments — now they had all abandoned her.
Yet she remained silent. She did not open her mouth to revile them. She, as it were, forgave them, for she had taken upon herself the measure of repentance to balance her sin, and so to atone for herself and her family.

The Rabbis have accordingly said of her:

> "Why was the adversity of the earlier righteous persons recounted? To inform the later generations, that even though the former were poor they trusted in their Creator. Hence they attained the life of this world and the life of the world to come. (Ruth Zuta 2,3)

*

For Naomi demonstrated her courage in her hope.
Inspired by that hope, she had arisen with her daughters-in-law to return to the land of Judah. — And precisely to Beth-lehem, her home city, and to her family.
At first, she herself did not know what hope there was for an old mother who had become bereft of all in a foreign land. Hence her inner struggle, concerning the advisability of taking them with her, was bitter and hard. Yet the spark of hope was rekindled in her — the hope of that "spiritual totality" which beckoned her to return to her land and birthplace and to her people, and to the loving-kindness of *Hashem* Whose mercies do not fail.

For the Lord had remembered His people in giving them bread.
And this also rekindled her hopes for her family. Perhaps she could redeem the dead who still lived in her memory from excision, and perpetuate them and their names on earth.

Her hopes were still dim and vague. For the Torah law of levirate marriage only devolved on one who was alive when his brother died. The ancient Sages of Israel, however, "knowing how important was this matter instituted the observance of this mitzvah even by other relatives." (Nahmanides, Gen. 38.1)

Could she, Naomi, expect that one of the relatives would perform this great act of compassion? They had withdrawn themselves from her, because of the sin committed against them by her and her household. Would they, then, undertake to rebuild her family? Furthermore, this daughter-in-law of hers was regarded as a gentile by them; was she not a daughter of Moab — — — ?

How far hope extends is attested to by the trustworthy King Solomon himself, in the Book of Proverbs.
[Rashi (Hullin 57a): He is trustworthy in this matter, and he stated this when divinely inspired.]

לֵךְ אל נמלה עצל ראה דרכיה וחכם (משלי ו, ו)

מה ראה שלמה ללמד לעצל מן הנמלה ?
רבנן אמרין : הנמלה הזו, שלשה בתים יש לה, ואינה כונסת בעליון מפני הדלף ולא בתחתון מפני הטינא (טיט שמרקיב את התבואה) אלא באמצע. והיא הולכת ומכנסת בקיץ כל מה שמוצאה ; חיטים ושעורים ועדשים. ואמר ר' תנחומא : ואינה חיה אלא ששה חדשים. וכל מאכלה אינה אלא חטה ומחצה. ולמה כונסת כל אלו ? שאומרת שמא יגזור הקדוש ברוך־הוא עלי חיים, ויהא לי מהיכן לאכול. (דב"ר ה, ב ; ילק"ש תתקלח)

"Go to the ant, you sluggard, consider her ways and be wise." (Prov. 6.6)

What led Solomon to derive a lesson for the sluggard from the ant? The Rabbis say: The ant has a three storeyed home. It does not store its food in the top story because of the dripping from the roof and not in the bottom floor because of the wet soil (the moisture making the grain rot), but in the middle.

It also goes about all summer, gathering whatever it can find: wheat, barley and lentils.

And R. Tanhuma said: It only lives for six months. Why? Because a creature that has neither sinews or bones lives only six months. And it only consumes a grain and a half of wheat. So why does it gather all this? It says: Perhaps God will ordain longer life for me, and I shall have what to eat. (Deut. Rabba 5.2; Yalkut Shim'oni 938)

Naomi's hope derived from the saints of earlier times; her inner strength was quite adequate.
The less her hopes could be sustained by logical and practical considerations, the more she devoted herself to prayer and drew her support from the source of life.

"The cords of death compassed me,
  and the straits of the nether world got hold upon me;
I found trouble and sorrow.
But I called upon the Name of the Lord;
  'I beseech You, O Lord, deliver my soul."
I was brought low and He saved me. — —" (Ps. 116.3,4,6)

*

Who knows whether Ruth herself was not attracted at first by this hidden spark of hope? Perhaps she clung to Naomi all the more in the hidden recesses of her soul, when Naomi revealed herself to be on the brink of despair, there, on the way —

Certainly Ruth was not consciously aware of this when she took her oath: "If aught but death part you and me." She did not know that she had by this means joined with Naomi to engender hope for life.

> "AND SHE LEFT OFF SPEAKING TO HER" — "SO THE TWO OF THEM WENT."

Together they walked in silence, in compassion and common suffering.
Till they came to Beth-lehem.

*

The acceptance, in love, of suffering is also one of the signs of hope.
Hence Naomi remained alone, in the midst of her people. She was silent, and did not open her mouth to revile her relatives. She forgave them, one and all. Perhaps, with the wish that they forgive her too.
She stayed and waited.

Hence Naomi was not put to shame when Ruth entered and stretched out the parched corn which she had left over from her meal. On the contrary, she awakened to joy, because in this morsel she saw the second spark of hope emanating from Boaz. She blessed God, and him as well, her husband's kinsman, the relative who had alienated himself from her.

> "BLESSED BE HE OF THE LORD, WHO HAS NOT LEFT OFF HIS KINDNESS, TO THE LIVING AND THE DEAD.
> AND NAOMI SAID TO HER: 'THE MAN IS NIGH OF KIN TO US, ONE OF OUR NEAR KINSMEN.'"

*

For three months she sat and waited. Every day Naomi's blessing would accompany Ruth as Ruth set out to glean. Every day Naomi waited in trembling for Ruth to return in the evening.
Every day hope would rise anew in her; and every evening it would be shattered.
Till the barley and wheat harvests were ended.

Then Naomi decided to send Ruth to Boaz to the threshing floor.
Why did Naomi herself not first go to seek his favor, to request him to accept Ruth and so to restore the name of the dead to his inheritance?

Was she too proud? Does pride stand in the way of a mother in seeking favor for her children?
Or was she too lowly and lacking in boldness in her own eyes?
Why was she so froward, then, in asking Ruth to undertake a dangerous mission, one which even seemed improper? And also illogical? — —
What would she have done had Ruth refused to accept such an assignment, even though Ruth had sworn to her in love?
What would Boaz say? He might find some cause to suspect her, and might have hurled a curse rather than a blessing at her?
What would the inhabitants say? And all the people?

Would not the two be driven out of the city the very next day — she together with this Moabitess, whom Naomi had brought with her to tempt a prince of a family in Israel to sin —

And yet here the heroism and greatness of Naomi becomes evident.

For here she placed all her expectations, all her hope through the performance of this mitzvah, upon the scale. For Naomi wanted the levirate union to be for the sake of the mitzvah, and she wanted to be sure that the seed would belong to her.

Therefore she put Ruth to the test to discover whether Ruth's intentions, and attachment and loyalty to her, were pure. She also put Boaz to the test to determine his feelings and attitude towards Ruth and herself, since he had been the first to extend solace to Ruth in the field of the reapers.

And in this daring manner Naomi intended to shatter the silence that had enveloped them since their return to Bethlehem.

Now she wanted to determine once and for all how the matter would end, to the extent that the man would not remain silent till he had completed the matter that day.

> And for this purpose, Naomi presented this proposal to her, one which suited her alone, in respect of its conditions, and which would not succeed if any one of those conditions would be lacking. Ruth's virtue, Boaz's noble spirit, his being her relative, his attitude, Naomi's consent — the combination of all these circumstances was the assurance that God's presence attended upon and consented to this union. The evidence — the results. (Akedath Yitzḥak — Ruth)

Trembling, Naomi sent out Ruth, but she was also sustained by her bravery and faith.

> "And get yourself down" — the *kethiv* is "I will go down". She said to her: "May my merit go down with you.—" (Yalkut Shim'oni 604)

*

"If he be destroyed from his place,
  Then it shall deny him: 'I have not seen you.'
Behold this is the joy of his way
  And out of the earth shall others spring.
Behold, God will not cast away an innocent man." (Job 8.18-20)

The joyful end of Naomi's long and arduous journey constitutes the last scene of the Book. Finally she reaped the reward for her hopes. She had won. The elders approved the levirate union, as did the rest of the populace, when they conferred the blessing of Rachel and Leah and Tamar, who bore Perez to Judah, upon Ruth.

And now the daughters of Beth-lehem, too, came to see her in her happiness, and they affirmed: "Blessed be the Lord who has not left you this day without a redeemer and let his name be famous in Israel — for your daughter-in-law, who loves you, has given birth to him.—"

And only now does Scripture account of Naomi that she took the child in her bosom, for only now was her soul at peace.

"AND NAOMI TOOK THE CHILD AND LAID HIM IN HER BOSOM
AND BECAME NURSE UNTO HIM."

When Naomi sat alone with the child in her bosom, she sang to him of that loving-kindness and favor, and of the sufferings and the hope. This was the essence of all her activity, the Divine service of her heart.

And the neighbor women listened and heard those songs of hers, echoing from the rafters of her house and the posts of the cradle. The end of her story now made the beginning intelligible to them.

Hence last of all, they came and they named the baby,*

"SAYING: 'THERE IS A SON BORN TO NAOMI';
AND THEY CALLED HIS NAME OBED,*
HE IS THE FATHER OF JESSE, THE FATHER OF DAVID."

*

And this was Naomi's recompense, that she too was a mother to David, the sweet singer of Israel.

"I beseech You, O Lord, for I am Your servant;
I am Your servant, the son of Your handmaid;
You have loosed my hands.

I will offer to You the sacrifice of thanksgiving,
And will call on the Name of *Hashem*." (Ps. 116.16-18)

SUPPLEMENTARY NOTES TO MOTHER OF ROYALTY

Page 1 In honor of King David.

The reason [for reading Ruth on Shavuoth] is explicitly stated by the Tosafoth (Ḥagigah 17b) citing the Yerushalmi (*Ibid.* 2.3): David died on Shavuoth; and we have it on authority that the Holy One, blessed be He, gives the righteous their full measure of years, to the very same day (Kiddushin 38a). Hence since David died on Shavuoth, his birthday must have been Shavuoth. ("Bchor Shor" Bava Bathra 14b)

Page 1 The first royal tree he had planted.

"He laid hold upon the skirt of his robe, and it rent." Whose robe was torn? Rav and Levi (offered opinions). One said: The skirt of the robe of Saul. The other said: The skirt of the robe of Samuel.
R. Samuel b. Naḥmani said: It appears rather that the skirt of Samuel's robe tore, since the righteous are accustomed to grieve when the shoots they plant do not turn out well. (Yalkut Shim'oni 123, Midrash Shemuel)

Page 2 With all that was precious and desirable in Israel.

"And Moses did as the Lord had commanded him; and he took Joshua . . .
And he laid his hands upon him." (Num. 27.22-23)
Rashi: Generously (in full measure), to an even greater extent than he had been commanded, for the Holy One, blessed be He, had said (v. 18): "Lay your hand" and he laid both hands. And

so he made Joshua become, as it were, the repository filled with a generous measure of his (Moses') wisdom. (See also Rashi, v. 16.)

Page 2 How can I go?

Cf. Pesahim 8, and also the commentary of R. Naftali Zvi Yehuda Berlin of Volozhin in his *Harḥev Davar* on (Exod. 32.26): "Whoever is for God, to me!"

Page 4 Two drops of oil.

Nabal said: His only surety is the two drops [of oil] with which Samuel has anointed him. Where is Samuel now and where are the drops? (Yalkut Shim'oni 134)

Page 5 The permanent Israelite monarchy.

"For I have provided for me a king among his sons." (1 Sam. 16.1) A king who will be for My name's sake. Wherever *li* ("for Me") is written, it implies permanent endurance, for ever and ever. (Yalkut Shim'oni 124, Midrash Shemuel)

Page 6 The progenitor of the Messiah.

In his *Shoresh Yishai,* R. Solomon Alkabetz quotes R. Shemaryah of Crete as asserting: "And I say that this Book [of Ruth], as a whole and in its details, was written to prove the legitimacy of King David, to show that a Moabitess is fit to enter the community of Israel—

Now if you argue that, since the Book was written to give the legal ruling in the case of Ruth, why was it not adduced as proof in the controversy between Abner and Doeg in Saul's time? Why did they have to accept Amasa's testimony, viz.: "So have I received it from the Beth Din of Samuel of Ramah, a Moabite male, but not a Moabitess" [is forbidden].

The answer: The book [of Ruth] had not yet been written at the time, for so the Rabbis have asserted that Samuel of blessed

memory wrote the Book of Judges and Ruth, as is stated in the first chapter of Bava Bathra, and Samuel had not yet written it, since, presumably, he only did so towards the end of his life.
I believe, and am convinced, that an inquiry was addressed to Samuel, of blessed memory, at that time concerning this law, whereupon he wrote this book to embody the legal decision which he had received by tradition, namely that a Moabitess is permissible."
Apparently the excerpt was copied down from R. Shemaryah's commentaries on the Five Megilloth which are extant in manuscript. (R. Judah L. Maimon, *Haggim Umo'adim*)

Page 6 The mitzvah of building the Holy temple.

"Since the day that I brought forth My people Israel out of the land of Egypt, I chose no city out of all the tribes of Israel, to build a house that My name might be there; but I chose David to be over My people Israel." (I Kings 8.16)
Three commandments devolved upon Israel on entering Eretz Israel: to appoint a king, as it is said (Deut. 17.15): "You shall surely set him king over you"; to extirpate the seed of Amalek, as it is said (Deut. 25.19): "You shall blot out the remembrance of Amalek"; and to build the Temple; as it is said (Deut. 12.5): 'Even unto His habitation shall you seek, and there you shall come." (Sanhedrin 20a; Maimonides, Laws of Kings 1.1)
From here it is possible to deduce what a privilege was bestowed upon Samuel and to understand his longing to fulfill all of the first three mitzvoth devolving upon the people of Israel upon their entry into the land of Canaan.
And if he at first refused to accede to the request of the people to appoint a king over them, this was the fault of the people, a result of his grief at "their not asking properly." (See Nahmanides, Gen. 49.10)
And by commanding Saul to go to war against Amalek, he formally declares himself a partner in the fulfilling of the commandment: "The Lord sent me to anoint you king over His nation, therefore hearken now to the voice of the words of the Lord."
Thus said the Lord of Hosts: I remember that which Amalek did to Israel..." (1 Sam. 15.1)

Page 12 How was it possible to flee from the Divine decree?

R. Berekhya said: Was it not the practice of the righteous to flee from famine? There were greater persons than Elimelech — Abraham and Isaac, who were richer than he — and the one fled to Egypt on account of famine, and the other to the land of the Philistines!

Said R. Berekhya in the name of Rabbi Isaac: The Holy One, blessed be He, caused these others to go away from evildoers, and gain renown in the world. He therefore had brought on the famine. Elimelech, however, lived in a locality [of righteous people] and of Torah study, and in great wealth. When a famine occurred, the poor began coming to him. He hid from them, and fled. Furthermore, he saw judgment coming upon the world and yet he went to live among the gentile nations. (Zohar Ḥadash 80)

Page 15 Ruth was the daughter of Eglon.

R. Bivi said in the name of R. Reuven: Ruth and Orpah were the daughters of Eglon, as it is written (Judges 3.2): " 'I have a message from God to you.' And he arose out of his seat." The Holy One, blessed be He, said unto him: You stood up from your chair for My honor, I shall cause to emerge from you a son who will sit on My chair, as it is said (1 Chron. 29.23): "Then Solomon sat on the throne of the Lord." (Yalkut Shim'oni, Ruth 600)

Page 20 And the woman was left of her two children — as if they had reverted to their childhood.

So we find in the case of Ishmael (twenty-seven years old at the time, according to Gen. Rabba) who was still called "child" by his father and mother, in their compassion for him: "Let me not look upon the death of the child." (So Akkedath Yitzhak, Gen. 21.14-16).

Reuben referred in similar vein to Joseph (who was seventeen then): "The child is not; and I, whither shall I go?" — "Do not sin against the child." (Gen. 37.29; — 42.22)

Page 22 Against her will, then, she followed her husband.

A similar difference of opinion between husband and wife is discussed in the Halakhah. If he desires to leave [Eretz Israel] and she refuses, he is pressed not to leave, and if he persists, he must give her a divorce and pay her her kethubah. (Kethubot 110b) Maimonides, Laws of Marriage, 13.18-20: And one is not to leave Eretz Israel and go to live abroad even from a bad dwelling to a good dwelling. The husband may not make his wife move from a city to a village, or from a village to city (17).

Page 23 So she became the remnant.

The "remnant" idea occurs extensively in the Books of the Prophets: See, for instance: Isa. chaps. 10, 11, 28; Jer. 23; Micah 2,5; Haggai 1; Zech. 8.

Page 28 She would be remembered too.

"I have surely remembered you . . . and they shall hearken to your voice." (Exod. 3.15-18)
This expression would be the sign that redemption was at hand. (Rashi; Exod. Rabba. See also Gen. Rabba on "And the Lord remembered Sarah.")

Page 29 Naḥal Yosef.

The author, R. Joseph Lipowitz, was one of the outstanding pupils of R. Nathan Finkel (*der Alter*) of Slobodka. I was privileged to make his acquaintance twenty years ago. His remarkable commentary on the Book of Ruth afforded me a pleasant surprise. I studied it, and learned from it, and rejoiced wherever I found that my views agreed with his. I deeply regret that I was unable to express my appreciation to him during his lifetime, for he died about a year ago. "Alas those who have departed."

Page 40 How strongly does this expression bring out the feelings of the two for each other.

As for clinging to God, the Torah admonishes us several times in this regard. "To love the Lord your God... and to cleave to Him" (Deut. 30-20); "To Him shall you cleave" (Deut. 10.20); "And unto Him shall you cleave" (Deut. 13.5).
David said: (Ps. 63.9): "My soul clings to You."
All these verses speak of one idea — of man clinging inseparably and immovably to God. (Mesillath Yesharim, The Path of the Just. Chap. 19)
"There is a friend that clings closer than a brother." (Prov. 18.24)

Page 46 Teaches us through His Torah.

To appreciate the beauty of this Midrash, one should note that the term "tents" does not denote physical property like sheep and cattle. Nor have we found the term "tents" employed in any such sense in reference to the patriarchs. Many other types of property were specified, but tents were not mentioned.
Of Abraham, Scripture has testified:

"And he had sheep and oxen, and he-asses and men-servants and maidservants, and she-asses and camels. (Gen. 12.16)
"And He has given him flocks and herds, and silver and gold, and men-servants and maid-servants and camels and asses." (*Ibid.* 24.35)

Of Isaac —
"And he had possessions of flocks, and possessions of herds, and a great household." (Gen. 26.14)
Of Jacob —

"And the man increased exceedingly, and had large flocks, and maid-servants and men-servants, and camels and asses." (*Ibid.* 30.43)
"And I have oxen, and asses and flocks, and men-servants and maid-servants. (*Ibid.* 32.6)

Page 51 She cleansed herself of the defilements of idolatry.

"Wash thyself therefore, and anoint thee, and put thy raimant upon thee."
Wash yourself — clear of your idolatry.
Anoint yourself — refers to good deeds and righteous conduct.
And put your raiment upon you — these refer to Sabbath clothes. (Ruth Rabba 5.12)

Page 52 Lot, as it were, ascended the mountain of the Lord.

"Who shall ascend into the mountain of the Lord? And who shall stand in His holy place?" (Psalms 24.4)
It has been previously stated: To ascend the ladder of goodness is not too difficult. Much more difficult and meritorious is the ability to maintain oneself there, to remain and not to descend...
"But the mountain falling, crumbles away" (Job 14.18) — this refers to Lot who fell from a mountain. (Gen. Rabba 52.1)

Page 53 The soul he had made.

(Gen. 12.5) R. Elazar observed in the name of R. Jose b. Zimra: If all the nations assembled to create a single insect, they could not infuse a soul in it. Yet you say: "and the souls which they had made"? It refers, however, to the proselytes whom they converted. If converted is intended, why "which they had made"? — It comes to teach you that anyone who wins over a gentile and converts him is regarded as having created him. (Gen. Rabba 39.14).

Page 62 "For I have known him."

This sense of "knowing" lends deeper meaning to the verse (Ps. 1.6): "For Hashem *knows* the way of the righteous, but the way of the wicked shall perish;" and the parallelism is properly balanced.

Page 64 Public Opinion.

Joseph's brothers furnish an example of this type of "general consent." They all concurred that Joseph had earned the penalty of death. Yet each in his heart did not want to kill Joseph. The proof is their immediately agreeing with Reuben's suggestion that Joseph be cast into the pit.
Then, afterwards, they agreed with Judah to sell Joseph. And our Rabbis have revealed even more to us by taking note of the juxtaposition of the verses:
"And Judah went down from his brothers" — his brothers demoted him from leadership. When they saw the grief of their father, they said to him: You advised us to sell Joseph. Had you advised us to restore him to our father we would have complied.

Page 66 From Naomi Ruth had most surely learned about the Jewish harvest laws.

Cf. Yevamoth 47a/b.

Page 68 And plans their course in advance to the last detail.

"And you shall 'appoint' (*hikrithem*)" — (Num. 35.11) — Rashi: The form *Hakrayah* denotes preparing as it is said (Gen. 27.20): "Because God prepared it for me."

Page 78 The greeting is in the Name of God.

Three enactments of the earthly Beth Din were approved by the Heavenly Beth Din, namely: Reading the Megillah, greeting and bringing of the tithes.
To greet using the Divine Name, and this does not constitute taking God's Name in vain (Rashi) — as it is said: "And behold Boaz came from Beth-lehem, and he said unto his reapers: *'Hashem* be with you.'" (Makkoth 23 Brachot 54a. See also Psalms 129.7-8)

Page 79 With an abundant harvest.

R. Israel of Salant would himself supervise the baking of matzah for Pesach. He watched the kneading, rolling and baking to make

sure that all was done strictly in conformity with all the legal requirements. Once, shortly before Pesach, he took ill and was not able to go to the bakery by himself.
His pupils went instead.
Before leaving they asked him, what they should particularly watch for. Take special care, he admonished them, neither to rebuke nor to vex the woman kneading the dough. She is a poor woman, a widow. ("Our Ancestors Told," M. Lipson)

Page 80 Did he expect them to come to his field to gather?

Cf. Mishnah Nedarim 4.8: If they were on a journey together and the first man had nothing to eat.

And "at the time of eating" (2.14) it is good to recall the halakhah.

Laborers, when taking a meal during the time that they are working for an employer, do not recite the blessing before the meal, so that they may not neglect the work, but only recite two after blessings after it....
If their employer takes the meal with them, they recite all the four blessings in complete form as everyone else does. (Maimonides Laws of Blessings 2.2)

Page 82 His remarks were verbose and vague.

We find many such passages in Scripture. They were not written in this manner for nothing. With all the interpretations that have been assigned to them, and there are many, we nevertheless believe that Scripture so presented the speakers' remarks to make us sense their mental and emotional states.
Examples:
(Gen. 21.26) Abimelech's answer to Abraham's rebuke.
(1 Sam. 15.15) Saul's answer to Samuel's sudden cross-examination.
(Ibid. 29.29) Jonathan's evasive answer to Saul concerning David's flight.
(2 Sam. chap. 14) The entire remarks of the woman of Tekoah.

Page 83 With public assent and approval.

Even a vow made with public knowledge can be annulled — for the performance of a mitzvah. Cf. Gittin 36a. (Mai. Laws of Oaths 6.8-9)

Page 85 I am of an alien people.

The Targum has given an excellent interpretation of "to take congnizance of me" (v. 10), similarly of "I am of an alien people" — and of (v. 19) "That took knowledge of you." Here the taking cognizance is to be understood in the legal sense — to legitimize, as opposed to those who were ignorant of the law, and had, therefore, alienated themselves from Ruth. So we find Rashi interpreting this verse (Gen. 42.8) in a reciprocal sense: "And Joseph recognized his brothers but they did not recognize him." — When they were at his mercy he took cognizance of their being his brothers; but when he was in their hands they did not take cognizance of his being their brother, and so to treat him accordingly.

Page 90 The Holy One, blessed be He, would have it recorded.

R. Cohen and R. Joshua of Sikhnin said in the name of R. Levi: In the past, when someone performed a good deed, the prophet placed it on record. Nowadays, when a man performs a good deed, who records it? Elijah records it and the Messiah, and the Holy One, blessed be He, subscribes His seal to it. (Ruth Rabba 5,6)

Page 92 What she had so longingly and carefully hidden away.

When teaching this verse, I usually relate this incident to my students — and thereby also fulfill the mitzvah of "Remember what Amalek did to you." During the Eichmann trial (Jerusalem, 1962), one of the witnesses, Prof. Gor Vels, a Frenchman, gave a horrifying account of the Dranci camp where 4,000 children were confined and from where they were to be transported to Auschwitz. In a shaken voice and with his hands trembling with emotion, he told of an incident involving a little boy by the name of Jacques Stern, one of the inmates of the camp. The story was received in tense silence in the hall, while all eyes were fixed upon the witness.

It happened when the witness, together with Renée Blum, brother of the French socialist leader Léon Blum, visited the children's rooms. At one of the doors stood a seven or eight year old boy, with "a clever, alert and good-looking face." "The quality of his clothes testified to their once having been good, even though they were old now." The child wore only one shoe, his jacket was torn, yet he was jolly.

The witness continued: "Blum addressed himself to the lad and asked him his age. The child answered that he was eight. Blum asked his name, and he answered: 'Jacques Stern.' When the child was asked who his parents were, he answered that his father worked in an office and that his mother played the piano well.

Then the child turned to us and asked us whether he would soon leave the camp to be reunited with his parents.

We used to tell the children that they would leave and rejoin their parents. We knew this to be false. We knew that after they were sent to Auschwitz they would never see their parents again. In spite of our knowing what would happen in Auschwitz, I nevertheless lied to the boy and said to him: Don't worry, You will rejoin your parents in a few days."

Here the witness became even more agitated as he unfolded the rest of the story: "Then the child Jacques Stern took a piece of half eaten biscuit from the pocket of his torn jacket and said to us: I have saved this for my mother, and I'll give it to to her when we meet.

Renée Blum turned to the boy and wanted to pat him on the head. The child suddenly burst out crying, shockingly, this same child who had been so jolly just before. We could bear it no longer and left the room." (From press reports and the transcript of evidence pp. 434-435)

Page 96 That bring good tidings.

"You did prepare in Your goodness for the poor, O God. The Lord gives the word; The women that proclaim the tidings are a great host." (Ps. 68.11-12)

Page 97 But set her thoughts right as well.

We find a similar correction in the Book of Numbers (chap. 32), in the section dealing with the tribes of Gad and Reuben. When Moses noticed that they had not formulated their remarks properly (They placed their herds before their children) [Rashi, v. 16], he corrected them.

R. Isaac Arama, author of the Akkedath Yitzhak, has discovered a similar instance in (vv. 17,20): "We ourselves will be ready armed," the tribes said, to which Moses replied, "If you will arm yourselves to go before the Lord and the land be subdued before the Lord." When they repeated their promise, they added Moses' amendment (vv. 25-27): "as my lord says."

Page 102 Man and Woman. Parenthood and inheritance — the Torah of Life.

Rabbi Akiva expounded: If husband and wife are worthy, the Shekhinah is in their midst. (Sotah 17)
Rashi: since God divided His name and shared it between them, the *Yod* in איש man, and the *Heh* in אשה woman.

Our Rabbis taught: It is said (Exod. 20): "Honor your father and your mother," and it is also said (Prov. 3): "Honor the Lord with your substance." Thus Scripture has made honoring father and mother comparable to honoring the Allpresent. (Kiddushin 30b)

Our Rabbis taught: There are three partners in man: the Holy One, blessed be He, father and mother. When someone honors his father and his mother, the Holy One, blessed be He, says: I account it as meritorious for them as if I had dwelt among them and they had honored me. (*Ibid*)

The extra *vav* (in ואת) is to include your older brother. (Kethuvoth 103a)

"And the Scribes have ordained that one is also obliged to respect his elder brother as he does his father." (Maimonides, Laws of Rebels 6.15)

Page 103 Waiting expectantly for the brother-in-law.

"His father kept the saying in mind" — waiting expectantly for when it would occur. (Gen. 37.11 — Rashi)

Page 105 Rich and respected but very old.

Boaz was eighty years old. (Ruth Rabba 6.4)
(See Ibn Ezra's calculation at the end of his commentary on Ruth).

Page 108 So Moses received it at Sinai and handed it down to Israel.

Even though the Book of Ruth was written by the prophet Samuel, as is stated in the Talmud (Bava Bathra 16a), yet it is known that the Holy One, blessed be He, revealed every generation and its Torah expositors, every generation and its Torah sages, to Moses. This being so, He foresaw the entire encounter of Ruth with Boaz, which indeed is an episode of significance to the whole people. — And Moses, our teacher, handed down to his disciple, Joshua, and Joshua to his disciples, and so on that the words should be recorded thus in the Book of Ruth. (Torah Temimah)

Only the person aware of the strictness of the laws handed down by Moses from Sinai (on which there is no disagreement — Maimonides' Introduction to his Mishnah Commentary) can contemplate and understand that the conversation between Ruth and Naomi was foreseen from on High. For it was most exactly transmitted, every letter being counted — those that were to be written down, and those that the prophet omitted from the *kethiv* and were only preserved in the *keri*. "Then they that feared the Lord spoke with one another; and the Lord hearkened and heard, and a book of remembrance was written before Him, for them that feared the Lord, and that thought upon His Name." (Malachi 3.16)

Page 114 Grace and humility commensurate with the mitzvah.

R. Berekhiah said: Cursed be the wicked. Elsewhere Scripture states (Gen. 39.2): "She caught him by his garment. saying: 'Lie with me.'" Ruth, however, said: "Spread therefore your skirt over your handmaid." (Ruth Rabba 6.3; Gen. Rabba 87, Yalkut Shim-'oni 606)
See the interesting note in the Torah Temimah. That corner (*kanaf*) indicates the mitzvath of levirate marriage (Yevamoth 49a).
See also Deut. 32.11; Ezek. 16.8.

Page 124 A leader and one of the Judges.

R. Nahman said: Ibzan of Beth-lehem is Boaz. (Yalkut Shim'oni 601; Bava Bathra 91)

Page 128 The law of conveyance by exchange.

This is one of the acts through which a legal transfer of property is effected.
It is most frequently employed when the article to be sold is not with the owner at the time.
Maimonides, Laws of Sale, 5.5: Land, slaves and all other movable articles are acquired through symbolic exchange, and this is called *kinyan* (transfer or delivery). The main manner of performance is that the buyer should give an article of any type to the seller and say: Acquire this article in exchange for the yard or the wine or the animal or the slave that you have sold to me for such an amount. Once the seller has raised the article and thereby acquired it, the buyer has acquired the land or those movable items, even though he has not yet drawn them to him or paid for them. And neither buyer nor seller can retract.
In the time of the Gemara, it was customary to hand a scarf (kerchief) and so this type of transfer has been called either acquisition by exchange or by kerchief. In our Book, the author prefaces his description of the incident, with the information that this act was performed in those times with a shoe, it being the "any type of article."
The reason for using a shoe was that this article was always readily available. (Ibn Ezra)

R. Isaac Arama, *Akkedath Yitzḥak*: The shoe, after all, has a function similar to a glove—hence, rationally, the law should have been that the seller gives his neighbor his glove as if to say "Just as I give you and let you acquire my glove, so I give you that piece of property." The legal ruling follows the opinion of Rav, however, that the transfer is effected with the possession of the buyer.

Page 128 The house of him that had the shoe loosed.

See the observation on halitzah quoted from the Malbim, p. 102. The entire note is based on our sensing the spirit of the law, but not on its actual legal requirements. In the Halakhah the levirate marriage cannot take place after halitzah. There was no actual halitzah involved here.

Page 130 Jacob had only become indentured... for the sake of Rachel.

This Midrash very effectively supplements Nahmanides' exposition of the verse (Gen. 44.27): "And your servant my father said unto us: 'You know that my wife bore me two sons.'"

Nahmanides poses this question: If he said that Benjamin was his mother's only son, then why should his father's old age be brought down in evil to the grave, since Jacob had many sons and grandsons, and Benjamin's mother was already dead and could therefore not weep over the son in the father's presence. The reason is, however, that Jacob had married only Rachel of his own free will. This is the reason for his saying: "My wife bore me two sons." Only two sons were born to me by the wife I married voluntarily, and my love for them is as if they were my only children.

It should be added here that this argument was advanced by Judah, the son of Leah. Possibly this admission by Judah may have roused Joseph to proffer the forgiveness he had denied his brothers so far. For had this not been the source of the sin of Leah's sons against him, and here was their confession.

The source of the sin of the sons of Leah.

The hatred and jealousy of the brothers did not begin with the giving of the coat to Joseph.
We can sense its root in Jacob's preference for Rachel over their mother. How great was their grief when Jacob placed "Rachel and Joseph last", the very last being cherished the most.

Page 131 Boaz upheld the ruling... by performing this demonstrative act.

"And he took ten men." (4.2) Why ten?
R. Nahman said: From here it follows that the blessing of the bridegrooms has to be recited in the presence of ten males.
R. Abbahu said: He took the ten to make it public knowledge that an Ammonite and not an Ammonitess, a Moabite and not a Moabitess were prohibited. (Kethuvoth 7b)

Page 131 The blessing conferred on Ruth that day.

I was led to this idea by a story involving the Ḥafetz Ḥayim, which I heard in my youth from Rav Roitbard, may God avenge him, rabbi of Luna near Grodno. The latter was one of the young, married, Talmidei Chachamim who studied the order of Kodashim under the guidance of the saint.

In his old age the Ḥafetz Ḥayim was unable to travel about to the small towns to sell his works, and so would delegate this assignment to "agents" who were also God fearing individuals. They would, in accordance with his instructions, preach in public, arouse the people to repentance and good deeds, and after his manner, would not accept more than the fixed price for the books and only sell the works to such persons as would study them.

It was during World War I. The "agent" was delayed and could not reach the Ḥafetz Ḥayim's locality. He had in his possession the money that had been paid for the books. During those years, the agent's family suffered great privation. His wife was ill and his children kept asking for food. He was forced slowly to spend the money in his possession for his household needs. When the roads were opened once more, the agent hurried to the Ḥafetz Ḥayim to ask forgiveness, since he could not now repay the money which he had used without permission.

The Ḥafetz Ḥayim hastened to comfort him and told him that he had acted correctly. He had acted with permission since the Ḥafetz Ḥayim had decided in his heart to give him the money as an outright gift, and he should therefore not think of repayment.

Towards evening when the agent was already in his wagon ready to return home, people were astonished to see the aged Ḥafetz Ḥayim hurry out to seek the agent. The Ḥafetz Ḥayim said he had come to say goodbye and give his blessing for the journey. He took out a woman's shawl which he importuned the agent to accept as a gift for his wife! —

Page 131 The fringes and the staff.

"And it was at that time that Judah went down" — "Before she travailed, she brought forth" (Isa. 66.7) — Even before the first enslaver had been born, the last redeemer had been born. (Gen. Rabba 85). See Rabbi Naftali Z. Y. Berlin's pertinent observation in his *Harhev Davar.*

Page 133 The messianic light breaks through...unexpectedly.

Three things come unexpectedly, namely: the Messiah, a finding and a serpent (Sanhedrin 97). The Gemara refers to the future, but we have referred the idea to the source of the Messiah.

Page 134 Petach Enayim.

The effrontery that will flourish during the age immediately preceding the advent of the Messiah will emanate from the inner craving for the supreme, inexpressible holiness, and this will ultimately be attained, for the people of Israel is destined to penetrate beyond the boundary of the ministering angels. The latter will then ask them: What has God wrought, what new idea has come out of the heavenly Academy?
Their sons are destined to be prophets of the highest category, of the same type as Moses our teacher and to receive the primeval light vouchsafed to Adam. The source of life in its fullest extent of goodness will be revealed in them and through them." (Rabbi A. I. Kook, *Oroth Hakodesh,* Hakodesh Hakelali 8, p. 308 and as recorded in a m. in the possession of the editor of the Rav's works, my teacher R. David Hakohen. See also Hokhmath Hakodesh — the radiation of the light of the Messiah — p. 135.)

Page 134 "I said: 'I will get wisdom'; but it was far from me."

Solomon said: I have stood and investigated all these and I have studied the chapter of the red heifer — but when I exerted myself over it, I said: I will get wisdom but it is far from me. (Eccl. Rabba 7)

Page 135 Since Jacob had married two sisters.

R. Abba b. Kahana opened his discourse: "Tremble and sin not" (Ps. 4.5). David said to the Holy One, blessed be He: How long will they tremble and rage against me and say: Is he not of tainted descent? Is he not a descendant of Ruth, the Moabitess? "Commune with your own heart upon your bed" (*ibid.*) Are you not descendants of a marriage with two sisters? Look at your own genealogy and be still. (Ruth Rabba 8.1)
But this was certainly the Divine will to extract the precious from the worthless, the good from the evil source, from the source of spoilage, since in this way the external obstructions allow them to emerge from the depths of the abyss. (*Knesseth Israel, Shoresh Yishai*).
(So the Ari, R. Isaac Luria, wrote in the Sefer Gilgulim — which is quoted by Malbim at the end of his commentary on Ruth).

Page 135 In God's life treasure....

The opening sentence of the first of the blessings of the Shema in the High Holiday morning service.

SUPPLEMENTARY NOTES TO THE SCROLL OF OBED

Page 170 The echo of the footsteps of the Messiah — in earlier generations.

"And Jacob sent messengers before him to Esau his brother unto the land of Seir, the field of Edom:
And he commanded them saying: 'Thus shall you say to my lord Esau: So said your servant Jacob
I have sojourned with Laban, and stayed until now. And I have oxen and asses and flocks, and men-servants and maid-servants;
and I have sent to tell my lord to find favor in his eyes.' " (Gen. 32.4-6)
("Act as if you were rich" — Rashi, Deut. 2.6-7)
Moses used similar language:
"And Moses sent messengers from Kadesh unto the king of Edom:
Thus says your brother Israel..." (Num. 20.14)

The expression "Thus says" resounds like a prophetic-historical proclamation. Accordingly the Midrash on the verse (Gen. 33.14) "until I will come to my master in Seir" becomes intelligible. —

R. Abbahu said: We have reviewed the whole of Scripture and do not find that Jacob our father ever went to Esau to the Mountain of Seir. Was it possible that Jacob was truthful and yet deceiving? Yet when would Jacob come to Esau? In the ultimate future. As Scripture avers (Obad. 1.21): "And saviors shall come up on Mount Zion to judge Mount Esau..." (Gen. Rabba 78.18)
See also the quotation from Midrash Tanhuma on the title page of the Scroll of Obed.

Page 175 As they journeyed forth from Egypt.

See Deut. 23.5. and compare with what was stated of Amalek:
"Remember what Amalek did unto you by the way as you came forth out of Egypt." (Deut. 25.17)

Page 177 The end of days.

This explains why the prophet mentioned the incident of Balak and Balaam in his prophecies dealing with the end of days (Mica 4.5,6).
"O my people remember now what Balak king of Moab devised,
And what Balaam the son of Beor answered him."
And this was Balaam's reply (Num. 24.14):
"Come and I will announce to you what this people shall do to your people at the end of days."

Page 179 From the field of Moab to Beth-lehem in Judah.

The Zohar Ḥadash distinguishes most sharply between Ruth and Balaam. Of him it is said: "And God happened to confront Balaam (*vayikar*)" (an expression denoting a casual, a shameful event — see Rashi).
And of Ruth it is said: "And it happened to her to light" — this denotes a noble event, as it is said (Ps. 36): "How precious (*yakar*) is Your loving-kindness, O God," (Zohar Ḥadash, 85)

Page 186 Hence the Torah preferred to use this example.

In describing individual cases the Torah seizes upon the most extreme, to allow us to apply it to the rest.
"If you meet your enemy's ox or his ass going astray, you shall surely bring it back to him again."
"If you see the ass of him that hates you lying under its burden, you shall forbear to pass by him; you shall surely release it from him."
Cf. the above instances with the similar verses in Deuteronomy (22.1-4).

Page 189 Knocking at the door of Elimelech only to find it locked.

See Chap. 2, p. 14, the excerpt from Yalkut Shim'oni: "Elimelech was one of the outstanding personalities of the country, as well as one of its leading providers."

Page 193 The detailed enumeration.

A blessing does not occur in things priced or weighed or counted, but in something that is hidden from the eye, as it is said (Deut. 28.8): "The Lord will command the blessing with you in your barns." (Barns — *asamekha; samui* — hidden) Interestingly, the exact number of livestock owned by the patriarchs is never explicitly mentioned.

Page 202 To attribute death and evil to Him.

"Have the gates of death been revealed to you? Or have you seen the gate of the shadow of death?" (Job. 38.17)
The Holy One, blessed be He, addressed this question to Job when He saw him puzzled by the justice administered by the Holy One, blessed be He. Come and see! Job had said: "Though He slay me, yet will I trust in Him" (*lo*). (13.15)
The word *lo* is spelled with an *aleph,* signifying "not"; but it is read as meaning "to Him".
"The Holy One, blessed be He, said to him: Am I the one who kills the sons of men? Have the gates of death been revealed to you?" (Zohar *Vayetze* 160)

Page 202 Distinguishing between friend and foe.

"For He breaks me with a tempest and multiplies my wounds without cause." (Job 9.17)
Rabbah said: Job blasphemed with a tempest and was answered with a tempest. He blasphemed with a tempest as it is said: "He breaks me with a tempest." Job said before Him: Master of the universe, perhaps a tempest has passed before You and has caused You to confuse *Iyov* (Job) with *Oyev* (foe)? (Bava Bathra 16a)

Page 205 I flee to the fortress of the Holy One, blessed be He.

Sensing the same idea, R. Solomon Ibn Gabirol culled expressions from both books and fused them in his love-poem to God:

> And if I do not wait on Thy mercies,
> Who will have pity on me but Thee.
> Therefore, though Thou shouldst slay me — yet will I trust in Thee,
> For, if Thou shouldst pursue my iniquity
> I will flee from Thee to Thyself

And I will shelter from Thy wrath in Thy shadow. (The Royal Crown, tr. Israel Zangwill, JPS ed., p. 118)

Page 221 The analogies of the potter and flax dealer.

"The Lord tries the righteous." (Ps. 11)

R. Jonathan said: When a flax-dealer knows that his flax is inferior, he does not knock it too hard or it will split.
When the flax is superior, he beats it more because it thereby continually improves.
Similarly, the Lord does not test the wicked since they cannot endure the trial. Whom does He test? — The righteous, as it is said: "The Lord tries the righteous."
R. Jonathan said: When the potter tests his furnace, he does not use the defective utensils. Why? — He could barely give them a single blow without breaking them.
What does he test? — The good utensils, for even if He were to beat these many times, he would still not break them. Similarly the Holy One, blessed be He, does not test the wicked but only the righteous. (Gen. Rabba 55.2)

Page 229 The women neighbors — they named the baby.

We previously explained the blessings conferred by the elders, the people and the women neighbors as an expression of joy at their forgiveness for the house of Elimelech (p. 153-4). Now we regard the women's blessing and naming the baby as signifying their approval of the levirate union, which had been the custom instituted in Israel in earlier times, in that the act devolved upon all heirs to the estate of the deceased (Nahmanides Gen. 38.8) See p. 100.
And perhaps Nahmanides had this in mind when he added "neighbor-women" at the end of his note.
"This was the matter of Boaz, and the reason for Naomi and the neighbor women. And the wise will understand."
If I have thought of the same idea as he did, then I am indeed gratified.

Page 230 "And they called his name Obed."

From the Hebrew root "avod" — "to serve."